A Cloud of Unknowing

A Cloud of Unknowing

*A Personal Survey of the
Great Issues of Religion*

Edward Celiz

VANTAGE PRESS
New York

The author gratefully acknowledges permission to include excerpts from the following:

The August 5, 1984, issue of *The Observer*. Copyright © 1984 by *The Observer* (London).

God and the New Physics, by Paul Davies. Copyright © 1983 by Paul Davies, reprinted 1983 and 1984. Reprinted by permission of J M Dent & Sons Ltd., Publishers.

The *Daily Mail* (London).

The World's Religions. Copyright © 1982 by Lion Publishing, P.L.C. Reprinted with permission by Lion Publishing, P.L.C.

Extracts from the *Authorized Version of the Bible* (the *King James Bible)*, the rights in which are vested in the Crown, are reproduced by permission of the Crown's patentee, Cambridge University Press.

November 30, 1987, issue of the *London Times* (article by Rabbi Ephraim Gastwirth). Copyright © 1987 by the *London Times*.

The July 10, 1986, issue of the *London Sunday Telegraph* article by Tom Stacey). Copyright © 1986 by the *London Sunday Telegraph*.

Published by Vantage Press, Inc.
516 West 34th Street, New York, New York 10001

Manufactured in the United States of America
ISBN: 0-533-08987-5

Library of Congress Catalog Card No.: 89-92915

1 2 3 4 5 6 7 8 9 0

To my wife, Viv, whose love and understanding made everything possible; and to my son, Peter, for whom this book is written.

Between us and our God there is ... a Cloud of Unknowing. ... Of God Himself can no man think. ... He may well be loved but not thought. ... The most godly knowing of God is that which is known by unknowing.

Unknown medieval mystic

Many would hold that, from the broad philosophical standpoint, the outstanding achievement of twentieth-century physics is not the theory of relativity with its welding together of space and time, or the theory of quanta with its present apparent negation of the laws of causation, or the dissection of the atom with the resultant discovery that things are not as they seem; it is the general recognition that we are not yet in contact with reality. To speak in Plato's well-known simile, we are still imprisoned in our cave, with our backs to the light, and can only watch the shadows on the wall.

The Mysterious Universe
by Sir James Jeans

Contents

Preface   xi
Acknowledgments   xiii
Introduction   xv

1. Does God Exist?   1
2. What Kind of God?   55
3. Where Is God?   108
4. What Is Time?   132
5. What Is Space?   151
6. Is the Future Predetermined?   180
7. How Do We Know That Wrong Is Wrong?   198
8. What Is Conscience?   219
9. What Is Faith?   236
10. Was Christ the Son of God?   266
11. Is There Any Future for Mankind?   298

Epilogue   319

Preface

All we can know is that we know nothing. And that's the height of human wisdom.

Tolstoy

A Cloud of Unknowing is a personal survey of the great issues of religion. One man's view of the Universe. One man's search for truth. In this latter regard, of course, it fails. For truth is beyond the reach of any human being. Truth is for seeking, not for finding. Only the Creator of Truth knows what truth is.

Man is approaching a critical stage in his evolution. Mind-boggling discoveries are being made in the fields of physics, computer technology and medical science. The last frontiers of knowledge are being breached. The walls of ignorance are coming down. Anything and everything are now possible. Or so it is believed.

Time to celebrate? Hardly. The forces of evil have never been so visible; man has never been more destructive. World-wide violence, terrorism, murderous religious fundamentalism and political and national fanaticism are a constant reminder that all is not well within the human soul.

Atheism, intellectual nihilism and agnosticism are rampant. Christianity is in a state of crisis. Modern liberal theology gnaws away at the vitals of the Christian faith, whilst conservative dogmatists unimaginatively retreat into the citadel of biblical orthodoxy. The Virgin Birth, the Miracles and the physical Resurrection are (in my view, quite rightly) debunked, but nothing is put in their place. The Christian faith is being fragmented and the liberal freethinkers are throwing out the baby with the bath water. Jesus, the star, has now become a walk-on extra in the greatest religious movie of all time.

The essential problem facing the Christian Church is this: How can the Jesus of history be demythologized without destroying the Jesus of faith? In other words, how can Christianity be brought into the scientific twenty-first century without relinquishing Christ as the definitive center of the Christian religion?

It is not for a layman to tell the Church how this can be done (if only for the reason that this layman doesn't know!); but perhaps they may find a clue in Chapter 10.

None of this is, of course, relevant to the question of the existence of God, which is the central theme of this book (though it is to the millions upon millions of Christians who worship God "through Jesus Christ"). I know that some physicists are saying that the new physics and the new cosmology have abolished God altogether; but then, physicists are not immune to saying silly things. Just because these scientists like playing at God doesn't mean that they are God.

However, it behoves me not to be arrogantly dogmatic. After all, the atheists may be right. Only God knows for sure whether he exists. And he's not telling!

If any contradictions are found in the philosophy expressed in these pages, it will be because the whole of existence is a contradiction; paradox is a universal truth. The point is repeatedly made herein that truth is subjective not objective; that relativity applies to material and immaterial alike; that life is a conglomeration of perceptions not absolutes.

There are absolutes, of course: love, truth, right, and wrong, for example. But having said that, I recognize that they are only absolute inasmuch as we perceive them to be absolute. And even then, it is the concepts themselves which are absolute not our personal judgements in relationship to those concepts.

God, the Universe, time and space, man, mind and soul, conscience, faith, right and wrong—everything is up for discussion. The scientists, the philosophers, the theologians, the intellectuals have all had their say. Now it is the turn of the ordinary man . . .

Acknowledgments

First and foremost, I would like to express my profound gratitude to all the authors of the source material I have so abundantly drawn upon in the preparation of this book, without which inspiration the book could not have been written.

I am also greatly indebted to my friend Marion Jack, for reading the manuscript and making invaluable comments which helped shape the final content.

Thanks too are due to Ann Holder who typed and retyped the manuscript more times than I or she can remember.

There is no need for me to thank my wife; the dedication says it all.

Finally, unfashionable though it may sound to the contempory secular ear, I humbly thank Almighty God for enabling me, in the words of Simone Weil, if only fitfully and in some small measure, "to see the true light and hear the true silence." And if God does not exist, then I thank God for blessing me with the imagination to imagine that he does.

Apology: As this book is not a work of scholarship or reference but one intended for quiet philosophical contemplation, the inclusion of an index was considered unnecessary and pretentious. The chapter headings are deemed sufficient to guide the reader back to areas of particular interest; nevertheless, should the omission of an index cause any inconvenience, the author apologizes.

Introduction

Each chapter in this book poses an unanswerable question, the kind that most thinking people ask themselves at some time or other during the course of their lives, and then sets out to try to answer it.

The author has studiously avoided the often incomprehensible jargon of the professional, believing that it is better to be understood than to appear learned. That is not to say that the reader will understand everything I have written. Because he won't. Some of what I have written I do not understand myself.

Most people, though perhaps not consciously aware of it, are, in one degree or another, interested in theology, philosophy, metaphysics, epistemology and anthropology (the words are grand but the meanings are simple, as we shall see anon); but find the works of professional thinkers too abstruse, too obscure, too heavy for their comprehension. This is a pity. For everyone should have right of access to philosophical debate.

It is for such people that this book is written: in other words, it is not for thinkers but for people who think.

Its aim is to interest and stimulate the imagination of that growing number of people who, in this ever-increasingly materialistic society of ours feel that something is missing from their lives; that there must be more to existence than cars, television, videos, and all the other delectations of modern consumerism (the consumer society is aptly named, for it consumes us all); that we weren't put on this earth simply to enjoy ourselves (if this is not apparent to us, the well-fed of the West, then it certainly is to the starving masses of the Third World).

Although not religious in the formal sense of the word, and probably only seeing the inside of a church at weddings and funerals, these people nonetheless have a deep-seated religious instinct, which no amount of scientific revelation can satisfy or subdue. Twentieth-century science may be king; but it isn't God. As Brian M. Stableford puts it in *The Mysteries of Modern Science*: "In so far as scientists have attempted to make science into a replacement for religious belief they have failed. Their wares are not attractive enough, the beliefs which they sell are not useful in the way that the customer wants to use them."

I make no bones about my own religious beliefs. I am a theist and a Christian. But undogmatic. I am interested only in truth—wherever it may lead. I do not pretend to have all the answers. Any answers I may have can only be provisional. The true test of philosophy is to ask the right questions; the answers must answer for themselves.

This book is not about religion; it is about God. If that sounds anomalous, I would refer the reader to Mahatma Gandhi. "God," he said, "has no religion." (Well, he couldn't have, could he? Whom would he worship?)

To the reader who would be overawed by those impressive sounding words—theology, philosophy, metaphysics, epistemology and anthropology, I would simply say: don't be, the meanings couldn't be more simple:

A theologian is one who speaks about God.
An anthroplogist is one who speaks about man.
A philosopher is one who seeks knowledge and wisdom.
A metaphysician is one who speaks about matters beyond physics. (*Meta* is Greek for "beyond.")
An epistemologist is one who speaks about the theory of knowledge.

Now anyone who has read thus far, is almost certainly one or all of these things. Everyone is a philosopher (you have to be to survive in this world!). And if Leibniz, Spinoza, Kant, Nietzsche, Hume, and all the others, can have a worldview, then so can Joe and Jill Bloggs.

Thinking is the greatest of human attributes. Thinking, and thinking about our thoughts, is what makes us human. "In 1666, at the age of twenty-three," writes Carl Sagan in his book, *Cosmos,* "Newton was an undergraduate of Cambridge University when an outbreak of plague forced him to spend a year in idleness in the isolated village of Woolsthorpe, where he had been born. He occupied himself by inventing the differential and integral calculus, making fundamental discoveries on the nature of light and laying the foundation for the theory of universal gravitation. The only other year like it in the history of physics was Einstein's 'Miracle Year' of 1905. When asked how he accomplished his astonishing discoveries, Newton replied unhelpfully, 'By thinking upon them.'"

By thinking upon them! Such is the power of thought.

As I have intimated, this book is God-oriented but not religious in the orthodox sense of the word. You will not be lectured. Or preached at. Or told how to lead your lives. I have no axe to grind. I am not an evangelist or a born-again Christian or a born-again anything else. I am an ordinary person, who, like millions of other ordinary people, thinks about extraordinary things. The subjects we shall be discussing here are far too important to be left to the intellectuals. Jesus wasn't an intellecutal. He was an ordinary person—just like (or rather not like) you and me.

We are living in an era of unparalleled scientific discovery. Soon, perhaps within the next five or ten years or so, scientists, will, they think, have solved the mystery of the Universe. A complete unified theory of creation will be ours, they say. "Our goal," says Stephen W. Hawking, one of the world's leading cosmologists (and they don't come more brilliant than he), "is nothing less than a complete description of the Universe we live in."

Well . . . yes. But will this "complete description of the Universe" tell us whether there is a God or not? And if there is, why he allows suffering? And who invented love? And who created evil? It will not. In other words, this "complete" theory will be incomplete. While telling us everything, it will tell us nothing.

To those who believe that science has all the answers, let me quote the words of the German existentialist philosopher, Karl Jaspers (*Philosophy is for Everyman*): "The trouble begins when the scientifically known is taken for Being itself, when everything not scientifically knowable is declared nonexistent. Science then becomes scientific superstition, a heap of nonsense in the grasp of pseudo science, containing neither science nor philosophy nor faith . . . The real world is appearance, not reality as such. We are thrown into the real world, where we orient ourselves with the aid of scientific knowledge, but we do not look beyond it. Only philosophical insight frees us from our imprisonment in the world."

If the reader is reluctant to take the word of a philosopher, I invite him to listen to that giant of science, Albert Einstein. "When I calculate and see this tiny insect that has flown on my paper," he said, "I feel something like: Allah is great, and we with all our scientific glory are miserable simpletons." (Quoted by Karl Jaspers, ibid.)

And miserable simpletons we shall remain—"unified theory" or no "unified theory." But in case the impression should be given that all modern physicists believe that they are now on the verge of omniscience, here is a message from our old friend, Stephen Hawking (*A Brief History of Time*): "Any physical theory is always provisional, in the sense that it is only a hypothesis: you can never prove it. No matter how many times the results of experiments agree with some theory, you can never be sure that next time the result will not contradict the theory . . . if there really is a complete unified theory, it would also presumably determine our actions. And so the theory itself would determine the outcome of our search for it! And why should it determine that we come to the right conclusions from the evidence? Might it not equally well determine that we draw the wrong conclusion? Or no conclusion at all?" It might, indeed!

To those who think it is the learned atheists who have all the answers, let me quote the words of that famous atheist-psychologist Sigmund Freud. "When I ask myself," he said, "why I have always aspired to act honourably, to spare others and to be kind whenever possible, and why I didn't cease doing so when I realised that in this way one comes to harm and becomes an anvil because other people are brutal and uncharitable, then I have no answer."

There is an answer, of course. But being an atheist, Freud couldn't have known it.

We live in a spiritually deprived environment in which God takes a back seat. I do not mean that our society is particularly wicked or immoral, but that the existence (or nonexistence) of God is regarded as of no importance. With science in the driving seat, what need have we of God? Well, now, even scientists are mortal. Like the rest of us, they grow old and die. Whether we like it or not, God is a part of our existence. We cannot do without him. If not God, then "God." If not "God," then gods.

Worship is as old as man himself. We have to worship something. Deprived of God, we turn to substitute gods. Drink, drugs, violence, and crime are as good a means as any of releasing our frustrations and expressing our feelings (or rather lack of feelings). Ephraim Gastwirth, Rabbi of the Manchester Home for Aged Jews, in an article in the *London Times* November 30, 1987, sums up the modern predicament thus: "Deprived of spiritual nourishment, the soul withers. It writhes and turns seeking some outlet for its spiritual energies. This hunger of the soul for spiritual sustenance is constant and insistent. But if the hunger is not assuaged from the true source of holiness, it will turn to false gods . . . Some seek mystical experience and relief from inner tensions by taking drugs to satisfy the yearnings of the spirit. Occasionally, the torments of the starved spirit will lead to mindless violence, a boiling over of frustration and lack of inner satisfaction. Man simply cannot live the placid existence of an animal. The divine in him will not be ignored. Boredom is spiritual hunger which cries out for satisfaction. . . . Those who preach and teach religion, must, like the prophets of old, hold up a vision of holiness combined with goodness. For without that vision, the people are lost."

The established Anglican Church is a feeble voice, preaching a feeble message. It seems to think that it can put the world right by putting the world right. Its illicit flirtation with humanism, if persisted in, will eventually reduce Christianity to just another code of ethics and human behavior, like Confucianism or Taoism, less popular than the more attractive Buddhism.

Humanism is an attempt by man to solve the world's problems without God. It cannot be done. God will not be excluded from his Universe. This is not to suggest that the Church should withdraw from the everyday lives of men and women or be unconcerned for their welfare. Far from it. For it is in this world not the next that we are instructed by Jesus to love one another, to love our neighbour as ourselves.

It is to the politicizing and humanizing of the Christian message that I am objecting. In a recent address (March 5, 1989), Dr. Runcie, Archbishop of Canterbury, said that the Church existed "to serve the whole nation, not just a section of it." With the greatest respect, the Church exists to serve God, not "the whole nation," nor even the whole of humanity. True, we cannot serve God without loving man (the two are synonymous), but we can and often do serve man without loving God. The patient cured of cancer by the skill of the surgeon, couldn't care less whether the surgeon is a theist or an atheist (the knife knows nothing of spiritual values), whether he is imbued with love or simply contemplating his nice juicy fee. But in eschatological terms (literally, in the last analysis) it is the love of the surgeon for his fellow man, not the surgeon's expertise, which is the universal saving force. Man can exist (and prosper) without the surgeon's skill, but without love the human race is doomed.

The Church's job is to change the hearts of men. If it succeeds in doing this, then the rest will follow. Jesus said, "My kingdom is not of this world." Why then does the Church insist that it is? Jesus did not preach against the evils of Roman imperialism. Or capitalism, or communism, or any other "ism"—evil though they may all possibly be. (Nor did he attempt to get a film about himself banned.) He tried to CHANGE THE HEARTS OF MEN. "Love one another" is such a simple injunction that it is seldom understood.

It is not my job to tell the Church how it should interpret the Gospels. If it wants advice it should go to the grass roots of its faith—to Jesus Christ himself—and ask itself what Jesus would be doing and saying if he were alive today. My guess is that he would be doing and saying what he was doing and saying two thousand years ago (is not his message eternal?). And the result would be the same. He would not finish up as Pope or Archbishop of Canterbury or Chief Rabbi but on the cross.

I would like now to touch upon a point that, although philosophically irrelevant to the discussion we are about to embark upon, nonetheless happens to be a particular hobbyhorse of mine. It concerns the use of the masculine gender when referring to

God, "mankind" when discussing the human race, and the pronoun "he" when addressing the reader. I want to assure my female readers that I am not a male chauvinist, simply old-fashioned. Having been brought up to intone the words "God the Father," I have difficulty in seeing God as "God the Mother." This does not mean that I regard God as masculine. Such an image is, in my view, grotesque and an insult to the female species. I have been a feminist all my life and have never considered the sexes as being other than of equal value. (Note: "equal value," not "equal"; a five-pound note and five one-pound coins are of equal value, but they are not equal.)

The female species is the womb of the world. How then can women be inferior? Whatever support the Church may think it can find in the Bible for sex discrimination, I can find none in my own heart. Admittedly, I am prejudiced in favor of women—you see, my mother was a woman and so is my wife. If that sounds frivolous—which it is, but nonetheless sincere—let me quote the words of Tom Stacey, in an article in *The London Sunday Telegraph*, July 10, 1986: "The spirit of the earth has always been perceived as female, the spirit of the Logos as male. Without the female, the male would be cut off from the cosmos. Woman is instinctually at one with creation, man at one with himself. In their unquenchable, and impossible, urge for union, they reach in to the mystery of their existence."

This book is the culmination of a lifetime's thought by the author. Over the decades his beliefs have changed and developed, not dramatically, but certainly not imperceptibly. Even during the course of preparing this work, his beliefs have been modified. So if he is right now, he must have been wrong before. And if he was wrong before, how does he know he is right now? The fact is, of course, he doesn't.

No individual thinks his thoughts and forms his ideas in a vacuum—there is no such thing as original thought (if you think there is, just try inventing an original joke). Even Einstein, an original thinker if ever there was one, did not produce his ideas in splendid isolation. Fellow-scientists and philosophers, and existent knowledge, all affected his thought processes. Nevertheless, the thoughts I express in these pages, though not original, are original to me. I slavishly follow no one, however great, however eminent, however revered.

I cannot close this Introduction without paying tribute to my late friend, D. H. Jack. Over a period of fifty years we discussed, on and off, every area of theology and philosophy. And it was these discussions more than anything else that stimulated me to produce this work. As I was nearing the end of my manuscript, I asked him if he would be good enough to read it before I had it typed.

"I shall regard it as a privilege," he replied. (Note: not a pleasure, but a privilege—he was that kind of friend.) Six months later, before having that "privilege," he died.

I know that this book would have interested him and given him food for thought. If it has a similar effect on the reader, I shall be satisfied.

Niels Bohr, one of the founding fathers of twentieth-century physics, used to commence each lecture with these words:

> "Every sentence that I utter should be regarded by you not as an assertion but as a question." (Source: *The Ascent of Man*, by J. Bronowski)

The present author would ask the reader to approach this book in the same spirit.

A Cloud of Unknowing

Chapter 1

Does God Exist?

The celestial order and the beauty of the Universe compel me to admit that there is some excellent and eternal Being, who deserves the respect and adoration of men.

Cicero

For my part, the being of God is so little to be doubted, that it is almost the only Truth we are sure of.

Joseph Addison

Anyone who thinks he can prove the existence of God is a fool. A Being that is clever enough to create the Universe and everything in it is hardly likely to allow his cover to be blown by any Tom, Dick, or Harry who happens to fancy his chances as a universal detective.

However, unabashed, unashamed, and unrepentant, the author will, in the course of this chapter, endeavour to demonstrate not only that God exists but that he cannot not exist.

Since the dawn of history and probably since man first became man, the majority of human beings has always believed in some kind of God. This, one might think, is hardly surprising, seeing that man, knowing that he himself did not create the world and everything in it, nor the sun and the moon and the stars that shine down so mysteriously from the heavens above, not unnaturally assumes that as he wasn't responsible for this awesome feat, then somebody else was. In fact, some might say that he would have to be exceptionally stupid (or a genius?) *not* to believe in God.

But belief is not proof, and the majority is not always right.

1

What was good enough for primitive, superstitious man, who worshipped everything under and including the sun, is not necessarily good enough for enlightened, twentieth-century man who might be expected to know better.

Many scientists see no incompatibility between modern physics and belief in God. Others, possibly the majority, do. They echo the oft-quoted words of French mathematician Laplace (1749–1827), who, when asked by Napoleon why he had not mentioned God in his *Traité de la Mécanique Céleste*, replied: "Sire, I had no need for that hypothesis."

But those of us who do have need for "that hypothesis" cannot dismiss the Creator of the Universe (if that is indeed what God was) with such airy indifference.

The scientific community believes that it is now on the verge of discovering the secret of the Universe—a complete theory of creation wrapped up in one simple mathematical equation.

"For the first time," writes Paul Davies, Professor of Theoretical Physics at the University of Newcastle upon Tyne, in his book *God and the New Physics*, "a unified description of all creation could be within our grasp."

All creation? But science investigates only the material world not the spiritual. So even if it does come up with a formula to explain "all creation," it will in fact explain only a part of creation. The spiritual, which many believe to be the most important part, can never be revealed in the laboratory, only in the hearts of men.

But this sort of talk cuts no ice with the scientists. Nor should it. For they search for the truth, the scientifically verifiable proof, that is, in the way that nature has equipped them best to do—by using their brains and their reason. After all, there must be a reason why we have been given a reason to reason with!

"No scientific problem," says Davies (ibid), "is more fundamental or more daunting than the puzzle of how the Universe came into being. Could this have happened without any supernatural input?" Davies goes on to say that quantum mechanics seems to suggest that it could. But a little later, as if to back it both ways, he adds: "It may seem bizarre, but in my opinion science offers a surer path to God than religion."

Now I am afraid that I couldn't agree less. The most that science can offer is a surer path to the *works of* God, not to God himself. To reach God, one needs a totally different approach, quite beyond the powers of science to provide. But that does not mean that religion necessarily offers a sure path to God. So much depends on the religious beliefs we hold, the manner in which we hold them, and the direction in which they lead us. It is difficult to believe, for instance, that the barbarous treatment of heretics by the Christian Church in the Middle Ages—the mutilation and burning alive of alleged blasphemers, even as recently as the eighteenth century—brought the perpetrators any nearer to God.

But this is to digress. My purpose here is not to discuss the shortcomings of believers, but to argue the case for a supernaturally inspired, supernaturally designed, supernaturally engineered Universe. A Universe, in short, conceived and created by God.

As with any investigation the best place to begin is at the beginning. "In the beginning," says the Bible, "God created the heavens and the Earth." Nothing equivocal about that! The scientists, on the other hand, tell us that in the beginning was the big bang, followed by billions of years of evolutionary progress from which man finally emerged. Theologians no longer dispute this scientific version. Indeed, why should they, as it in no way conflicts with the religious belief in God the Creator of everything. If God created everything then, ipso facto, he created the big bang. Every human being is conceived in an orgasmic burst of energy, so why shouldn't the Universe have begun the same way?

Those scientists who believe they are now on the verge of solving the riddle of the Universe, do not know how long the remainder of their journey might take. Close as they may be (or think they may be) to their goal, they cannot be certain that the last few yards will not take infinitely longer than the many miles already travelled. Nor can they be sure that when they do come to the end of their search and fling open the door, that what they will find is not the answer to everything, but the answer to nothing—just another big, fat question mark!

The Answer, the Final Explanation, the First and Last

Truth—call it what you will—is not susceptible to scientific formulae. It lies deeply embedded in the spiritual "gene," and has done since the dawn of creation. Every answer the scientists find is followed by another question. Truth is one big merry-go-round. When we think we have reached the end, we find ourselves back at the beginning.

Let us assume that the big bangers are right, that the Universe, including time and space, were brought into existence with one almighty explosion of energy some 18,000 million years ago. So what? That only explains how it happened, not why. What we really want to know is, who lit the fuse that triggered off the big bang? Who put the spark in the primeval sludge to set it off on its long and tortuous evolutionary journey, and cause it one day to evolve into an Albert Einstein, a Michelangelo, a Mozart . . . a Jesus Christ? And, even more important, who had the IDEA of lighting the fuse?

Before the starting pistol is fired someone has to have the idea of firing it. The idea of flying existed in someone's mind long before the first airplane was invented. Man went to the moon in his imagination long before the first rocket was designed. When we look at a beautiful cathedral, what do we see? We see an idea. Before the mason cut the first stone, before the architect drew up the first plans, someone had to have the idea of erecting a building in which to worship God. Nothing can happen until the idea has been conceived. In the beginning was—THE IDEA.

An idea cannot create itself. Nor can it be created in a mindless vacuum, by a mindless creator. An idea presupposes a mind, creation a creator. Not so, says the skeptic; there is no Mind, there is no Creator. "Physicists," writes Paul Davies (ibid.), "are now talking about 'the self-creating Universe': a cosmos that erupts into existence spontaneously." Maybe it did. But that is not the same as saying that the *idea* of a spontaneously erupting Universe erupted spontaneously. And if the skeptic says that an idea is simply the product of electrical impulses vibrating in the brain, then I have to ask: who had the idea of creating electrical impulses? If I am then told that in a self-creating universe electrical impulses don't need a Creator, they create themselves, I can only reply that that wasn't the question. The question was:

4

who had the idea that self-creating electrical impulses should be able to create themselves, that self-creating electrical impulses would be a good idea? You see, I am not talking about electrical impulses, I am talking about the idea of electrical impulses.

The idea of electrical impulses had to exist before electrical impulses could be created. Human minds conceive ideas, they do not create them. Nor do they create the possibility of there being ideas to be conceived. Before the wheel was invented, the idea of the wheel existed independent of the mind in which it was conceived. Wheels did not exist, but the possibility of wheels being conceived did. We should not confuse the idea with the conception and fructification of the idea.

Then there are the mechanics of evolution. And what mechanics! To ensure that the primeval sludge would be receptive to, and supportive of, life; to ensure that one form of life would evolve into another, then another . . . then another . . . ad infinitum, suggests an engineering feat of miraculous proportions. But that was the easy bit! The hard bit was having the idea in the first place!

Then there is the question of design. And what design! The atheist-biologist, however, disagrees. The existence of chance variations in life's structures, he says, caused by the endless struggle for survival, proves that design (and therefore a designer) does not exist. Not so, say I; it proves no such thing. Why should design itself not evolve? Why should it be static and immutable? The possibility of chance variations could have been built into the grand design in order that the Grand Design itself would evolve and survive. So that what we call "chance" variations, may in fact be "planned" variations, inasmuch as the possibility (or rather, certainty) of them occurring by "chance" may have been incorporated into the Original Design by the Original Designer. If, however, the biologists are right then what we see as design is not design at all, but something else; though I have to say that from where I stand it does look suspiciously like design!

"Look at the fact of design!" says Michael Green in his book *You Must Be Joking*. "At every level the world of nature shows evidence of design. Think of the focusing equipment of an eye,

5

of the radar of a bat, of the built-in gyroscope of a swallow, of the camouflage of a nesting pheasant. Or think of the perfect harmony of the laws of physics. Reflect on the marvel of conception and birth. At every point there is evidence of a great Designer. Even John Stuart Mill, a strong opponent of Christianity, came to the conclusion at the end of his life that 'the argument from design is irresistible.' . . . Einstein, too, spoke of his 'humble admiration for the illimitably superior Spirit who reveals himself in the slight details which we can perceive with our frail mind.' After Einstein had propounded his theory of relativity, and after its general acceptance following the Michelson-Morley experiment, the experiment was repeated and gave different results. But nobody doubted the relativity theory! Everyone assumed (rightly as it turned out) that the results must be due to experimental error, because the theory was too good, *too rational,* to be false. In other words, the physicists themselves were operating on the assumption of design in the Universe, however much they might have claimed to be following merely experimental results."

It is possible, of course, for something to resemble design without actually being design. One can throw a pot of paint onto a canvas and produce a "design." But to suggest that the fantastic design that runs through the whole fabric of creation only resembles design, that it was thrown onto the cosmic canvas by a pseudo-artist who knew nothing about art, is grotesquely absurd. We only have to compare a design produced by one of those modern artists who hurls paint onto a canvas in random fashion, with, say a Rembrandt, to see that the former, though perhaps attractive to the eye, lacks the verisimilitude and purpose of the latter. It is for the reader to decide whether the Universe is a work of art (a signed original at that) or just a purposeless smudge of paint.

According to the Oxford Illustrated Dictionary, evolution is "the origination of species of animals and plants by process of development from earlier forms." Note the words "from earlier forms." Evolution is the process by which one thing evolves into another. It is not the evolving of nothing into something. Nothing can come from nothing, even though it may sometimes look that way. (This is not to dispute the Judaeo-Christian belief that

6

God created the Universe out of nothing. Rather to point out that before God could create something from nothing, he had to have the *idea* of creating something from nothing. And as an idea is not nothing, then in that sense it cannot be correct to say that the Universe was created out of nothing).

Something cannot be created by *nothing*. Existence cannot be created by nonexistence. Can a table be created by nothing? A silly question. But is it any sillier than asking if the Universe could have been created by nothing? The Universe is no different from a table. It consists, like the table, of a collection of atoms. We know that the table was fashioned by a carpenter, even though we didn't see him do it. How do we know? Just take a look at it. And how do we know that the Universe was designed and fashioned by a Master Designer and an Original Creator? Same way. Just take a look at it. "Voltaire," says Besterman *(Voltaire)*, "examined the laws of nature, the mechanics of the senses and ideas, and concluded that none of these things can exist in themselves and must be a part of a prime cause."

How could something—a table, a mountain, a universe—anything—which did not exist, be influenced to exist if there were a total absence of any thing or any influence whatsoever? Everything that exists, exists because someone or something or some influence has caused it to exist. Whatever it is that caused the Universe to exist, may be physical or spiritual, material or immaterial, a universal law, an abstract thought, a truth, a word or an idea. But it cannot be nothing. And even if the Universe were uncaused or caused itself, there would have to be a reason why it was uncaused or caused itself. And reason is not nothing.

The "most far-reaching, deepest and most fundamental of all questions," according to Martin Heidegger (1889–1976), German existentialist philosopher, was first formulated by Gottfried Wilhelm Leibniz (1646–1716), German mathematician and philosopher: Why is there something rather than nothing, i.e., why does the Universe exist rather than not exist?

This unanswerable question is answered by the theist without a moment's hesitation. There is something rather than nothing, because God ordained that it should be so. This irrational response serves only to irritate the scientist. To him, the attribution to God of everything that cannot be explained rationally, is the ultimate cop-out. The trouble is, however, that the theist's answer is the only one (apart from "I don't know") that makes sense.

We may be sure that there is a reason why there is something rather than nothing—even though we cannot guess what the reason is. But suppose we turn the question around: what if there were nothing rather than something? Well, first, the question couldn't be asked, because there would be no one to ask it. Second, no reason is required for there to be nothing. Only something requires an explanation for its existence. Nothing is simply the absence of something. It would not be sensible, for instance, to ask why there aren't any five-legged dogs with four heads and three tails. There aren't because there aren't. And it would be equally senseless to say that there must be a reason why there is nothing whatsoever. Because if there were nothing whatsoever then reason itself would not exist. Which is absurd because—and here I frankly admit that I am taking a leap of faith—reason has a necessary existence, it cannot not exist.

So for me, the logical (with a dash of faith thrown in) answer to Liebniz's question is: There is something rather than nothing because it could not be otherwise; which is another way of saying because God ordained that it should be so. Which is another way of saying that God, like reason, has a necessary existence.

If this answer, Mr. Scientist, is not acceptable to you, then pray, let us have yours.

But how does evolution fit into all this? Didn't Darwin disprove the existence of an original creator? No of course he didn't. The theory of evolution concerns only a tiny fraction of the history of planet Earth, and even then only the evolution of species not the origin of life itself. To put Darwin into perspective, the history of Earth (depending on which book you read) goes something like this: Earth was formed about 4,500 million years ago from interstellar gas and dust particles. For a million years or so, its surface consisted solely of molten rock, volcanos and boiling lava, enveloped in poisonous gases. The sun was unable to penetrate Earth's atmosphere. It was dark, perpetual night. There were no oceans, lakes or rivers; no life of any description. Slowly, the surface cooled down and solidified. Steam turned into water, and it rained virtually nonstop for hundreds of thousands of years. Gradually the atmosphere cleared. It stopped raining. The sun came out. And, lo and behold, 700 million years or so later, life, in the form of bacteria-like cells, started to appear in the newly formed oceans of the world. Evolution had begun!

Just what caused these first microscopic stirrings of life is unknown, although a small band of cosmologists (small in number, that is, not in stature) believes that the germs of creation did not originate here on Earth, but in outer space. "Life had already evolved to a high information standard long before the Earth was born," say Fred Hoyle and N.C. Wickramasinghe, in their book *Evolution from Space*. However, be that as it may, it is not relevant here and will be discussed later in Chapter 9.

These primitive germs remained unchanged for over a million years, before evolving into the simplest forms of marine plant life—single-cell algae, fungi, mosses, liverworts, etc. Nothing much happened for another 2,000 million years, until the first minute forms of protozoa (animal life) started to appear in the sea. These resembled tiny blobs of jelly, some of which later grew protective shells. Then came corals, sponges, polypods, flatworms, trilobites and various shrimp-like creatures. Then crabs, spiders and a multitude of insects.

Fishes—the first true vertebrates—appeared roughly 700-800 million years ago, followed by more complicated forms of life. Amphibians left the water, discarded their fins, grew legs and gave rise to saurians (the lizard family), of which there were hundreds of species—from the enormous dinosaurs weighing up to 100 tons, to small creatures no more than a few inches long. From the saurian species, birds gradually evolved. The first mammals arrived on the scene about 650 million years ago, and slowly evolved along various branches of the evolutionary tree, until finally, in the last few seconds of cosmic history, man emerged!

There is no unanimity of opinion as to when man first arose. Calculations made by scientists at Yale University, based on the rate of change in the DNA structure of humans and chimpanzees, estimate that the divergence of man and ape occurred about seven million years ago. But fossil evidence, which anthropologists regard as more reliable, suggests that the time scale could be more like twenty-five million years.

The oldest, most complete and best-preserved skeleton of any erect-walking human ancestor was discovered by Don Johanson, Curator of Physical Anthropology and Director of Scientific Research at the Cleveland Museum of Natural History, in a remote part of Ethiopia, on November 30, 1974. It was estimated to be 3.4 million years old, and Johanson named it "Lucy," after the Beatles record "Lucy in the Sky with Diamonds," which was being played on the camp tape recorder at the time. (Source: *Lucy: The Beginnings of Humankind*, by Donald C. Johanson and Maitland A. Edey.) This female skeleton shows that human beings (or near-human beings) with some apelike features (thigh bone, pelvis, for example) were walking upright on two legs nearly three and a half million years ago. But it gives no clue as to when the divergence between man and ape first occurred. Lucy's ancestors may have been in that stage of development for millions of years, the time span could have been vast indeed. Donald C. Johanson and Maitland A. Edey (ibid): "We can picture human evolution as starting with a primitive apelike type that gradually, over a long period of time, began to be less and less apelike and more manlike. There was no abrupt crossover from ape to human, but probably a rather fuzzy time of in-between types that would be difficult to classify either way. We have no fossils yet that tell us what went on during that in-between time. Therefore the handiest way of separating the newer types from their ape ancestors is to lump together all those that stood up on their hind legs. That group of men and near-men is called hominids.

"I am a hominid. I am a human being. I belong to the genus *Homo* and to the species *sapiens*: thinking man. Perhaps I should say wise or knowing man—a man who is smart enough to recognize that he is a man ... *Homo sapiens* began to emerge a hundred thousand—perhaps two or three hundred thousand —years ago ... If one goes back far enough, one finds oneself dealing with a different kind of creature. On the hominid line the earliest ones are too primitive to be called humans."

There is a vast grey area of which we know nothing; a period of some twenty million years about which we can only speculate. But what is clear is that man was an unconscionable long time a-coming! From boiling sludge to modern man in 4,500 million years.

The question that immediately springs to mind is: Why so long? Why was the main character brought on so late in the play? But how do we know that man is the main character? And how do we know that it's late in the play?

We seem to exist in a hazardous time,
Driftin' along here through space;
Nobody knows just how we begun,
Or how fur we've gone in the race.

Ben King (*Evolution*)

Perhaps man isn't the leading man after all, only his understudy. Maybe in a few million years' time our successors will look back on us with the same degree of distaste that we look back on our apelike ancestors. As for it being late in the play, perhaps we have only just seen the first act, with the main plot yet to unfold. The Universe is reckoned to be 18,000 million years old. Which, to man, with his time-obsessed view of existence, is a long time. But to an Infinite Being, with an infinite past, an infinite present and an infinite future, with an infinity of moments between one moment and the next, it may be just an instant. Any period of time, however long, would be no time at all to a Being for whom time did not exist. With all the time in the world at his disposal, why should God be in a hurry?

At what point the divine spark first entered man, is the most intriguing question of all. My guess is that it was already there, in code form, when the big bang banged.

Man's transformation from ape to *Homo sapiens* didn't happen overnight. It took millions of years for the evolutionary process to work its magic. "Fossils exist of an apelike creature, a possible remote human ancestor known as Ramapithecus, dating from around nine million years ago," says Elaine Morgan in *The Aquatic Ape*. " . . . [But between nine million and three and a half million years ago] comes the gap [of five and a half million years] in the fossil record that Richard Leakey, the famous American anthropologist, aptly described as 'a yawning

11

void.' And it was during this blank period that man's ancestors apparently embarked on the divergent evolutionary path leading to their separation."

Evolution doesn't proceed in a single straight line, at a slow steady pace. When life originally began, it took off in many different directions, and traversed many different routes. Plants went one way, animal life another. Fish, insects, reptiles, birds and mammals, all "selected" the routes that suited them best, the routes they had been programmed to take. Not all species made it; some fell by the wayside and failed to survive.

Fred Hoyle (*The Intelligent Universe*) believes that evolution progresses in fits and starts: "Perhaps the mutations, and the evolution from species to species which the mutations produce, came in bursts. Perhaps there are short periods when all hell is let loose, with comparatively long periods of quiescence between? The fossil record is not complete, perhaps because these periods are largely missing . . . In my view evolution proceeds, not in small steps but in major leaps."

Is this what happened with man? Was he one of Hoyle's "major leaps" at a time when frenzied activity was taking place? There is an enormous span in the planet's history when one or more of these extraordinary evolutionary "leaps" could have occurred, although it would be wrong to deduce from this that man's predecessors did not travel along the same branch of the tree of life for millions of years hand in hand with a species of ape.

Long before *Homo sapiens* evolved, there was a parting of the ways. Man took the high road and apes took the low. Men are not monkeys; but men and monkeys did evolve from a common stock.

The biological connection between men and monkeys is obvious for all to see. Whereas there is no way that man could be directly related to, say, the crocodile, the giraffe, the ant or the flea, one only has to look at the ape and observe its behaviour to see that we both share a common ancestry. Of course man was never an ape. For when he was an ape, he wasn't man!

Even among modern primates there are many disparate species. The ape family, for example, comprises five different types: chimpanzees, gorillas, orangutans, gibbons, and siamongs. All these animals have, in varying degrees, the ability to walk upright on two legs. Monkeys, tarsiers and lemurs on the other hand do not. Monkeys have longer spines than apes and are consequently better runners. Apes are good "swingers," and cleverer than monkeys. Orangutans are "four-handed"—they use their legs like a second pair of hands. The gorilla spends most of his time on the ground, tarsiers and gibbons most of theirs in the trees.

In a Dutch TV documentary, a family of chimpanzees was filmed in its natural habitat in a zoo in Holland, unaware that it was being observed. The chimpanzees' antics were quite extraordinary and bore an uncanny resemblance to the behaviour of human beings. The film clearly showed that these animals are not just adept at copying human behaviour, or doing what they are trained to do. It demonstrated that they possess innate intelligence, the perspicacity to overcome problems and the ability to make and use primitive tools. (The chimp incidentally, is the only animal apart from man to be able to recognize itself in a mirror).

Fred Hoyle (*The Intelligent Universe*) tells us that the chromosomes of a chimpanzee are little different from those of a man, and need refined techniques to tell them apart. But before we press the point too far, let us listen to Elaine Morgan (*The Aquatic Ape*):

"In 1871 Charles Darwin published *The Descent of Man* proposing that man and apes are descended from a common ancestor. No anthropologist today questions his basic premise. There is total agreement about how to explain the similarities between men and apes. The impression is sometimes given that there is an equal consensus on how to explain the differences between them. This impression is misleading. Considering the very close genetic relationship that has been established by comparison of biochemical properties of blood proteins, protein structure and DNA and immunological responses, the differences between a man and a chimpanzee are more astonishing than the resemblances. They include structural differences in the skeleton, the muscles, the skin, and the brain; differences in posture associated with an unique method of locomotion; differences in social organization; and finally the acquisition of speech and tool

13

using, together with the dramatic increase in intellectual ability which has led scientists to name their own species Homo sapiens sapiens—wise wise man. During the period when these remarkable evolutionary changes were taking place, other closely related ape-like species changed only very slowly, and with far less remarkable results. It is hard to resist the conclusion that something must have happened to the ancestors of Homo sapiens which did not happen to the ancestors of gorillas and chimpanzees."

Yes, indeed! Something did happen! But what? One or more of Hoyle's "major leaps"? As has been remarked, there was plenty of time for these to have taken place.

The evolutionary road from ape to man is not without its twists and turns. It has been a bumpy ride, as the anthropologists testify. John Reader (*Missing Links*): "The fossil record shows, [Louis Leakey] said, that most, if not all, vertebrate lineages have their dead branches along which related forms have evolved to extinction, and he saw no reason why the *Homo* lineage should be any different. In Leakey's view, the hominid line, leading to man, and the pongid line, leading to the apes, branched away from their common ancestral stock about 20 million years ago (Leakey, L.S.B., 1969), and he believed there have been many more branches since then."

Richard E. Leakey and Roger Lewin (*Origins*): "It is now apparent that the ancestral line that led to modern humans stretches back five, perhaps six, million years. And it is clear that for a large part of that time our ancestors shared their environment with two types of creatures with whom they were closely related but who eventually became extinct. These evolutionary cousins are called the australopithecines, one of whom was slightly built while the other was much more robust.

"The two forms of australopithecine and the *Homo* ancestor shared at least two things: first, they shared a common ancestor, a small ape-like creature called *Ramapithecus* who first appeared at least twelve million years ago . . . and second, they all stood and walked upright . . . these three evolutionary cousins [were] known collectively as hominids."

The term *hominid* is used to describe that species of creature that is loosely regarded as "half-ape, half-man." From the nu-

14

merous fossils that have been found, the most recent hominids are believed to have been short in stature (about four to five feet tall), completely erect, with "man-like" bodies and "ape-like" heads. Mary Leakey, in her book *Olduvai Gorge,* writes: "Recent discoveries of fossilized hominid footprints in the Pliocene deposits at Laetoli, dated 3.6 million years ago, show that the Pliocene hominids were entirely upright and bipedal. Furthermore, the structure of their feet is indistinguishable from the feet of living peoples who habitually walk bare footed. . . . The evidence from the hominid foot-prints . . . leaves no doubt . . . that even in Pliocene times man's ancestors walked with a free-striding, fully upright, bipedal gait."

The creatures who made the fossil footprints, which were preserved in volcanic ash and discovered in Laetoli, Tanzania, in 1978, undoubtedly walked upright, and so were well on the way (evolutionarily speaking) to becoming fully human. What we don't know, however, is: How large were their brains, and did they use tools? (It is assumed by most experts that their brains were bigger than an ape's, although only slightly larger than a modern chimpanzee's, and that they did not use tools—but more of this anon.)

There has been considerable disagreement among anthropologists as to which of the three uniquely human attributes—bipedalism (walking upright on two legs), brain expansion, and speech—came first. In 1912 Grafton Elliot Smith, a distinguished professor of anatomy at the University of London who pioneered work on the function and evolution of the vertebrate brain, was convinced that "the brain led the way," but subsequent fossil findings have apparently proved him wrong. John Reader *(Missing Links)*: "The human-like characteristics of the Laetoli footprints imply that hominids acquired the bipedal gait considerably more than 3.6 million years ago, says [Dr. R. J.] Clarke [in the *South African Journal of Science*]. Yet the Afar fossils [skeletons discovered in the Afar region of northeastern Ethiopia, and believed to be about three million years old] show that a small-brained hominid with some ape-like cranial features was still living three million years ago. So that if bipedalism had developed while wholly ape-like features were retained, the very early ancestors of mankind are likely to have been creatures whose skulls would merit classification as apes while their feet could have belonged to a hominid, says Dr. Clarke.

"The Laetoli footprints [says Reader] are entirely human. Unlike the form of the ape footprint, they show a well-developed arch to the foot and no divergence of the big toe. The size of the feet and stride suggests the larger individual [there were two sets of footprints] stood about 140 centimetres tall, and the smaller about 120 centimetres . . . there can be no doubt that the Laetoli hominids had already acquired the habitual, upright, bipedal, free-striding gait of modern man 3.6 million years ago."

The evidence that bipedalism came before brain expansion is compelling but by no means conclusive. If hominids were walking on two feet more than 3.6 million years ago, yet had the brain of an apelike creature three million years ago, this would indeed suggest that bipedalism came first. ("The hypothesis of bipedal precedence was confirmed"—Reader; ibid.) However, it must be pointed out that Reader and Clarke are comparing *footprints* of one creature with *skeletons* of another. We have no way of knowing how large or small the brain was of the hominid who made the footprints. Footprints only tell us that the creature who made them walked on two legs, they do not tell us the size of his brain. (If only the skeleton of the creature that made the footprints had been found too!) Also, it may be pertinent to ask: How certain can we be of the accuracy of the dating processes? If either one or the other of the fossil finds has been incorrectly dated, then the conclusions drawn will be invalid.

But an even bigger mystery is: "Why, of all the mammals that have ever walked the earth, did only one group choose to walk erect? . . . [Bipedalism] is not really the best way of getting around in a hostile world. And yet it is the way our ancestors chose in order to become human. Why?" (Donald C. Johanson and Maitland A. Edey; *Lucy: The Beginnings of Humankind*).

And why did the brain start to expand? The answer to this latter question, although pretty obvious, only begs the question. The brain had to expand to accommodate the thinking process. The question begged, of course, is: Why did man start to think?

Speech must have followed hard on the heels of brain enlargement. To a thinking animal speech is essential. Apes, who

16

can't think, have no need to speak. The linguistic requirements of a nonthinking animal are very modest. To squeal when you're hurt, chatter when you're excited, roar when you're angry, and purr when you're happy, do not require articulate speech and an extensive vocabulary.

Once the thinking process really got going and there were thoughts to be expressed, speech became inevitable. One day man would be required—because his brain would grow so large, and his heart so big—to express the most fantastic thoughts to his fellowman. And unless at some time or other he could find a way of communicating his thoughts and ideas to those around him, words like the following could never have been written:

> The quality of mercy is not strain'd;
> It droppeth as the gentle rain from heaven
> Upon the place beneath; it is twice blest;
> It blesseth him that gives and him that takes;
> 'Tis mightiest in the mightiest; it becomes
> The throned monarch better than his crown;
> His sceptre shows the force of temporal power,
> The attribute to awe and majesty,
> Wherein doth sit the dread and fear of kings;
> But mercy is above this sceptred sway;
> It is enthroned in the hearts of kings,
> It is an attribute to God himself;
> And earthly power doth then show likest God's
> When mercy seasons justice.
>
> Shakespeare, *The Merchant of Venice*

Imagine having those kinds of thoughts in your head, and those kinds of feelings in your heart, and not being able to express them! There is no mystery as to why man learned to speak. Had he not, his head would have exploded and his heart would have burst!

Brain enlargement, thinking and speech, form a cranial continuum. Thinking is inseparable from language; and language is inseparable from speech. So, to those who (vide Elaine Morgan's *The Aquatic Ape*) are puzzled as to "why men speak and

17

apes do not," I would simply say: Men speak because they have something to say; apes don't because they haven't.

When our ancestors started to think, it was like putting a match to tinder. Their brains had already begun to grow to enable them to think; and now that they could think, it was "humanly" impossible for them to keep their thoughts to themselves. Language and speech followed as surely as night follows day. Within no time at all (cosmically speaking), these "intelligent" creatures were up on their feet and talking with their friends. Talking because for the first time in their evolution they had something to say. Up on their feet because—well, we'll come to that in a moment.

At what stage man acquired a soul is the biggest mystery of all. Perhaps it evolved in the same way that the body did, and is likewise still evolving. Maybe it has been there since day one waiting for man to grow into it. If biological man evolved, why not spiritual man?

What we do know is that somewhere in the murky mists of time, *Homo sapiens* emerged. The original seed, planted in the fertile pastures of the primeval sludge four and a half thousand million years ago, finally flowered. The transition from ape to hominid, and from hominid to man, may possibly have taken twenty-five million years. Then again, it may have taken only two or three million. We shall probably never know.

Before *Homo* (man) became *sapiens* (wise), when he was still in his hominid teens, something caused him to stand erect. What?

The brain had enlarged to accommodate the thinking process (or the thinking process had caused the brain to enlarge). Perceptual thinking (the sort that chimpanzees are capable of) had evolved into conceptual thinking (the kind that is unique to man). The tool user had become the toolmaker and tool designer (it obviously requires a higher degree of intelligence to design and make tools than it does to use tools that already exist; it also takes foresight). It was time now for "man" to stand up and be counted!

Several theories have been advanced to explain why man made this fantastic leap forward—the three most popular of which are as follows:

1. *"Man" stood up in order to see over the tall grasses on the savannah (treeless plains) onto which he had decided to move.*

Towards the end of the Miocene Age, about five million years ago, severe climatic changes caused the vast bands of forests around the tropical and subtropical regions of the Earth to shrink and decline. This forced our apelike ancestors (so the story goes), who, by this time, had adopted a semi-upright posture, to venture out onto the savannah in search of food. Having lost some of their vegetarian source of nourishment in the shrunken and denuded forests, which had also become rather overcrowded, they began to hunt and devour the animals that roamed the plains. And by adopting a fully erect posture, they were better able to see over the tall grasses and detect their prey.

Frankly, I do not find this at all convincing. If that was the reason, then why didn't the animals they were hunting follow suit and stand up to see *their* predators coming? Also, if "man's" brain at the time was, as we have been told, no bigger than an ape's, how did he manage to work out that standing up was a good idea? And why didn't his ape cousins, whose brains were supposedly commensurate with his, do the same and follow him out onto the plains?

Surely the truth is that this creature, who was clever enough to change the habits of an evolutionary lifetime, and brave enough to venture out of the security of the forests into what was, to him, the great unknown (a feat in its way equal to Columbus's journey to America, and Armstrong's to the moon), was no ordinary ape; that his brain, if not bigger than an ape's, certainly worked a whole lot better!

2. *"Man" stood upright in order to escape his predators.*

This theory is even less convincing. For "man" was much slower on his two legs than his predators were on their four. It was only by using his superior intelligence that "man" managed to overcome his lack of mobility. To escape his predators he would have done better to have remained on all fours.

3. *"Man" stood upright in order to free his hands to use tools and to carry weapons.*

A likely story! "Man" didn't need to be fully upright to use tools. He could have used them just as well sitting on his haunches. As for carrying weapons, if he hadn't been so foolish

19

as to adopt an inefficient method of locomotion, he wouldn't have needed weapons to defend himself; he could more easily have run away. (It was the necessity to defend himself *after* he had given up quadrupedalism that induced him to invent weapons.)

"The idea [that 'man' originally stood up in order to have his hands free to carry tools and weapons] never did make sense," says C. Owen Lovejoy, an American locomotion expert. So far, so good. But listen to what follows! "Now it is exploded by the Laetoli and Hadar fossils. Those animals were bipedal, but that had nothing to do with tools. They were walking that way maybe a million years before their descendants began using tools" (quoted by Donald C. Johanson and Maitland A. Edey, ibid).

This I find quite astonishing. To assert that a manlike creature was walking upright on two legs *a million years before* he began using tools is, in my view, complete nonsense. Is it conceivable that this creature, having uniquely adopted a method of locomotion no animal had ever done before or has ever done since, walked around *with his hands free* for a million years before learning how to use tools? *A million years?* I don't believe it!

John Reader *(Missing Links)* goes even further: "Yet although hominids were bipedal and free to develop manipulative skills at Laetoli 3.6 million years ago not a single artifact or introduced stone has been found anywhere among the eighty square kilometre deposits. The earliest tools known to date are about two million years old. Hominids, it seems, were walking erect with their hands free for at least 1.6 million years before the advent of stone tools."

What on earth did "man" do with his hands during this vast time span of 1–1.6 million years? Why had evolutionary pressures freed them? To do what? He no longer needed them for swinging from branch to branch. He didn't require them for running. So what did he use them for? For picking fruit off trees? For fetching and carrying? For putting food into his mouth? Big deal!

It doesn't make sense. For remember, we are not talking about a minor mutation—or even a major one—we are talking about a quantum leap forward! If the experts tell us that the fossils indicate that this unique, free-striding creature took 1–1.6

million years after his hands had been freed to make and use tools, then all I can say is that the fossils have been misinterpreted or wrongly dated.

To appreciate the magnitude of this mutation, and its implications for the human race, we only have to consider what would have happened (or rather, not happened) had our ancestors not made it. If our hands had not been freed, we would still be living in the jungle. Everything a civilized community possesses, needs hands to make it and hands to use it. Without hands there'd be no houses, no furniture, no clothes, no food, no shops, no TV, no cars, no airplanes, no artists, no writers, no poets, no musicians. "The hand when it uses a tool," wrote J. Bronowski (*The Ascent of Man*), "[is] an instrument of discovery . . . We see it every time a child learns to couple hand and tool together—to lace its shoes, to thread a needle, to fly a kite or to play a penny whistle."

Only man with his freed hands is capable of producing and using the paraphernalia of civilization. A pig, however intelligent, could not make or drive a car. A horse, however musical, could not make or play the violin. An elephant, however artistic, could not paint a picture. "The hand," said Bronowski (ibid), "is the cutting edge of the mind. Civilization is not a collection of finished artifacts, it is the elaboration of processes. In the end, the mark of man is the refinement of the hand in action."

It is the devastating combination of hand and brain that has made the human species what it is. Is it likely, then, that the two vital concomitants of the human condition—brain enlargement and bipedalism—evolved separately? No. These attributes, which uniquely set man apart from the rest of the animal kingdom, are interrelated and interdependent. Does it not make philosophical as well as biological sense that they evolved together?

There are over one and a quarter million species of animals living on Earth, some of them stretching back over 500 million years (compare this with man's measly few million), yet none of them, not one, with the exception of man has developed intelligence, speech and upright walking. Why? Why did man's brain, and not the chimpanzee's, the crocodile's, the beetle's or the bug's, start to get bigger? Why don't cockroaches compose sonatas, write poems and paint pictures? Why does no other animal walk upright on two legs? And why do men—and men alone—contemplate their existence and worship their Creator? Could it be that man is, after all, a special creation?

Once our hominid ancestors felt the first stirrings of intelligence, the die was cast. There was no way that they would be content to spend the rest of their history up a tree. One day this intelligent creature would be required by his evolutionary stars to travel the world, explore the continents, sail the seven seas, climb the highest mountains, even hurtle himself into space and walk on the moon. He had to start some time, and his genes told him that this was the time!

Let us try to imagine what this primitive creature must have felt as he descended from the trees and gradually became aware that he was different from the other animals around him. At first he would not be conscious of his superior intelligence. His thinking would be very basic—only marginally more perceptive than an ape's. Shuffling around in the forests, adopting a semi-upright posture for much of the time, he would perceive the need for tools. So he would set about making them. His first efforts, crudely worked pieces of flint, were so primitive that they would have been virtually unrecognizable as tools to modern eyes. Later they would become more sophisticated; and the need to eat meat would lead this perceptive creature to invent weapons to kill animals. And so, "man" the hunter was born. As he became more aware of himself and his environment, his curiosity grew. He began to wonder what lay on the other side of the hill, beyond his own little world, his own little community, his own little cave . . . So he set off to find out!

But before he set off, he stood up. Why? What made this ancestor of ours give up efficient quadrupedalism, which had held him and his long line of antecedents in good stead for millions of years, for inefficient bipedalism? It must have been something important, something philosophically and psychologically significant, and not just a *biological* mutation. What?

I think it was this: slowly, imperceptibly, this intelligent creature came to realise that he was a "superior" creation. His newly acquired intellectual status (a grandiose term, but that is what it was) told him that he was different from the other

22

animals around him. He could think; they couldn't. He could speak; they couldn't. He could make and use tools; they couldn't. He was organised; they weren't. He knew he was not just another animal—he was superior!

It was at this point that he began to experience a new kind of sensation, something he had never experienced before—PRIDE!

Now what happens when we are filled with pride? That's right, we pull back our shoulders, chuck out our chests, and draw ourselves up to our full height. Walking tall, we call it. (If anyone doubts the physical effect that pride has on a human being, let him compare the heads-held-high, shoulders-back marching of a victorious army, with the hang-dog shuffling of a defeated one.) And what did our remote ancestors do? You've guessed it. They did the same. Pride welled up inside these "superior" creatures. They felt the instinctive urge to pull back their shoulders and stand erect. (It's difficult to feel superior when you're shuffling around on all fours.) There is no way a unique, intelligent, thinking, speaking, self-conscious creature would be content forever to look at the ground and not feel the need to stand erect and stare up into the heavens above.

"Man" had now reached a crucial juncture in his evolutionary history. He was cleverer than the other animals. And he knew it. This feeling of superiority was insidious, and would have a profound effect on his future spiritual development. Although intelligent, he wasn't intelligent enough to ask himself why he had been endowed with this special gift, and who had done the endowing. He regarded himself as superior *in kind* to his less gifted, less intelligent cousins, little realizing that whether he was superior or not, depended on how he used the gifts with which he had been endowed. Not knowing for what purpose he had been created, he had no means of knowing whether or not he was superior. If man is superior, it is because the Creator of all species, who alone knows why we have been created, thinks he is, not because man thinks he is. We are undoubtedly special, but that does not mean we are superior. A broken-down old car that won't go is not superior to a spark plug that does its job properly; an evil pervert who preys on little children is not superior to the lowly silkworm assiduously spinning its cocoon of silk.

To be puffed up with pride, to be filled with a sense of self-importance, is to worship oneself. (By *pride* I mean "the overweening opinion of one's own quality, merits, etc., which expresses itself in arrogant bearing and conduct," and not the laudable sense of satisfaction one feels in a job well done, a mission accomplished, a mountain climbed—always provided, of course, that it does not lead us to a sense of superiority of our own intrinsic worth.)

The first and ultimate sin is to believe and to act as if we are better than our Creator. And it was when man first experienced the arrogance of pride, and succumbed to its temptations, that he "fell." (They do say, don't they, that "pride goeth before a fall"?) Pride—"the overweening opinion of one's own quality and merit," the belief that one race or creed or individual is superior to another—has, throughout the ages, led to the most heinous crimes. Had the Nazis not believed that the "master race" was superior to Jews, gypsies, and Slavs, they would not have murdered these peoples in their millions. (The Nazis did not kill them because they hated them; they killed them because they considered them inferior.) Had the white races not believed that they were superior to the blacks, they would not have enslaved them for hundreds of years. Had the medieval Christians not believed that their faith was superior to that of others, they would not have persecuted and burnt at the stake thousands of their fellow theists.

To believe that one is superior, is to believe that others are inferior—a judgement we have no right to make. One person may be taller and stronger, more handsome and more intelligent than another. But he cannot be superior. One nation may be cleverer and more advanced than another. But it cannot be superior. Human beings are unequal physically, mentally and spiritually. But they are all equal in the sight of God, all equally entitled to his love. No one is superior and no one is inferior. In judging ourselves superior, we place ourselves on a higher pedestal than God. We usurp his position, and in effect set up in business on our own account. If I were God, I think I would be disposed to forgive man anything, except him thinking and acting as if he were better than me.

Pride, not sex, was the "forbidden fruit," man's first and

most insidious false god. When God made men and women, he knew that they'd be more than just good friends. Indeed, had they not been, the human race would never have got started. We were programmed to go forth and multiply in the only way available to us. And when God gave us the necessary equipment and the desire to use it, he knew perfectly well that he was making us an offer we couldn't refuse.

At some stage in man's evolution, back in the mists of time, he looked up into the sky and was filled with an overwhelming sense of awe—and the need to worship. Anything: the sun, the moon, the seasons, thunder and lightning, his ancestors, the spirits, fire, graven images, the phallus . . . anything that he couldn't understand. It was then that he first experienced humility. But it was too late! Having eaten the forbidden fruit of pride, he had acquired the taste and has been enjoying it ever since.

In 1859 the imagination of Victorian England was captured by the publication of Darwin's theory of evolution by natural selection, which caused one of the greatest upheavals in modern philosophical thought. But the Church was not amused! To suggest that God's special creation—man—was nothing more than a "glorified monkey," was not only obscene but downright blasphemous. And it was a long, long time before the theologians could bring themselves to accept the biological fact that man did not begin life in the Garden of Eden but up a tree. Even now there are some believers who will not accept this unpalatable truth.

Like it or not, the evolutionary story has to be (broadly) true. Fully grown men and women didn't suddenly drop out of the skies or land from spaceships. Even if they did, that wouldn't explain how they came to be created in the first place. To make human beings, you need sperm and eggs—and a womb in which they can incubate. Now, there may possibly be sperm and egg banks in outer space; but there certainly aren't any womb banks. And a womb cannot function on its own; it has to be located inside the body of a woman. "Women with wombs" evolved over aeons of time, just as "men with sperm" did.

Why is it that some people find it so difficult to come to terms with the evolutionary facts of life? Clearly they regard the notion

25

of our having evolved from monkeys disgusting. Why? Do they find it disgusting that only a few weeks (not a few million years!) before we were born, we were a foetus? And a few months before that, a shapeless blob of jelly? And before that, a speck of spermatozoon and an egg mating in the uterus? And before that. . . ?

Living in some remote corners of the globe today are primitive peoples who bear more than a fleeting resemblance to our early ancestors. Do they disgust us? If they do then there is something wrong with us not with them. The most primitive person on Earth has the potential of a genius or a saint, whereas an ape has the potential of . . . an ape. Human beings, however primitive, however uncultured and uncivilized, can and do love their fellow humans. And can and do fall down on their knees and worship God, something no ape has ever done in the twenty-odd million years it has inhabited the earth. If man is nothing more than a "glorified monkey," if man is not a special creation, why hasn't the monkey, with so much more time at its disposal, developed intelligence, speech, and upright walking? And learned how to compose music, write poetry, paint pictures, and build hospitals and churches? Biologically, man did descend from a monkey-like species. But biology is only part of the story. There is more to man than flesh and blood and chromosomes and earthly appetites.

Darwin's theory of biological evolution describes the changes taking place in existing organic life, it makes no attempt to explain the existence of life itself.

The weakness of the Darwinian theory is that it doesn't explain where the various species come from. There is an obvious connection between members of the same species, but none between members of different species. No direct link, for instance, has ever been suggested between the ant and the elephant, the spider and the horse, the dragonfly and the dog.

"There is a misapprehension," said Fred Hoyle in the Border Television Series and book, *Revelations: Glimpses of Reality,* "about what Darwinism or the theory of biological evolution really amounts to. The idea in many people's minds is that it's natural selection. It simply says that the varieties and forms which are best suited to survive will survive. But it does absolutely nothing for evolution. If you had a truck load of potatoes you could select them for their sizes, shapes and smoothness but you wouldn't be able to convert them into a truck load of tomatoes, which is the sort of thing involved in the idea of evolution."

No evidence has yet been found to suggest that one species evolved into another.

"Over ten thousand fossil species of insect have been identified," says Hoyle *(The Intelligent Universe)*, "over thirty thousand species of spiders, and similar numbers for many sea-living creatures. Yet so far the evidence for step-by-step changes leading to major evolutionary transitions looks extremely thin. The supposed transition from wingless to winged insects still has to be found, as has the transition between the two main types of winged insects, the paleoptera (mayflies, dragonflies) and the neoptera (ordinary flies, beetles, ants, bees)."

So, Darwinism isn't the last word in biological evolution (as we have seen it isn't even the first). Too much is left unexplained. Evolution *within* species has been established, but not evolution *between* species. It looks very much as if there has been separate biological development from the beginning. Come to think of it, isn't that what Genesis says?

The biblical story of Adam and Eve is a glorious example of man's creative imagination. It is a myth; but like so many beautiful myths, it is based on a beautiful truth. "Then the Lord God formed man from the dust of the ground and breathed into his nostrils the breath of life; thus man became a living being." (Genesis 2:7).

Is that so very far from the literal truth? Is it not a biological fact that man's material body is little more than dust? And are we not entitled to believe that God quickened man's soul by (metaphorically) breathing life into his genetic "nostrils"—the spiritual kiss of life, as it were?

> A fire-mist and a planet,
>   A crystal and a cell,
> A jellyfish and a saurian,
>   And caves where the cavemen dwell;
> Then a sense of law and beauty,

And a face turned from the clod—
Some call it Evolution,
And others call it God.
             W. H. Carruth, *Each in His Own Tongue*

But this means little to the biologist. Crystals and cells, jellyfishes and saurians, are right up his street. But a sense of law and beauty, and quickening man's soul and breathing into his nostrils the breath of life, are quite beyond his terms of reference. Things like mind and soul, morality and ethics, music, art and literature, do not figure in his investigations. But these things exist, and the reason they exist cannot be explained by any theory of biological evolution.

It is a fact that our biological beginnings were spawned in the primeval slime, but it is certain that our spiritual beginnings were not. (Slugs can wallow in slime; love can't.) The worship of one's Creator is not a biological activity, the soul is not a biological entity. Biology can tell us everything about the body, but nothing about the spirit.

Does the theory of evolution preclude meaning and purpose behind the Universe? As so many things in nature appear to happen fortuitously, are we to conclude that that is how the Universe began—by chance? Or do we not think, perhaps, that God is as entitled to say about his Universe, what George Eliot's Priscilla Lammeter in *Middlemarch* said about her culinary arts: "My pork pies," she grandly remarked, "don't turn out well by chance."

Let us examine the evidence and see whether we cannot arrive at a reasonable conclusion, which, although unprovable, bests fits the facts as we perceive them. There is no direct evidence. No one was here to see the Universe begin (or not begin). So we shall have to rely on a reasonable interpretation of the circumstantial evidence available to us.

Suppose we take a journey to another planet on the other side of the galaxy. Suppose that when we arrive and step out of our spaceship, there, standing in front of us, is a gleaming new motorcar. What would our reaction be (apart from one of surprise)?

Would we assume that it just happened to be there by

chance? That it evolved out of nothing without cause? That its component parts manufactured and assembled themselves into a coherent and sophisticated working pattern, without the aid of a designer and an engineer? Or would we, do you not think, come to the conclusion that it proved the existence of an intelligence similar to our own?

Now if it takes the intelligence of a human being to make a motorcar, what kind of intelligence does it take to create a human being? (We are not so naive, I take it, as to believe that when a man and a woman get together, they actually create a child, any more than when we switch on the electric light, we create electricity?)

But if man did not create man—who did?

To say, as biologists do, that man's germinal beginnings evolved from inanimate matter through a series of physico-chemical processes, is to say precisely nothing. One might just as well say that a baby is created by sexual intercourse! The question is: who had the *idea* of creating the germinal beginnings and inanimate matter from which man evolved, and the physico-chemical processes which did the evolving?

Furthermore, in the inconceivable (to me) event of biologists ever succeeding in creating life itself (fertilising an egg in a test-tube is light-years from actually creating life), it has to be pointed out that they would not be performing an original act of creation. To do this one would have to use original materials that one had created oneself. The biologist uses existing matter and existing energy, and his brains, all of which were created from him by somebody else. (The fact is, of course, scientists never create anything; they simply reveal what is already there).

How and why did LIFE come into existence? Not how did it evolve, which is what Darwinian evolutionists are concerned with, but how and why did it begin? Was it just an accident; did it just happen by chance?

When something is not amenable to scientific experimentation, we are obliged to use our reason and powers of logical deduction in order to arrive at a conclusion which a reasonable person can accept as reasonable (remembering, of course, that we are dealing with possibilities and probabilities, not with cer-

29

tainties). Is it not reasonable, therefore, to ask how such a productive accident could have occurred in the absence of a positive motivating force? In short, can positivity be created by negativity? An affirmative answer would surely be an illogical absurdity.

Life an accident? Design an accident? The Universe an accident? My, how accident-prone everything is! (As Winston Churchill might have said: "Some Universe; some accident.")

Was the Mona Lisa an accident? St Paul's Cathedral? The works of Shakespeare? The symphonies of Beethoven?

When we look at things with which we are familiar, we apply common sense reasoning and immediately see how ridiculous the accident scenario is. But when the atheist looks at the Universe, common sense goes out of the window, and what is obvious to the rest of us is regarded by him as naive superstition.

But if it is as simple as that, why aren't the atheist-scientists (who, after all, are no fools) the first to acknowledge the existence of a Creator?

I think there are two reasons: first, scientists know that common sense is not an infallible guide; things are not always what they seem. (Who would have thought, for instance, that time was elastic, that it can shrink and stretch, speed up and slow down? Common sense tells us that this is absurd; nevertheless, as we shall see in Chapter 4, it is true. We all know that the sun rises in the east and sets in the west. Except, of course, that it doesn't. It doesn't rise and set anywhere; it only appears to).

Secondly, by their very nature and training scientists are agnostic, loathe to accept anything that cannot be verified by scientific experimentation. Skepticism is their religion; science their faith.

The problem is, however, that if we are to believe only those things that can be confirmed by scientific experimentation, then we will not believe many of the things we know to be true. For example, I cannot prove that Napoleon lived (his existence could be a gigantic hoax on the part of historians). But I know that he did. I cannot prove that a sunset is beautiful. But I know that it is. I cannot prove that I am writing these words. But I know that I am. I cannot even prove that when I look in the mirror the reflection I see is mine. But I know that it is.

Common sense may not be infallibly right, but it is more often right than wrong. That is why it is called *common* sense. Some things have to be taken on trust, and we should have no hesitation in believing those things which, whilst not amenable to scientific proofs, our whole instinct and reason and common sense tell us to be true.

Many scientists are incapable of seeing the (spiritual) wood for the (material) trees. They are reluctant to take the necessary leap of faith. Because leaps of faith are alien to their temperament and training, and cannot be placed under the microscope, or put into a test tube, or translated into mathematical formulae. And so, because design, purpose and meaning cannot be scientifically proven to exist, exist they do not. Or if they do, then they exist by accident. Accident, forsooth!

It seems to me that the evidence we see all around us points ineluctably to the existence of an Original Creator. If it doesn't then one has to ask: What quality does evidence have to have for it to qualify as proof? If my fingerprints are found in a room, that fact alone is deemed sufficient proof of my having been in that room. To whom, then, do the fingerprints belong that lie around the Universe in such profusion?

"Ah," says the skeptic; "they aren't fingerprints at all, simply random patterns caused by chance." He cites the unpredictable behaviour of the subatomic world to cast doubt on the belief that for every event there is a cause. For if something in the micro-world of the atom can be proven to happen by chance, then bingo! the same could be true of the macro-world of the Universe. After all, what is the Universe but a collection of atoms? Paul Davies *(God and the New Physics)*: "In the 1920s it was discovered that the atomic world is full of murkiness and chaos. A particle such as an electron does not appear to follow a meaningful, well-defined trajectory at all. One moment it is found here, the next there. Not only electrons, but all known subatomic particles—even whole atoms—cannot be pinned down to a specific motion. Scrutinized in detail, the concrete matter of daily experience dissolves in a maelstrom of fleeting, ghostly images. Uncertainty is the fundamental ingredient of the quantum the-

31

ory. It leads directly to the consequence of *unpredictability*. Does every event have a cause? Few would deny it. The quantum factor, however, apparently breaks the [cause-effect] chain by allowing effects to occur that have no cause. Is nature inherently capricious, allowing electrons and other particles to simply pop about at random, without rhyme or reason—events without a cause?"

Events without a cause! Now if it could be demonstrated that just one event could happen uncaused then why shouldn't the Universe have happened uncaused? For what is true for a single atom could also be true for a whole series of atoms (i.e. the Universe). So that, scientifically speaking, we could dispense with the need for a First Cause (i.e. God).

A subtle argument. And a sobering thought indeed for those theists whose belief in God rests solely on the conviction that every event (which is what a subatomic particle is) must have a cause, and that if we trace the cause-effect series right back to the beginning we inevitably arrive at a First Cause.

And what if events *do* happen within the atom uncaused?

Back to Paul Davies (ibid): "Some (a minority) physicists have not taken kindly to this idea. Einstein dismissed it in a famous retort: 'God does not play dice.' These physicists desire that every event should be caused by something or other, even at the subatomic level. Amazingly enough, it is possible to perform an experiment to demonstrate that, unless influences can travel faster than light, atomic systems are indeed inherently unpredictable—'God' *does* play dice . . .

"Most scientists, under the leadership of the Danish physicist Niels Bohr, accepted that atomic uncertainty is truly intrinsic to nature: the rules of clockwork might apply to familiar objects such as snooker balls, but when it comes to atoms, the rules are those of roulette . . . Many ordinary systems, such as the stock market or the weather, are also unpredictable. But that is only because of our ignorance. If we had complete knowledge of all the forces concerned, we could (in, principle at least) anticipate every twist and turn."

Professor Davies then goes on to show how the Bohr-Einstein controversy was finally settled. An experiment was carried out in 1982 at the University of Paris by Alaine Aspect and colleagues. The details are too technical for inclusion here, but the upshot was that Bohr was proved right, and Einstein wrong: "The Paris experiment, taken together with other less accurate experiments performed during the seventies, leaves little room for doubt that the uncertainty of the microworld is intrinsic. Events without causes, ghost images, reality triggered only by observation—all must apparently be accepted on the experimental evidence."

Einstein, who died in 1955, long before the experiments which were to "prove" him wrong took place, would not accept that events in the microworld could happen uncaused. In a letter to the distinguished German physicist, Max Born, April 29, 1924, he wrote: "I find the idea quite intolerable that an electron exposed to radiation should choose *of its own free will,* not only its moment to jump off, but also its direction. In that case I would rather be a cobbler, or even an employee in a gaming house, than a physicist." (Source: *Einstein: A Centenary Volume,* Edited by A. P. French.)

If Einstein were alive today, I wonder what he would have to say? My guess is that he would be unrepentant. "Proof" or no "proof," I doubt whether he would accept that the Universe is a "gaming house," and God a "croupier." Who, then, is right—Einstein, or the modern physicists who have "proven" him wrong? Does God *in fact* play dice—or does he just *appear* to play dice?

It may be remembered that Davies's exact words were: "unless influences can travel faster than light, atomic systems are indeed inherently unpredictable." Now, it is an accepted tenet of physics that nothing can travel faster than light. The only known particles that travel at a speed equal to that of light, are the mysterious, electrically neutral neutrinos. Hypothetical faster-than-light particles, called tachyons, which could be responsible for retroactive causation (i.e. effect coming before cause), have been mooted, but their existence is purely speculative. So, until such time as it can be scientifically proven that faster-than-light particles do exist, the question of their possible existence must be left open.

However, just because we cannot, *at present,* predict the behaviour of atomic particles, doesn't mean that such behaviour is *inherently* unpredictable. What is unpredictable today may well be predictable tomorrow. Today's knowledge is yesterday's ignorance—that is the verdict of the scientist not the mystic. It would be extremely unwise to be dogmatic when dealing with the "ghost images" of the atom. Einstein may yet be proved right!

A further point: assuming that Einstein *was* wrong, and that there *is* an intrinsic measure of uncertainty in the behaviour of the atom as experiments indicate, could this not suggest that an Original Designer deliberately designed it that way as a fail-safe device for ensuring that "clever-dick" man would never be able to predict future events, thus placing a permanent veto on our powers of prediction? The importance of this is that if man *were* able to predict with certainty the future, he would effectively be usurping God's position as an omniscient Being (and would, moreover, cease to be a free-will agent—a subject we shall be looking at in Chapter 6).

It is not unusual for physicists to speak about earthly matters in unearthly terms. Scientific talk often borders on the mystical. "The world of physics," said the legendary Erwin Shrödinger, "is a world of shadows, we were not aware of it; we thought we were dealing with the *real* world." And this from philosopher Karl Jaspers *(Philosophy is for Everyman*; trans. by R. F. C. Hull and Grete Wels): "Like the Universe, matter has been transformed for us by conclusive scientific knowledge. The discovery of radioactivity in the nineties of the last century, of atomic decay, was a revolutionary event. Atoms do exist—indeed, today their existence is more evident than ever before—but they are not the ultimate elementary particles; they are composed of smaller ones, of protons, neutrons, electrons, and so on. Matter has to be conceived as something fundamentally different from what it had been thought to be.

"First, there are no longer any visibly demonstrable ultimate elementary particles at all . . . Second, new elementary particles (mesons and others) are constantly being discovered and still we have not got to the last and smallest parts of matter . . . [matter] is no longer conceived as a primary substance. All substances are phenomena, not fundamental realities. The nature of matter remains indeterminable."

Phew!

It should also be borne in mind that "influences" need not necessarily be physical particles. There may be influences that are nonphysical, and therefore inaccessible to scientific investigation. We do not know where the borderline (if there is one, which probably there isn't) between the physical and the nonphysical lies, where matter dissolves into nonmatter, and concrete reality fades into the "ghost images" of the atom. That there are influences that travel faster than light, I am certain. Truth is one of them. Love another. Truth and love travel faster than light, for the simple reason that they don't have to travel, they are already there. What is true at one end of the Universe, is simultaneously true at the other; and the love shared by two people, though they may be thousands of miles apart, doesn't have to travel from one geographical location to another, or through a jungle of atomic structures, it exists everywhere at the same time, irrespective of where the lovers happen to be.

Truth and love have nothing to do with atomic systems; and it is not impossible that there exist other nonphysical influences of a different order from those already known to science, which could be responsible for the unpredictable behaviour of the "ghostly" atom (unpredictable only because it is *presently* unpredictable, not because it is *inherently* unpredictable).

If this sounds a bit too metaphysical for those interested only in scientifically verifiable truths, I recommend that they listen to Einstein, one of the most creative physicists that ever lived: "The products of his [the theoretical physicist] imagination," he said, "appear so necessary and natural that he regards them . . . not as creations of thought but as given realities" (*On the Method of Theoretical Physics.*) Given realities!

In spite of what the physicists say, I believe that there is a reason why subatomic particles behave the way they do, why they fling themselves around with such gay abandon—just as there is a reason why a lunatic runs amok without apparent reason. Maybe atomic particles enjoy a modicum of free will, which they are allowed to exercise within certain limits—like a prisoner who is permitted to go where he likes, provided he keeps within the boundaries of the prison walls. Or perhaps, as

35

I think more likely, they simply obey laws that so far we have not been able to discover.

Everything that happens in the Universe—whether in the micro-world of the atom or in the macro-world of "real things"—happens within a framework of possibilities. In other words, it is possible for an accident to happen—but not by accident. In the casino, for example, no one can predict where the roulette wheel will stop or how the dice will fall (unless, of course, the wheel is fixed and the dice loaded). But the casino was not built by accident. Nor were the rules of the house created by chance. Of course, the roulette wheel and the dice don't know this. But the casino owner does—because he built the casino and invented the rules.

Even if the Universe was an accident, someone or something or some influence was responsible for creating the conditions whereby such an accident could happen. (A multiple crash on a motorway could not happen if the vehicles involved were not all at the same spot at the same time. The accident itself may be an accident; but the fact that the vehicles are all present at the same time isn't.)

We cannot conclude that because a subnuclear particle *appears to* erupt spontaneously from nowhere, that the Universe *definitely did* erupt from nowhere. In the first place, we don't actually know that the particle does come from nowhere. All we know for certain is that suddenly something exists which did not appear to exist before—"nowhere" could be "somewhere" which hasn't yet been discovered. In the second place, if a subnuclear particle (and by implication the Universe) can appear from "nowhere," what greater proof do we need of Original Creation? Anyone can make something appear from somewhere. But it takes the miraculous genius of an Original Creator to make something appear from nowhere!

What is the argument for blind chance? Is the Universe, as John Locke *(An Essay Concerning Human Understanding)* asserts, "a blind, fortuitous concourse of atoms not guided by an understanding agent?" Was Saintine ('Picciola') right when he said, "Chance is blind and is the sole author of creation"?

"The essential feature of Darwinian evolution," says Paul Davies *(God and the New Physics)*, "is its accidental nature.

Mutations occur by blind chance, and as a result of these purely random alterations in the characteristics of the organisms nature is provided with a wide range of options from which to select on the basis of suitability and advantage. In this way, complex organized structures can arise from the accumulation of vast numbers of small accidents . . . Today's beautifully fashioned creatures sit atop a family tree festooned with genetic disasters." (In other words, if at first you don't succeed, try, try, again!)

It seems to me that nature is not so blind after all! If "complete organized structures can arise from the accumulation of vast numbers of small accidents," does this not suggest that there is an Intelligence at work arranging these "vast numbers of small accidents" into "complete organized structures"? Is it not a strange coincidence that "nature is provided with a wide range of options" from which to choose "on the basis of suitability and advantage," as if there were an Intelligence making absolutely certain that the "right" options would eventually be chosen?

In his book *Causality and Chance in Modern Physics*, David Bohm, Emeritus Professor of Theoretical Physics, Birbeck College, London, writes: "One of the most characteristic features of chance fluctuations is that *in a long enough time* or *in a large enough aggregate,* every possible combination of events or objects will eventually occur, even combinations which would at first sight seem very unlikely to be produced." (Bohm's emphasis.)

But what exactly does "in a long enough time or in a large enough aggregate" mean? If it means that it would take an infinity of time and/or an infinitely large aggregate for every possible combination of events or objects to occur, then by definition there are some things that will never occur. (There is no end to infinity; so there is no end to the things that could happen in an infinitely long period of time or an infinitely large aggregate.)

The mathematical odds of chance fluctuations causing the works of Shakespeare to occur anywhere but in the mind of Shakespeare, are not just infinitely small, they are nonexistent. It is no good saying, "given enough time and a large enough aggregate," they would occur, because they wouldn't. No time would be long enough and no aggregate large enough. If a thing is impossible then length of time and size of aggregate have no relevance.

To assert that an enterprise as colossal as the Universe could have happened by accident, without cause, for no reason; that it simply, as it were, fell off the back of a truck, is to stretch credulity to breaking point. Instinct and reason rebel. It is a theory of intellectual despair. What kind of mind is it that says, in effect: "I don't know why or how the Universe happened so I think I'll play safe and bring in a verdict of 'accidental life?' " The skeptic, it seems, is prepared to believe anything, provided he is not asked to believe in something. "For God's sake don't ask me to believe in God," he says, "anything but that!"

Of all the explanations of the origin of the Universe, the accident theory is the most crackpot. If the reader is still not convinced, let him ponder these words from Paul Davis (ibid): "The accumulated gravity of the universe operates to restrain the expansion [of the universe], causing it to decelerate with time. In the primeval phase the expansion was much faster than it is today. The universe is thus the product of a competition between the explosive vigour of the big bang, and the force of gravity, which tries to pull the pieces back together again. In recent years, astrophysicists have come to realize just how delicately this competition has been balanced. Had the big bang been weaker, the cosmos would have soon fallen back on itself in a big crunch. On the other hand, had it been stronger, the cosmic material would have dispersed so rapidly that galaxies would not have formed. Either way, the observed structure of the universe seems to depend very sensitively on the precise matching of the explosive vigour to gravitating power.

"Just how sensitively is revealed by calculation. At the so-called Planck time [10^{-43} seconds, the earliest moment at which the concept of space and time has meaning] the matching was accurate to a staggering one part in 10^{60}. That is to say, had the explosion differed in strength at the outset by only one part in 10^{60} [i.e. one part in 1,000,000,000,000,000,000,000, 000,000,000,000,000,000,000,000,000,000,000,000] the universe we now perceive would not exist."

Can it seriously be suggested that such fine(!)-tuning was an accident; that the matching of the explosive vigour to the gravitating power just happened to be precisely right? What are the odds in favour of picking the right formula out of a hat containing 10^{60} wrong formulas? Not, I would suggest, the sort that a betting man would put money on. And even if it were argued that in an infinity of time the right formula would eventually be chosen, was it an accident that the right formula just happened to be in the hat waiting to be chosen?

And if that is not enough, just consider this: it would need only one infinitesimally tiny accident to occur within the structure of the atom for it to fly apart, the consequence of which would be the instant disintegration and annihilation of the Universe. It would seem hard to resist the conclusion that whoever it was that created the Universe KNEW WHAT HE WAS DOING.

Let the late great C. S. Lewis (*Miracles*) have the last word: "No philosophical theory which I have yet come across is a radical improvement on the words of Genesis, that 'In the beginning God made Heaven and Earth.' "

Many philosophers and theologians, from Cicero (106–43 BC) onwards, have used what is sometimes called the "simile of the watch" to postulate the existence of God. Voltaire (1694–1778), the French deist philosopher, expressed himself thus (*Epigram*):

Sir Richard Blackmore (1650?–1724), the English physician and writer, put it this way (*The Creation*, published 1712):

> The world embarrasses me, and I cannot think
> That this watch exists and has no Watchmaker.
> In all the parts of Nature's spacious sphere
> Of art ten thousand miracles appear;
> And will you not the Author's skill adore
> Because you think He might discover more?
> You own a watch, the invention of the mind,
> Though for a single motion 'tis designed,
> As well as that which is with greater thought,
> With various springs, for various motions wrought

This from William Paley (1743–1805), English prelate and theological writer (*Natural Theology,* published 1802):

> Suppose I had found a watch upon the ground . . . The mechanism being observed . . . the inference we think is inevitable that the watch must have a maker; that there must have existed, at some time, and at some place or other, an artificer or artificers, who formed it for the purpose which we find it actually to answer; who comprehended its construction, and designed its use.

And this from a character in Tolstoy's *War and Peace* (translation by Louise and Aylmer Maude):

> And thou art more foolish and reasonable
> than a little child, who playing with the parts
> of a skillfully made watch dares to say that,
> as he does not understand its use, he does not
> believe in the master who made it.

These philosophical dissertations have prompted the following imaginary conversation between a watch and a passer-by who happens to come across the watch lying on the ground.

Passer-by: Who are you?
Watch: I'm a watch.
Passer-by: Where did you come from?
Watch: I don't know.
Passer-by: What are you doing here?
Watch: I don't know.
Passer-by: Come now, surely you can do better than that?
Watch: It's all right for you, you have a mind, you can figure these things out. I'm just a watch; I can't think.
Passer-by: Sorry, I didn't mean to be rude. Now let's see if I can help. Judging by your finely balanced mechanism, your delicately coiled springs, your exquisite design, and the way your hands move with perfect precision, I would say that you have been

	made for a specific purpose. Now, just think (sorry), have you no idea what that purpose is?
Watch:	Haven't the foggiest!
Passer-by:	What actually do you do?
Watch:	I don't do anything—except tick away all day and turn my hands.
Passer-by:	Ah, now that could be a clue! Has it occurred to you that there could be a reason for all this ticking and turning?
Watch:	No, it hasn't.
Passer-by:	And have you not noticed that one of your hands is longer than the other . . .
Watch:	Come to think of it, yes I have!
Passer-by:	. . . and moves more quickly?
Watch:	By George, you're right!
Passer-by:	Now, it's quite clear to me that there is a reason for this. And you still have no idea what that reason is?
Watch:	No, I haven't. And what's more, I can't stand here all day talking to you.
Passer-by:	That reminds me—what's the time?
Watch:	It's a quarter past . . . Oh, I see what you mean!
Passer-by:	Not to worry, we humans have the same problem.

Unlike the watch, we know that it was designed for a purpose—if for no other reason than that we designed it. But we didn't design the Universe. So in that respect we are in the same boat as the poor old watch. Except, of course, that we can think and have the power of reason. Now if our reason tells us that the Universe happened without reason, then in my opinion our reason is not functioning correctly. Reason that reasons that there is no reason, is not the kind of reason that I find reasonable.

Suppose hominid-man had come across a watch, what would he have made of it? Like the watch in our little dialogue, he would have been completely baffled. And if one of his friends had said to him, "I don't know what it is or what it does, but I wouldn't mind betting that in a few million years' time we will understand why it was made and what its purpose is," he would probably have replied: "If we've got to wait a few million years

41

to find out what it's all about then it can't be very relevant to use here and now." But of course, he would have been wrong. The "concept of the watch" was as relevant then as it is now. It's just that hominid-man didn't know it at the time.

Similarly, modern man is baffled by the "concept of the Universe." The Universe is shrouded in mystery, and, irrespective of what the scientists may or may not discover in the future, it always will be. But reason tells us that there is a reason for its existence. It doesn't exist just for the sake of existing. When the atheist sees a watch, he knows that there is a watchmaker. But when he looks at the Watch, his imagination deserts him. "There is no Watchmaker," he declares. The theist, however, argues that if the watch did not design or make itself, then neither did the Watch. The watch is an intricate piece of machinery that demands the existence of a watchmaker. Is the Watch less intricate than the watch? If it isn't then why does it not require the existence of a Watchmaker?

The atheist will reply: "We can prove" (how?) "that the watch was designed; but we cannot prove that the Universe was designed." But this won't do. No one asks for scientific proof before accepting that the watch was designed. We know that it was because we believe the evidence of our eyes and the judgement of our reason. Nor do we ask for scientific proof before acknowledging that the watch was designed for a purpose. We know that it was, the proof is there every time we tell the time.

Agreed that, however obvious a truth may be, we still need faith to believe it. But I would suggest that a smaller leap of faith is required to believe that something (a watch, the Universe—anything) was created by someone or something for some reason, than that it was created by no one or nothing for no reason. Frankly, that degree of faith I do not possess.

The Universe is the manifestation of an Idea created in the womb of creativity. In the words of Schiller, it is "a thought of God." Universal laws were created to facilitate the birth, evolution and eventual death(?) of the Universe. Without these laws the Universe could neither exist nor evolve; it would have been stillborn or stifled at birth. The big bang (if that is indeed the way it all began) was no ordinary explosion. It was a paroxysm of creation not an orgy of destruction. Everything that is, was, and will be was encoded in that single act of creation. The whole history of the Universe, past, present, and future, was present in the original Universe "gene."

There is a unity, a oneness about the Universe, which led Marcus Aurelius (121-180), Roman emperor and religious philosopher, to declare *(Meditations)*: "One Universe made up of all things; and one God in it all, and one principle of Being, and one Law, one Reason, shared by all thinking creatures, and one Truth."

The structure of the Universe, the way it works, the manner in which it is organized, and the exquisite laws that govern its existence are too well thought out, too ingenious, to be other than a deliberate act of creation by an infinitely intelligent and infinitely creative Mind. But if we are looking for scientifically verifiable proofs, we can forget it. God wouldn't be God if we could prove he was God. For my part, I would cease to believe in God the day science proved that he existed.

Suppose, however, that God does not exist, that the scientifically verifiable Universe is all there is, that there was no supernatural input—what then?

In that case, the reason for its existence must lie within the Universe itself. And the accident scenario still doesn't make sense. Because an accident is something that is not meant to happen. It is unplanned, and indicates that something has gone wrong. Now, is it likely that something as exquisitely designed, as beautifully engineered, as efficiently organized as the Universe, is unplanned, wrong? No! The Universe is not wrong; it is right; it is as it should be, as it was meant to be. How do we know this? Well, just consider what happens when there is an explosion. There is chaos and disorder. Now just take a look at the Universe. What do you see? Unity, order, beauty, and symmetry. Funny sort of explosion, peculiar kind of accident that reverses the natural order of things in such an outrageous manner and turns nothing into something. More like a miracle, I would say!

The Universe was a planned creation, the embodiment of the Creator's ideas, and a demonstration of his creative ability and imagination. The Universe is not a small-time production by a small-time producer. It is a big creative event that required a big creative input. And nothing less than "God" could have provided an input of that magnitude. The only legitimate question is: What is God?

The nature of God is something we shall be discussing in the next chapter. At present I am concerned only with the question of his existence (or nonexistence). That there is something other than what our senses can perceive is beyond dispute. Albert Einstein, a scientific genius, knew this as well as the most ardent theist: "In every true searcher of Nature there is a kind of religious reverence; for he finds it impossible to imagine that he is the first to have thought out the exceedingly delicate threads that connect his perceptions. The aspect of knowledge which has not yet been laid bare gives the investigator of feeling akin to that experienced by a child who seeks to grasp the masterly way in which elders manipulate things." (In Herbert Hörz's *Philosophical Concepts of Space and Time, Einstein: A Centenary Volume.*)

This sense of mysticism was also felt by the German philosopher and metaphysician, Immanuel Kant (1724–1804). "Two things," he wrote, "fill the mind with ever new and increasing wonder and awe, the oftener and more steadily we reflect on them: the starry heavens above me and the moral law within . . . I associate them directly with the consciousness of my own existence." *(Second Critique.)* And this from the Apostle Paul: "The things that no eye has seen and no ear has heard, things beyond the mind of man." (1. Corinthians 2:9).

To suggest that the Universe came into existence uncaused is, in my view, illogical and absurd. Causation is a universal law. Nothing within the Universe can come into existence uncaused. And as the Universe is the sum total of everything within the Universe, the universal law of causation applies equally to the Universe itself.

However, "caused" or "uncaused," only a supernatural input could account for the Universe. Not everyone, however, would agree. Paul Davies *(God and the New Physics):* "The first instant of the big bang where space was infinitely shrunken, represents a boundary or edge in time at which space ceases to exist. Physicists call such a boundary a *singularity*. . . . A singularity represents the ultimate unknowable in science. It is an edge or boundary of spacetime at which matter and influences can enter or leave the physical Universe in a totally unpredictable fashion. If a singularity is 'naked' then anything can apparently come out of it without prior causation. Some cosmologists believe that the Universe emerged without cause from a type of naked singularity. If these ideas are correct, a singularity is *the interface between the natural and the supernatural*" (my emphasis).

Well, now, if the border between something and nothing, and somewhere and nowhere, is "the interface between the natural and the supernatural," then this is getting remarkably close to Genesis. Could it be that the physicists are about to discover what the theists have known all along: that God alone created the Universe? No. Only the spiritual can prove the spiritual. The ear cannot do the work of the eye; and the eye cannot do the work of the ear. And what if it could be proved that God created the Universe; would that bring us any closer to God? Of course not. We would be as far away as ever.

For the physicist, the beginning is the end—the end of his search, for there is nowhere left for him to go. But for the believer, his search has only just begun. He may not know what lies on the "other side" of the singularity, but that there is "something" he may be sure.

I implied earlier that we had a duty to use our reason when examining the evidence. Enoch Powell, in his *No Easy Answers,* says this: "We are not required by our religion to deny what our intellect takes for truth . . . it would be a kind of blasphemy to suppose that we are ever called upon to deny it." However, it is also true that the more we indulge in intellectual gymnastics, the less chance we have of finding God. We do not find a beautiful painting by analysing the paint on the palette, or by examining the properties of the canvas, or by studying the brush strokes of the artist. Nor do we discover the nature of the artist by reading the critical reviews of his work.

Reason is an intellectual pursuit. It can help put us on the right road, but it cannot show us the way. Those who "find" God intellectually, do not find the real God. If the way to God were through the intellect, then only the finest intellects would discover God, which would disqualify almost the entire human race! As often as not the intellect is an impediment to finding God.

It is through the heart, not the head, that God reveals his presence. I was reminded of this when a young blind Vietnamese boy was being interviewed on television. He had been brought to Britain in the aftermath of the Vietnam war by a charity organization, and placed in the care of an English family with a strong Christian commitment, who subsequently adopted him.

Unable to speak a word of English, and in spite of receiving an abundance of love from his foster family, the boy did not settle in at all well. Nothing went right; there were problems from the start.

He was very destructive, extremely uncooperative, wouldn't eat and couldn't communicate. Looking after this problem child was a daunting task, but being the warmhearted Christian folk his new parents were, they stuck to it and, after an unhappy period when it had begun to look as if the adoption would end in failure, suddenly everything changed! The boy responded to the love of his new family (which included a son and a daughter, as kind and affectionate as the parents themselves), got on well at school—in fact, so well that he is now assured of a place at university—and learnt to speak English without a trace of ethnic accent. Among his many talents is the ability to create music ("the notes are just there in my head"). He was totally unconcerned about his blindness, and said: "God has made me blind (correcting this to "God has allowed me to be blind") in order that I might use the special gifts that he has given me." He was clearly a very religious boy and deeply affected by the generous love of his adopted family. One could not help wondering how he would have turned out had he not fallen into the loving hands of such kind and caring people.

My purpose in relating this story is not to suggest that God looked down on this unfortunate boy and promptly performed a minimiracle, but to demonstrate how God reveals himself to us through the heart. The love this family showed the boy, and which had such a dramatic effect on his life, especially in helping him to find God, came via the heart not the intellect.

Also, and this is even more important, this story would have no meaning or relevance IF THERE WERE NO GOD. The love and compassion which so relentlessly wore down the boy's resistance and transformed his life, have meaning only in the context of the existence of a living and loving God. Take God out of the equation, and we are left with a lovely little story that, for some reason or other (or rather, for no reason whatsoever), warms the cockles of our heart. Apart from that it is meaningless.

Unless we accept the existence of a living and loving God, we have here an inexplicable mystery. Why should these people persist with this troublesome boy, who could speak no English, showed no sign of gratitude, and to whom they owed no responsibility? They were under no obligation to take on the difficult and unrewarding task of bringing up a disabled orphan thrust into an alien environment. Nor were they to know that their love and affection would eventually bear fruit, and that everything would turn out so well. So why did they do it?

The atheist will say that they were good humanitarians. That their actions had nothing to do with God and all that nonsense. That they acted out of a sense of duty to a fellow human being. And that their actions gave them a feeling of satisfaction.

The question I would put to the atheist is this: Why should it give them a feeling of satisfaction? And to what did that feeling of satisfaction relate? It would only have relevance in relationship to an existent and a loving God. It could have no relevance *on its own and by itself.* Because if there is no God then there is nothing to which it can relate. We can relate one thing to another, one entity to another, one value to another. But if there is nothing apart from everything, to what do we relate everything? We know what love is, because we know what hate is. And we know what hate is, because we know what love is. But how do we know what love and hate are, if there is nothing to which they can *both* relate?

This loving family were more than good humanitarians. They were in tune with the "miracle of love"—something that God performs every time one human being helps another without thought of gain or self-interest. The "miracle of love" would have no meaning were there no God of love to whom it could relate. And the atheist's subjective standards of humanitarianism would have no validity were there no objective standard against which all subjective standards could be measured.

Plato believed that there is an absolute standard of right,

just as there is one—and only one—absolutely right answer to any mathematical calculation. I believe that the absolute right answer to all questions—mathematical, physical, moral and spiritual—is God. God is absolute—absolute truth, absolute good, absolute love—the absolute standard against which all things are judged. In his book *Mere Christianity*, C. S. Lewis writes: "The moment you say that one set of moral ideas can be better than another, you are, in fact, measuring them both by a standard, saying that one of them conforms to that standard more nearly than the other. But the standard that measures two things is something different from either. You are, in fact, comparing them both with some Real Morality, admitting that there is such a thing as a real Right, independent of what people think and that some people's ideas get nearer to that real Right than others."

Whether we realize it or not, we acknowledge the existence of God every time we obey the moral law (any moral law—even if it is immoral). Because by doing so we recognize that morality per se exists. Morality exists because God exists—AND FOR NO OTHER REASON.

Many famous theologians and philosophers have attempted to prove the existence of God by sophisticated philosophical deduction. Most theists, however, do not feel the need for God's existence to be philosophically demonstrated, let alone scientifically proven. God demonstrates his own existence, as the following words, written over two hundred years ago by the Irish bishop and idealist philosopher George Berkeley (1685–1758), attest *(Berkeley's Principles)*: "But though there be some things which convince us [that] *human* agents are concerned in producing them, yet it is evident to everyone, that those things which are called the works of nature, that is, the far greater part of the ideas or sensations perceived by us, are not produced by, or dependent on the wills of men. There is, therefore, some other spirit that causes them, since it is repugnant that they should subsist by themselves. But if we attentively consider the constant regularity, order and concatenation of natural things, the surprising magnificence, beauty, and perfection of the larger, and the exquisite contrivance of the smaller parts of creation, together with the exact harmony and correspondence of the whole . . . we shall clearly perceive that they belong to the [Eternal] Spirit 'who works all in all,' and 'by whom all things consist.'

"Hence, it is evident that God is known as certainly and immediately as any other mind or spirit whatsoever, distinct from ourselves. We may even assert that the existence of God is far more evidently perceived than the existence of men; because the effects of nature are infinitely more numerous and considerable, than those ascribed to human agents."

To add to the above would diminish its meaning; comment is superfluous.

When I read the great atheist philosophers, Nietzsche and Schopenhauer in particular, I am appalled by their massive pessimism. I am sure we were not meant to be like this. There is no emotion more universal, more persistent, than hope. We clutch at straws when there are no straws to be clutched at. We refuse to give up hope even in the most hopeless situations.

"Hope is itself a species of happiness," said Samuel Johnson, "and, perhaps, the chief happiness which this world affords." This also, from the same source: "The natural flights of the human mind are not from pleasure to pleasure, but from hope to hope." From Emily Dickinson: "Hope is the thing with feathers/That perches in the soul." The Greek poet Sophocles wrote: "It is hope which maintains most of mankind." And from the New Testament: "Hope to the end" (1 Peter, i, 13). "Who against hope believed in hope" (Romans, iv, 18). The American poet Paul Moon James expressed himself thus: "Hope—that star of life's tremulous ocean." And the poet William Wordsworth: "Hope, the paramount duty that Heavens lays / For its own honour, on man's suffering heart."

What excrutiatingly miserable lives we would have to endure if we were wholly devoid of hope! The hope that "springs eternal in the human breast" does so for a reason. We were meant to hope. And if that is so, what is the point of hoping if there is nothing for us to hope for?

If, however, the nihilists are right, if there is indeed nothing then life is meaningless. But this cannot be—BECAUSE IT DOESN'T MAKE SENSE.

A meaningless Universe presupposes a meaningless Creator. Does this make sense? Could intelligent creatures have been created by a Creator who was not himself intelligent? Can the Creator be less creative than the created? The Perfect less perfect than the perfect? In other words, does nihilism make sense? In my opinion, it does not—at least, not on the basis of the evidence that I see around me. Everything in the Universe is positive. Even the elements that are destructive are positive. The negativity of nothingness has no place in a positively charged, positively induced Universe.

The senselessness of nihilism should be repudiated by any sensible person. As I see it, the difficulty for the nihilist is this: If there is no God then how did it all happen? This Universe? Vibrant, exotic life? The fertility of nature, matched only by the fertility of the human mind? Intelligence, logic and reason? Human beings who can think, and think about their thoughts, and contemplate their existence? Minds so brilliant that they can conceive that nothing can cause something, that everything, including man's intellect and artistic talents, can spring uncaused and unaided from that most creative of all phenomena —NOTHING? And other minds—oh, so naive, so blinded by unreasoning faith—that actually believe—don't laugh—that it didn't all come from nothing for no reason, but from something for some reason?

Lastly, if I were a nihilist, my biggest difficulty, I think, would be this: If there is no God then who invented love?

I believe that God exists. Not because I want to (though I do). Not because I need to (though I do). But because every fibre of my being—my heart, my mind, my reason and my instinct—tell me that God cannot not exist, that God is the ultimate constituent of reality which would be a contradiction to deny. "If we fully understand *what* God is," says C. S. Lewis (*Miracles*), "we should see that there is no question *whether* He is. It would always have been impossible that He should not exist." This from Michael Green (*The Empty Cross of Jesus*): "The most compelling argument for the existence of God . . . is Jesus Christ." Voltaire, the deist, said: "If God did not exist, it would be necessary to invent him." Quite. But if God did not exist, we would not have the ability to invent him.

What does God mean to the believer? "God is to me," wrote

Henry Sloane Coffin *(Newton, My idea of God)*, "that creative Force, behind and in the Universe, who manifests Himself as energy, as life, as order, as beauty, as thought, as conscience, as love." Henry George, in a speech in New York in 1887, said: "I believe in God the Father Almighty, because wherever I have looked, through all that I see around me, I see the trace of an intelligent mind, and because in natural laws, and especially in the laws which govern the social relations of men, I see, not merely the proof of intelligence, but the proof of beneficence." To the German mystic Jean Paul Richter (1763–1825), God was "an unutterable sigh, planted in the depths of the soul." To a character in a John Galsworthy novel: "infinite invention going on in infinite stillness. Perpetual motion and perpetual quiet at the same time." Plato said: "God is truth and light his shadow." In Anna Karenina, Tolstoy wrote: "There is one evident, indubitable manifestation of the Divinity, and that is the law of goodness which is made known to men through revelation." St. Anselm (1033–1109): "That good through which all good things are good . . . that existent through which all existents exist . . . that truth through which all true things are true." (Source: Antony Flew's *A Dictionary of Philosophy.)* St. John: "God is love; and he that dwelleth in love dwelleth in God, and God in him." The immutability of God was expressed by Charles Kingsley *(The Saint's Tragedy)* thus: "All but God is changing day by day." The nearness of God was expressed by Tennyson *(The Higher Pantheism)* like this:

    Speak to Him, thou, for He hears, and Spirit
       with Spirit can meet—
    Closer is He than breathing, and nearer than
       hands and feet.

Richard Chenevix Trench *(Notes on the Parables: The Prodigal Son)* wrote "None but God can satisfy the longings of an immortal soul; that as the heart was made for Him so He only can fill it." Seneca: "Nothing is void of God; He Himself fills his work" *(De Beneficiis)*. Finally, from St. Augustine: "God is more truly imagined than expressed, and he exists more truly than is imagined" *(De Trinitate)*.

The believer is often accused (and often quite rightly) of arrogant dogmatism. "You believers are all the same," the skeptic will say; "you never 'think' or 'believe'; you always *'know'*."

Fair comment. But unfortunately, that is the nature of faith—though there is never any excuse for arrogance. As a believer myself, I know (sorry, believe) that God exists, in the same way that I know (believe?) that I exist. I recognize, of course, that I may be wrong. Perhaps God doesn't exist. Perhaps *I* don't exist. Perhaps everything—you, me, the Universe and the content of the Universe—is just a dream, a grand hallucination. Maybe I shall wake up tomorrow and find myself a nonexistent being in a nonexistent Universe. So to that extent the skeptic is right. I do not *know* that God exists. However, if the skeptic is allowed to say that he knows that he exists then I am entitled to say that I know that God exists. I rest my case.

But this degree of certainty places an enormous burden on the believer. Being "privileged" in this way, he is obliged to face up to the responsibilities of his beliefs. The question "Does God exist?" ceases to be profound, and suddenly becomes important. As important to him as it would be to an orphan who suddenly discovered that he wasn't an orphan after all.

What the individual does about it is up to him. I cannot help. If he wants advice he must go to the Great Adviser. But how? where? "God enters by a private door into every individual," said Emerson. But what if we lock the door, how is God to get in? Well, that's a problem. God doesn't use force. Either we let him in of our own accord or he'll remain outside. (I was tempted to say that he won't remain there forever. But of course, he will. You can't "out-patience" God; he has a lot more time than we have!)

If we run out of time then that's just too bad. We may be given another chance, in "another world," in another life in this world. On the other hand, we may not. *This* may be *it*. All I know is that the longer we leave it, the harder it gets. And if we leave it to the "next world" then we may find it harder still! But that's a different story.

It is now make-your-mind-up time. Time to retire to the jury room of your hearts and minds to consider your verdict. "Does God exist?" is the most profound question that can be asked. Because it goes right to the heart of our existence. Yet like all profound questions it cannot be answered. But that is not quite true. It can be answered—but only by the person who asks the question. We all have to provide our own answer, because God's existence can only be experienced subjectively; it cannot be demonstrated objectively. Belief in God is intuitive; it wells up from within. No matter how convincing the evidence, unless one has the inner faith that supercedes reason, one cannot believe. It was that kind of unreasoning faith that led Rousseau to assert that nothing could make him doubt immortality and a benevolent providence. "I feel it, I believe in it, I desire it, I hope for it, I will defend it with my last breath." (Source: Theodore Besterman's *Voltaire*.) That kind of faith is unashamedly subjective; it has nothing to do with reason.

The evidence has been put before you. Design, purpose and intelligence are all there in the universe in abundance—only a fool would deny it. Faith, hope, and love are there too—in the hearts of men. The laws that govern the Universe are scientifically demonstrable. The moral law that governs (or rather, should govern) the hearts of men is spiritually demonstrable.

What proof is there that God does *not* exist? None. There is plenty of evidence to suggest that the loving and just God worshiped by Christians, Jews and Muslims does not exist. But none to support the view that there is no original creator, whom theists call God. At best, the "atheistic" universe created itself. In which case the Universe is God.

But how credible is this deist belief? It is difficult to see how unself-conscious, nonthinking Nature could have produced conscious, thinking man. One could surmise that there exists a universal consciousness infinitely greater than the limited self-consciousness enjoyed by man. But is it *superior?* This "thinking reed," as Blaise Pascal (1623–1662), French mathematician, physicist and engineer called man, is so insecure that "a vapour, a drop of water is enough to kill him." Nevertheless, "if the Universe were to crush him, man would still be nobler than his slayer, because he knows he is dying and the advantage the

Universe has over him. The Universe knows none of this."
(*Pensées*: vide Hans Küng's *Does God Exist?*)

It has not been my purpose to try to convert the reader to my point of view. What you believe is up to you. Whether or not you believe in God is none of my business. All I have tried to do is to share my beliefs with you. I personally have never not believed in God—for the simple reason that it has never occurred to me that God doesn't exist. Blind faith? Of course not; it is the atheist who is blind.

And so, having answered (or rather, not answered) the question "Does God exist?" we shall now move on to the equally (did I say equally? I should have said even more) important question: What kind of God?

Chapter 2

What Kind of God?

God is incorporeal, divine, supreme, infinite Mind, Spirit, Soul, Principle, Life, Truth, Love.

Mary Baker Eddy

A God defined is a God who is finished.

French saying (anonymous)

"To say that you 'believe in God,' " says Enoch Powell *(Wrestling with the Angel)*, "means nothing; for you can give the sound 'God' any meaning you please. You must say *what* God."

"God" has a long history. There would appear never to have been a time when man did not worship some kind of God. "In the whole long history of mankind," writes Hans Küng *(Eternal Life?)*, "no people or tribe has been found without any traces of religion . . . religion and belief in immortality have existed always and everywhere."

Ake Hultkrantz ("Religion Before History", *The World's Religions)* says: "The prehistoric era of religion stretches from the beginning of mankind—probably about two or three million years ago—until approximately 3000 BC . . . Earlier evolutionists thought that there had been an original nonreligious phase in human history. Their information has, however, proved to be false."

We have no direct evidence as to whom, what, or how, earliest man worshipped. But we may confidently conclude that he worshipped something. It would be quite extraordinary, to say the least, if a thinking animal (however crude) did not think (however crudely) about his origins; about who or what created the sun and the moon and the stars; and who or what caused the sun to shine and the rain to fall. Even early hominid-man would have had an intuitive belief in someone or something greater than himself. If a creature is intelligent (if he can design and make tools and think and speak then he is), he must be aware of creation and the creative instinct. It follows then that he could not see something that he himself did not create, without wondering who did. He could not look at the sun without wondering who put it in the sky; a river without wondering who made it flow; a tree without wondering who caused it to grow. He could not experience thunder and lightning without an immanent sense of wonder and awe. In short, he would be aware that there was a creator. And being aware, he would worship and take part in some kind of religious practice, however primitive, even if only the breaking open of the human skull and eating the brain.

Religion and worship have evolved over millions of years. Man's spiritual evolution has been no less dramatic than his biological—from a primitive fear of the dark unknown through to the single Creator-God of the Hebrew prophets.

The ancient primal religions that preceded the great universal religions of the world, all had a belief in a spiritual world, many in supernatural deities, some even in a universal God for all peoples (vide Harold Turner, *World of the Spirits,* ibid).

The history of religion is replete with deities—gods and goddesses of war, healing and fertility, storms, deserts and disorder, winds and hurricanes, earth, sun and sky, fire, thunder and lightning, fishes and the sea, corn and agriculture, beauty and love. (It is not difficult to see what man's preoccupations have been over the millenia.)

It is also full of acts of bloody sacrifice. "If we could look down on the ancient world in about 1500 BC," says Robert Brow *(Origins of Religion*; ibid), "we would see ordinary men and women still offering animal sacrifice as their normal way of approaching God or the gods."

It has to be said that the unprovoked killing of an animal does seem a pretty barbaric way of paying homage to one's God. But before we start to get too superior let us listen to the Rev. Brow (ibid): "The very idea of animal sacrifice conjures up revolting images of dark, superstitious rites and gory victims. It is important to realize that before the rise of Jainism and Buddhism in the sixth century B.C. men were meat eaters, as they still are in most parts of the world. If animals are to be eaten, they have to be killed, and most races have agreed that the blood should be drained out from the carcass. This happens in our Western civilization in thousands of slaughterhouses. We turn away our eyes, but for early man each 'sacrifice' had a spiritual significance. When we read of thousands of animals being sacrificed by Solomon, we could simply paraphrase 'he gave a big feast for all the people.' In both Greek and Hebrew the same word is used for sacrifice and killing animals.

"The important thing about animal sacrifice in the Bible is that God used the joyous occasions of eating meat as visual aids to teach spiritual truths. There is nothing more primitive or obnoxious about attaching spiritual truths to animal sacrifice than to bread and wine."

I am afraid I cannot agree with the Reverend's last remark. The use of bread and wine in the Christian communion service may be primitive (though I would prefer to say mystical), but it isn't obnoxious. The killing of a harmless animal as a means of sucking up to one's God is, in my view, both primitive and obnoxious. It is true, as the Reverend Brow says, that if animals are to be eaten they have to be killed, and that this is what happens in the slaughterhouses of our Western civilization. But there is a difference. The butcher kills the animal for it to be eaten; and we eat it as a means of sustenance. Neither of us regards the killing and eating as a means of pacifying our God, or as an easy route to redemption. Personally, I do think there is something obnoxious about killing an inoffensive animal purely for the gratification of our palates and stomachs. Feeling this way, why am I not a vegetarian? I suppose it is because I am not wholly convinced that it is morally wrong to kill animals for human consumption. Nonetheless, it bothers me. I mean, why should I have the right to life, and not the cow, the pig, the chicken or the lamb? Agreed that I am (presumed to be) a higher form of life than they. But surely that only makes it worse? If I am superior, why am I not concerned on their behalf? Why do I allow them to be sacrificed on the altar of my appetite? If I have the right to kill and eat them, why have they not the right to kill and eat me? What does my superior mental and moral condition have to say about that? Nothing, I am afraid. Having being brought up as a meat eater, I see nothing wrong with the "superior" animal (man) killing and eating the "inferior" animal (whatever happens to land up on my dinner plate). Yet the thought of the converse fills me with horror. Someone once asked: "Why do we love our dogs and eat our cows?" I suppose the answer is, because our cows taste better.

Our ambivalent treatment of the animal kingdom gives cause for concern. Discussing the morality of vivisection, for instance, Colin Morris *(Get Through till Nightfall)* writes: "In the God-ordained order of things, beasts may have, regrettably, to be sacrificed for the good of man who is made in the divine image. But what is this saying about the nature of God? If in the pecking order of the Universe man has the right to torment animals because of superior status, then must not one infer the right of higher beings, even God himself, to torment man according to the same hierarchical principle? If on the other hand we deny man a unique status and classify him as the cleverest of the anthropoids, why in logic is it right to experiment with some anthropoids in the laboratory but wrong to practice upon others in the concentration camp or psychiatric ward?"

Mr. Morris acknowledges that the question "defies a morally unambiguous answer," and that there is a contradiction here "which cannot be resolved by theological casuistry."

It seems to me that man is not quite the superior animal he likes to think he is. To kill a fellow creature, to cut it up and eat it, is a pretty disgusting habit. (We would certainly think so if the rôles were reversed.) The fact that we don't see it that way, simply demonstrates the point I am trying to make. I myself eat meat with not the slightest feeling of revulsion. Yet were I required to cut the throat of the animal myself, I would be a vegetarian. Which says a lot for my fastidiousness, but little for my unique status and superior imagination. "Man," said Samuel Butler *(Notebooks)*, "is the only animal that can remain on friendly terms with the victims he intends to eat until he eats them."

We are undoubtedly the cleverest of the anthropoids. We

probably do have unique status. But we still have a long, long way to go before we can claim divinity.

Our antecedants not only slaughtered defenceless animals in order to appease their gods, they also ritually slaughtered their fellowmen.

"Sacrifices in many forms played an important part in the Maya religion," says George Bankes ("Land of the Aztecs and Incas: America before Columbus," *The World's Religions*). "They could consist of one's own blood or that of human or animal victims . . . Human sacrifice involved extracting the heart while the living victim was held down by the arms and legs. The rain gods preferred small offerings . . . and in the case of human sacrifice the preferred victims were children."

The Aztecs, too, had a pretty gruesome idea of what their gods required of them. "In order to keep the sun moving on its course it had to be fed every day with human blood. The Aztecs regarded sacrifice as a sacred duty towards the sun. Without this the life of the world would stop. Therefore constant human sacrifices—mainly of war captives—had to be provided. It is thought that more than 20,000 were slain each year . . . The Toltec method of human sacrifice was continued by the Aztecs. The victim was held down on a low stone block, his chest opened with a knife and the heart torn out." (George Bankes; ibid.) Many other state religions, too, demanded human sacrifice.

The actions of these primitive peoples were indeed barbaric. But were they so very different from those of a modern civilized state that wages war and sacrifices millions of human lives in order to worship their chosen god—the god of hate, pride, greed, selfishness, and fear? If modern man truly believed, as did the Aztecs, that without a bloody human sacrifice the sun would go out, can it be doubted that his response would be the same as the Aztecs'? The only difference between us and the Aztecs is that we are intellectually advanced enough to know that a sacrifice of human blood is not required to keep the sun moving on its course. Which is just as well considering the means of destruction available to modern man. We had a taste, did we not, of what modern man is capable of when six million Jews were murdered, not by primitive Aztecs who knew no better, but by civilized Germans who ought to have known better. Intellectually and technologically modern man inhabits a different planet from primitive man, but morally and ethically we still play in the same grubby backyard.

Humankind spiritually "came of age" when the Jews first conceived of a single, personal, living God transcending the whole of creation. "Judaism," writes David Harley ("Chosen People: Judiasm," *The World's Religions*), "is the oldest of the world's three great monotheistic religions and is the parent both of Christianity and Islam. At the heart of Judaism is the belief that there is only one God, who is the creator and ruler of the whole world. He is transcendant and eternal. He sees everything and knows everything. . . . The pious Jew seeks to love God with his whole being and that love is expressed in practical obedience to the law of God in everyday life. Hence 'the Law' is of paramount importance to the Jew. This Law is found in the first five books of the Bible . . . which record the revelation of God to Moses on Mt. Sinai 3,000 years ago. . . . These instructions, summed up most succinctly in the Ten Commandments, have proved the foundation of many of the subsequent great legal codes of the world."

The Ten Commandments (Exodus 20) are the bedrock of the Jewish faith. They depict God as jealous, stern and wrathful; yet just, merciful, and loving. "Thou shalt have no other gods before me . . . I, the Lord thy God, am a jealous God punishing the children for the sins of the fathers to the third and fourth generation of those who hate me, but showing love to thousands who love me and keep my commandments." He is a righteous God: "Thou shalt not kill. Thou shalt not commit adultery. Thou shalt not steal. Thou shalt not bear false witness against thy neighbour. Thou shalt not covet thy neighbour's house. Thou shalt not covet thy neighbour's wife, or his manservant or maidservant, his ox or donkey, or anything that belongs to thy neighbour."

The God of the Jews demands absolute love and absolute obedience. Judaism is a reward-punishment religion—reward to those who keep God's commandments; punishment, even eternal damnation, to those who do not.

Judaism is intensely "nationalistic"; it is not for export. Unlike Christianity, which is truly international, the religion of no one nation, Judaism cannot be divorced from the Jewish people. To embrace Judaism one must be a Jew. Gentile converts can never be other than outsiders. Judaism is not just a religion, it is the history of the Jewish people.

Judaism gave birth to Islam, which was founded by Muhammad in Mecca about AD 610. "Many of the laws of Islam are derived directly from, or adapted from, Judaism. Its strict monotheism, its opposition to idolatry, the practice of facing a holy city (Mecca) in daily prayer, regular fasting, the avoidance of pork and the observance of a weekly holy day all reflect the influence of Judaism upon Islam." (Marvin Wilson; "The Influence of Judaism," *The World's Religions*.)

Muhammad believed that he was receiving messages from God; and it was these messages that were later to form the Qur'an. "They asserted," says Montgomery Watt ("The Way of the Prophet," *The World's Religions*), "that God was *One* (Allah) and that he was both merciful and all-powerful, controlling the course of events. On the Last Day he would judge men according to their acts and assign them to heaven or hell. Muhammad sincerely believed that these revelations were not his own composition, but were the actual speech of God conveyed to him by an angel. This is still the belief of Muslims. Muhammad died in 632 [and on his death] left both a religion and a state. Raiding their neighbours had been a normal occupation of the nomadic Arab tribes, and Muhammad and the first caliphs realized that they could not keep peace within the federation unless they found some outlet for the energies of the tribesmen. They therefore organized raiding expeditions (razzias). . . . The aim of these was to obtain booty, including domestic animals."

According to Lothar Schmalfuss *(Muhammad*, ibid), Muhammad was "a caravan leader who had grown up in bitter poverty, a father who lost most of his children, a moderately successful business man. Above all, a man who perceived in everything that God is in close control, that God is the beginning and end of this world and that he holds in his hands the life of every human being. Early in life Muhammad lost his parents. First he was looked after by his grandfather and then by an uncle. At the age of twenty-five he led the caravans of a businesswoman, Khadija, so successfully that she offered him her hand in marriage. He was now rich and became a respected and influential citizen of Mecca. But Muhammad was not satisfied by material security. Early on he had shown a love of solitude. Questions oppressed him. Restlessness drove him round in circles, and before long he came to a severe crisis point in his life. Increasingly he withdrew from business and family and sought the loneliness of the desert. It was there that the event occurred which was to change his life and to affect the history of the world."

Schmalfuss goes on to quote the prophet's first biographer, Muhammad Ibn Ishaq, who records that one night whilst alone and lying asleep on the Hira mountain, an angel spoke to Muhammad. After a traumatic verbal exchange with the angel, Muhammad awoke, came out of the cave and stood on the mountainside. Then he heard a voice calling to him from heaven: 'Muhammad, you are God's messenger and I am Gabriel.'

"From then on," says Schmalfuss, "Muhammad was sure that he had been called to be the prophet of the one God. He returned to Mecca and on the street corners preached about the resurrection of the dead and God's judgement. 'God will judge you according to your works,' he called to the town traders, and he challenged them to submit their lives to God and to practice love towards the poor and imprisoned, to slaves and foreigners."

Muhammad was regarded by many of the citizens of Mecca as a dangerous revolutionary, and he "and his small group of followers [were forced] to live in a ghetto. When his wife died and, soon afterwards, the uncle who had protected him, Muhammad left Mecca . . . and went to Medina . . . From then on Islam was no longer just a religion but also a distinct political power. In Medina the community of believers became a state, with Muhammad as its religious and political head, and the social and religious practices of Islam were developed.

"Muhammad expected that the Jewish inhabitants of the town would recognize him as God's prophet, but he was disappointed. So he drove out and destroyed the Jewish clans. Enlisting the help of the nomadic Arab tribes, Muhammad began armed raids on Mecca and in 630 he took the town with ease. Surrounded by jubilant followers he rode on a camel straight to the centre of pilgrimage, the Ka'ba. Mecca was quickly cleared of all images and symbols of pagan belief. Then Muhammad raised himself on the saddle and formally announced the end of idolatry and the start of a new age of the one God." (Lothar Schmalfuss; ibid.)

Two years later, Muhammad died.

In complete contrast to Islam, Judaism and Christianity, there is no God at the centre of the Buddhist religion. Buddhism, atheistic in content, was founded in about 560 BC by an Indian sage, Siddhartha Gautama, who became known as the Buddha (the enlightened one). Buddha did not believe in God or any kind of gods. However, as one of the foremost belief-systems in the world, which has spread from India across Asia, China and Japan (and into the West), Buddhism cannot be ignored in any discussion about spirituality.

At first Buddhism restricted its teaching to ethics and meditational exercises, but gradually developed into a full-blown system of philosophy (vide Antony Flew's *Dictionary of Philosophy*).

Buddha taught that the principal cause of suffering was desire; that desire should be suppressed by mental and spiritual discipline, and that the reward for achieving this would be nirvana—a state where the individual existence is absorbed into the supreme spirit. But Buddhism concerned itself with more than the spirit. "Whatever else Buddhism is or is not," writes Trevor Ling *(The Buddha)*, "in Asia it is a great social and cultural tradition. It has encouraged equality of social opportunity but without frantic economic competition. Buddhist values have inculcated a respect for the environment and a realistic attitude towards the importance of material things, an attitude which sees the folly of plundering and extravagantly wasting what cannot be replaced. Neither exploitation nor colonialism have any place in Buddhist civilization; the key word is cooperation, at every level of being." In fact, you could say that the Buddhists were the original Greens.

Buddhism is first and foremost a way of life, a philosophy of being, a belief system that rejects the idea of a personal, all-creative God and the individuality of the human ego. "It is [says Ling] a theory of existence which is in no way dependent on the

63

idea of a divine revelation to which, ultimately, all men must submit in faith."

Like all religions, Buddhism is a living tradition. It has evolved over the centuries in different countries, in different ways. Its essential character, however, has remained the same: gentle, nonviolent, compassionate, tolerant, humanistic.

Gautama, founder of Buddhism, was born a prince and was "brought up . . . in the present luxury and splendour," writes Wulf Metz in "The Enlightened One: Buddhism" *(The World's Religions)*. "He was educated in the arts and sciences and encouraged to do physical exercises; as he later admitted, according to the Buddhist scriptures: 'I was spoiled, very spoiled. I annointed myself only with Benares sandalwood and dressed only in Benares cloth. Day and night a white sunshade was held over me. I had a palace for the winter, one for the summer and one for the rainy season. In the four months of the rainy season I did not leave the palace at all, and was surrounded by female musicians.'

"The prince married a girl called Gopa or Yashodara. He also had a harem of beautiful dancers. Yet he called his only son Rahula which means 'chain,' for in the midst of all this luxury he felt as if he were in chains. Life gave him no satisfaction, and so he decided to leave and become homeless. [He stole away in the night] while his wife and child were asleep [and] began to search for knowledge in the traditional Hindu way, striving through constant yoga exercises to unite his self *(atman)* with the origin and meaning of the world *(brahman)*. But this method, under the guidance of two Brahminic teachers or gurus, did not satisfy him, or appear to lead to true knowledge." After much travelling, many vicissitudes and ill health, he "resolved to direct all his energies to achieving holiness and meditation. Immersed in contemplation under a fig tree . . . he finally reached the highest knowledge, and became the Buddha. After his enlightenment, Gautama travelled about India for about forty-four years, living as a beggar monk and teaching." He died at the age of eighty.

According to Buddha, the individual self is an illusion. "The reality," says Metz (ibid), "is a constantly changing arrangement of the different elements which make up the world. Belief in the self is rejected; 'I' and 'my' are concepts bearing no relation to truth. The Western mind finds it hard to grasp this doctrine of the nonself . . . nevertheless it has been described as the most important contribution of Buddhism to the field of religious thinking."

The goal of life, according to Buddha, is nirvana. *"Nirvana,"* continues Metz, "is commonly described as 'nothingness,' but this is totally inappropriate. The Tripitaka, an early Buddhist scripture, describes it thus:

" 'Nirvana is the area where there is no earth, water, fire, and air; it is not the region of infinite space, nor that of infinite consciousness; it is not the region of nothing at all, nor the border between distinguishing and not distinguishing; not this world nor the other world; where there is neither sun nor moon. I will not call it coming and going, nor standing still, nor fading away, nor beginning. It is without foundation, without continuation and without stopping. It is the end of suffering.' "

Buddhists believe that nirvana can only be completely realized in death, but may be partially experienced in life by deep meditation—a kind of self-induced hypnotic trance in which, it could be said, nothing exists except existence itself. As we have seen, it can only be properly described by the liberal use of negatives.

It is interesting (though not surprising) to note that, like the theistic religions, Buddhism embraces the conventional moralities: murder, hate, malice, theft, lying, adultery, sensual desire are forbidden, nobility of thought, truth, reconciliation, good deeds extolled. Evil impulses must be suppressed, good impulses encouraged.

Although Buddha did not believe in God, he subscribed to the same moral values, the same moral law that theists insist emanate from God. He believed in the works but not in the Creator of those works—rather like believing in Marxism but not in the existence of Marx. As Metz remarks: "[Buddhism] offers the chance to be an atheist without having to dispense with religion."

Buddhism has great philosophical appeal. It offers man everything he needs—everything, that is, except that which he needs most, the knowledge that he is not alone, that there is someone who cares for him, someone he can turn to in his hour of need, someone who will be waiting for him when he reaches the end of his journey.

"The Buddhist system," says Metz, "may be just, but it is without mercy or grace. Buddhism is a religion of self-redemption. According to Christian teaching, however, man is not in a position to save himself. We can look to God alone for salvation. So Christians speak not only of God's justice, but above all of his grace and mercy."

Christianity is the only religion to point to an historical figure as the unique revelation of God IN THAT PERSON. Christ did not show the way; he was the Way: "I am the way, the truth, and the life: no man cometh unto the Father, but by me." (John 14:6.)

Christianity is steeped in Old Testament tradition, rituals and beliefs; and Christians should not forget the enormous debt they owe to the Jews. However, "the sense of supreme justice," writes Richard Wurmbrand, himself a Christian Jew, in his *Christ on the Jewish Road,* "does not come from the Jews, whose ultimate revelation is the Old Testament (a very valuable book but one which contains commands to utterly destroy innocent people). It comes from Jesus. Jesus was the first to preach a just and impartial God, who reveals Himself through love to every nation that seeks Him."

The Jewish influence on the Christian religion is paramount and all-pervasive. As Wurmbrand reminds us, Jesus was a Jew, his father was a Jew, his mother a Jewess, his disciples were Jews, and every single word in the Old and New Testaments was written by a Jew. (It may be pertinent here to remark that not only should Christians acknowledge the tremendous debt they owe the Jews for inheriting their religion, they should also recognize that they have a special duty towards the Jews. For it is Christianity more than anything else that has, throughout the ages, by demonizing the Jews, set the tone for anti-Semitism. Christianity's historical encouragement of anti-Semitism, and the anti-Jewish rhetoric of many of its leaders and much of its propaganda, led indirectly to Auschwitz. It was, after all, a so-called Christian nation that embarked on the Final Solution —Hitler's soul-vomiting euphemism for genocide against the

Jewish people. And it was other so-called Christian nations that, by refraining from wholehearted and unambiguous condemnation of the evil of anti-Semitism, by default helped the whole ghastly process to be set in motion. This may be (and indeed is) a libellous slur on many good Christians (including Germans) who spoke up against Nazism in the thirties and risked their lives to help save Jews, but the unpleasant fact is that at the time much of institutionalized Christianity preferred to look the other way and pretend that what was going on in Germany was not in fact going on rather than condemn the National Socialist regime, which many regarded as a "Christian bulwark" against "atheistic Jewish Bolshevism." No, I am not blaming Christianity for the Holocaust, but whenever the word is mentioned we Christians should hang our heads in shame. If Christians are outraged by these remarks, they would do well to study the history of the Christian Church. It wasn't only pagan Nazis that persecuted Jews. All over Europe, for many hundreds of years, with monotonous regularity, Jews were hounded, tortured, killed, humiliated, and dispossessed by followers of Christ. I do not, however, want to end this interjection on a sour note of recrimination. It is for forgiveness and reconciliation that I pray. My hope is that one day, however impossible it may presently seem and however distant it may be in the future, Christianity and Judaism will unite (reunite?) in one universal monotheist religion. It is a pity they were ever divorced in the first place.)

Jesus was reared in the Mosaic religion, the religion of his forefathers. And his sacred book was the Old Testament (Christians need hardly be reminded that the Gospels were not written until several decades after the death of Jesus). The many gods of Greece and Rome had given way to the single God of the Jews. Now Jesus was revealing a new interpretation of that God which the Jews had uniquely given the world. Jesus did not invent a new religion. He came to "fulfill the Law" which God had given to Moses on Mount Sinai.

But first, a little historical background to the life and times of Jesus.

"Born just before the death of Herod the Great, king of Judea, in 4 B.C.," writes Richard France ("Jesus," *The World's Religions*), "Jesus lived for little over thirty years, scarcely travelling outside Palestine throughout his life. The Jews were a subject people living either under local princes appointed by the Roman emperor, or under the direct rule of Rome itself. A priestly party, the Sadducees, accepted Roman rule, to which they owed their influence. The Pharisees, who later became the dominant party, were mostly less concerned with politics, and concentrated on the study and application of the Old Testament Law. But there were many Jews who resented Roman rule, and from time to time revolts broke out, leading eventually to the disastrous 'Jewish War' of A.D. 66–73.

"The Jews had long hoped for 'the day of the Lord,' when God would act to save his people. There were several different hopes of a 'Messiah,' a savior, whom God would send, and such hopes ran high at the time of Jesus. Some saw the Messiah in more spiritual terms, as a priestly or prophetic figure, but in popular expectation he was to be a political liberator . . .

"Jesus was born in Bethlehem . . . but was brought up in Galilee, and most of his public activity was in that region. His family was respectable, if not affluent: he was a 'carpenter,' or general builder, an important figure in village life. . . . But, along with the very down-to-earth circumstances of his birth, the Christian Gospels record the fact that it was far from ordinary. Angels proclaimed him the promised savior, and his parents maintained that he was not conceived by human intercourse, but by the power of God. This bringing together of earthly poverty and obscurity with a miraculous birth is typical of the Gospels' portrait of Jesus, as truly human but also uniquely the Son of God."

And so it is claimed, this "ordinary" Galilean Jew, born of simple Jewish parents in a remote corner of the Roman Empire, was not ordinary at all, but uniquely extraordinary, conceived in a miraculous, scientifically impossible way.

There is virtually no record of Jesus' early life, but it is safe to assume that he received a sound religious education in the Old Testament scriptures. Jesus began preaching when he had been baptized by his relative, John the Baptist, and his ministry, it is thought, lasted approximately three years, during which time he preached, taught and healed.

"As a preacher he drew large crowds, who followed him

constantly," says France (ibid). "He taught with a vivid simplicity and an authority which contrasted sharply with other Jewish religious teachers." Jesus is also reputed to have displayed supernatural powers, curing sickness and infirmity by a word or a touch, driving out the devil, walking on water, calming a stormy lake, turning water into wine, feeding a multitude of people with a few loaves and fishes, and bringing the dead back to life.

Jesus became very unpopular with the religious establishment. He reinterpreted the Old Testament Law and rejected the heartlessness of the scribes and the Pharisees.

The people were expecting a Messiah, a leader who would free them from their oppressive Roman masters. But Christ rejected violence as a means to political and social ends and of achieving national liberation. The revolution he proposed was in the hearts of men; the freedom he sought was the freedom from sin in the human soul.

And so, the people were doomed to disappointment. Not only did Jesus refuse to lead them into political and military insurrection against their national enemies, he actually insisted that they loved them!

"Ye have heard that it hath been said, An eye for an eye, and a tooth for a tooth: But I say unto you, that ye resist not evil: but whosoever shall smite thee on thy right cheek, turn to him the other also. And if any man will sue thee at the law, and take away thy coat, let him have thy cloke also. . . . I say unto you, Love your enemies, bless them that curse you, do good to them that hate you, and pray for them which despitefully use you, and persecute you." (Matthew 5:38–44.)

Eventually the religious and political establishment decided that they had had enough of this troublesome fellow. Jesus was arrested, charged with blasphemy, found guilty and sentenced to death. Under Roman law it was necessary for the sentence to be confirmed by the Roman governor of the province. So Jesus was taken before Pontius Pilate who, not without certain misgivings ("I find no fault in this man," Luke 23:4; "I am innocent of the blood of this just person," Matthew 27:24), confirmed the sentence. In point of fact, it would have been extremely foolhardy, even suicidal, for Pilate to have gone against the wishes of the Jewish establishment.

And so, Jesus was duly executed.

Throughout his ministry Christ preached repentance and forgiveness, love and compassion. He condemned sin but not the sinner. He hated hypocrisy, spoke about faith and salvation and the kingdom of God (or of heaven).

What is the kingdom of God? "[The kingdom of God]," says Richard France (ibid), "is more accurately the reign of God . . . an activity not a place or a community." Hugh Kingsmill (quoted by Richard Ingrams in his *God's Apology*) says: "The kingdom of heaven . . . cannot be created by charters and constitutions, nor established by arms. Those who set out for it alone will reach it together and those who seek it in company will perish by themselves." To Simone Weil *(Waiting on God)*, the kingdom of God was "the complete filling of the entire soul of intelligent creatures with the Holy Spirit." But the words I find most illuminating are from Matthew (18:1–4): "At the same time came the disciples unto Jesus, saying, Who is the greatest in the kingdom of heaven?" (Whom, I wonder, did they expect Jesus to name? Moses? Elijah? Abraham? The disciples, perhaps?) "And Jesus called a little child unto him, and set him in the midst of them. And said, Verily I say unto you, Except ye be converted, and become as little children, ye shall not enter into the kingdom of heaven. Whosoever, therefore shall humble himself as this little child, the same is greatest in the kingdom of heaven."

And this from Luke (18:16–17): "Suffer little children to come unto me . . . for of such is the kingdom of God. Verily I say unto you, Whosoever shall not receive the kingdom of God as a little child shall in no wise enter therein."

This is one of the most intriguing utterances ever to fall from the lips of Jesus. What did he mean? *In what way* are we to become as little children? *How* are we to humble ourselves as little children?

I believe that Jesus was pointing to the utter innocence of a little child. Its freedom from sin. Its absolute purity and total absence of hypocrisy, pride, envy, jealousy and hate. Its untouched-by-the-worldness. Its unquestioning trust. Look into the eyes of a child and you will see (am I imagining this or do others

70

see it too?) WISDOM. Not the wisdom that comes from knowledge, learning and experience, but from knowing God.

Christ's vision of, and relationship to, God were implicit in the way he lived and the things he said: "He that hath seen me hath seen the Father" (John 14:9). "I and my Father are one" (John 10:30). What could be more explicit? No wonder the Jews regarded (and still regard) Jesus as a blasphemer!

The God of Jesus was not the "vindictive," "tyrannical," "arbitrary" God of the Old Testament who slaughtered his enemies by the thousands, but the merciful wholly good God of the New, who loves *all* his children, not just the children of Israel. "Who," in the words of Hans Küng: *(Does God Exist?* trans. by Edward Quinn), "forgives instead of condemning, liberates instead of punishing, leaves grace to rule instead of law; who rejoices at the return of a single unrighteous person more than over ninety-nine righteous, who prefers the prodigal son to the one who stayed at home, the tax collector to the Pharisee, the heretic to the orthodox, the prostitutes and adulterers to their judges, the lawbreakers and outlaws to the guardians of the law. This preaching of Jesus is certainly offensive and scandalous, not only for that time but particularly also for today; nor was he content with words, going on to practice, to an equally offensive, scandalous practice, to fellowship with sinners."

Offensive and scandalous indeed! I think that Christians would do well to pause for a moment and reflect on the kind of God that Jesus was proposing: a God who was more concerned with the ungodly than the godly—which, in plain English, means murderers, terrorists, hoodlums and perverts, rather than decent, upstanding, God-fearing citizens. And with common prostitutes rather than Mother Teresa!

Although Christ's kingdom was not of this world, he was very much concerned with the way people conducted themselves in this world. When Peter asked him how many times he should forgive his brother—seven times?—Jesus replied: "I say not unto thee, Until seven times: but, Until seventy times seven." (Matthew 18:22.) In other words, indefinitely! "Judge not, that ye be not judged," said Jesus (Matthew 7:1.) "Thou shalt love thy neighbour as thyself." (Matthew 22:39.) "Whosoever shall exalt

71

himself shall be abased; and he that shall humble himself shall be exalted." (Matthew 23:12.)

There is little doubt whose "side" Christ was on—the poor not the rich, the humble not the proud, the lowliest not the highest, the meek not the mighty, those who pray and do their good deeds in secret not the hypocrites and the outwardly righteous. "No man can serve two masters," said Jesus. "Ye cannot serve God and mammon." (Matthew 6:24.) To the rich young man who asked what he should do that he might inherit eternal life (Mark 10:17–20), Jesus said: "Sell whatsoever thou hast, and give to the poor, and thou shalt have treasure in heaven: and come, take up the cross, and follow me." (10:21.) The disappointment of the young man can be immediately felt. "And he was sad at that saying, and went away grieved: for he had great possessions." (10:22.) Jesus knew this, and, turning to his disciples, said: "How hardly shall they that have riches enter into the kingdom of God!" (10:23.) And, to top it all: "It is easier for a camel to go through the eye of a needle, than for a rich man to enter into the kingdom of God." (10:25.)

Scholars have pondered these words over the centuries, wondering whether Jesus meant them literally or metaphorically. If the former, then a rich man would not just find it difficult to enter the kingdom of God, but impossible. Which does seem a little hard on the rich man. After all, there must be many rich men who are just as kind and caring and compassionate as many poor people. Poverty is not a virtue, and wealth not a vice. In any case, poor and rich are comparative terms—the poorest person in the West being inordinately rich compared to the starving masses of the Third World.

Nice try! But unfortunately for those who, like myself, are rich, not very comforting. For I believe that Jesus meant exactly what he said—literally! However kind and generous a rich man may be, he cannot enter into the kingdom of God—*whilst he is rich*. (Of course, Jesus did not say that rich men alone would find it impossible to enter into the kingdom of God; presumably many others would find it impossible too.)

It has been pointed out (quite correctly) that Jesus was talking to a specific person, who had asked a specific question—"What shall I do that I may inherit eternal life?"—and was therefore given a specific answer: "Sell whatsoever thou hast, and give to the poor." Our rich friend had apparently led an exemplary life, observing all the commandments from his youth. But Jesus told him that there was one thing he lacked, and that was "treasure in heaven," which he could only acquire by first divesting himself of his wealth and giving the proceeds to the poor; and then (said Jesus) he must "take up the cross, and follow me."

Now it is often said (I have said it myself) that Jesus obviously did not mean that we should all sell everything we have and give the proceeds to the poor. Of course not; the idea is ridiculous. For if this were implemented on a universal scale, the world economy would collapse. Just imagine the chaos if everyone who owned a house tried to sell it, if all investments were suddenly disposed of, if everyone sold everything they possessed—their cars, their TVs, the contents of their homes, the shirts off their backs. No, no; Christ did not mean that!

No, no, indeed! But I am afraid we can't get out of it so easily as that. It is quite true that Jesus was speaking to one particular person. But unfortunately that person was *me*. We get this all the time with Jesus. Humanly speaking he could not be taken literally; but his commandments were meant literally (vide Enoch Powell's *No Easy Answers*). And when he spoke to others, he was in fact speaking to me—and, of course, to you.

When Jesus said, "Sell whatsoever thou hast, and give to the poor," he was not making a political or social statement. Christ was not interested in politics or economic systems. He knew nothing about GNPs, balance of payments surpluses and deficits, the price of gold, etc. The Dow Jones and FT indices would have meant nothing to him. The reason why Jesus told his reluctant listener to get rid of his wealth, was because it was an impediment to "taking up the cross and following me." And that is the real kicker! Had the rich man simply sold everything he had, distributed the proceeds to the poor and let it go at that, he would have been no better off. The sting in the tail of Christ's remarks was the almost throwaway line: "TAKE UP THE CROSS, AND FOLLOW ME."

You see, Jesus was concerned with the hearts of men, with laying up "treasure in heaven," with "eternal life." He was not, as some modern Churchmen seem to think, a political activist or social reformer. To suggest that he was is to pervert the message he came to preach. (Clearly, of course, if we were to follow the teachings of Christ—"Love one another." for example—one would expect this to have a dramatic effect on the way we treat the old and the sick, the poor, the homeless, and the hungry. To call ourselves Christians whilst allowing derelicts to sleep in cardboard boxes in the heart of one of the richest capital cities in the world is an affront to the founder of the Christian religion. But this is a personal statement, not a political one. When Mother Teresa last visited Britain, she was deeply moved by the plight of the down-and-outs sleeping rough on the streets of London. Asked in a TV interview whom she blamed for these dreadful conditions, her reply, much to the surprise (and discomfort) of the interviewer, was not "the Government" or "the local authorities" or "society," but "you and me." That, unfortunately, is where the buck stops. It stops with ME. With Jesus, *I* am the bottom line.)

The crux of our problem is this: we are told by Jesus to do things that are diametrically opposed to human nature. Knowing how deficient human nature is, why did Jesus command us to do those things which he knew we would find impossible to do? I think the answer is this: in Christ there can be no compromise; universal truth is absolute. How we come to terms with the absolute; how we attempt to overcome the impossible; is up to us. In the supernatural world of absolutes, deviation is not possible. Tough luck on us, but that's the way it is!

Christ told his disciples that when he was no longer with them in the flesh, the Holy Spirit, "whom the Father will send in my name, he shall teach you all things." (John 14:26.) Clearly Christians have a duty to listen to the Holy Spirit and to interpret its message in the light of current circumstances and current knowledge, and in the spirit of Jesus, and not just slavishly and unthinkingly accept every word that is printed in the gospels. Jesus wrote no books; he left no recorded works. The words he uttered come to us via his apostles, who (intentionally or unintentionally) no doubt misreported some of his original words. It would be amazing if the apostles had got it all right. But it would be more amazing still if they had got it all wrong.

There are, most certainly, other ways to God than through

the Christian religion. But Christians believe that if these ways are the right ways, leading to the right God, then Jesus will be our companion on the journey and will be waiting for us at the end of the journey—whether we know it or not.

The continual evolving of truth is inevitable. Truth itself doesn't change, but our perception of the truth does. Over the centuries, the Christian faith has slowly evolved, though Jesus himself is eternal. Christianity has been revisited and revised. Traditional dogmas and beliefs are constantly being questioned. The nature of Christ, his birth and resurrection, have been discussed—much to the discomfiture and alarm of many conservative theologians—on TV, radio and in newspaper articles concerned with new and radical strands of Christian thought.

In a BBC "Poles Apart" series on radio 4, the controversial Bishop of Durham, the Rt. Rev. Dr. David Jenkins, said: "I am bothered about what I call God's conjuring tricks. I am not clear that he works miracles through personal responses and faith. A conjuring trick with bones only proves that it is clever as a conjuring trick with bones. Because I am a passionate Christian believer and a responsible Christian leader, I am naturally taking the opportunity open to me to invite people to explore the Christian faith. If people want to explore, they can listen to the programme and go on from there. If they are afraid to explore, they can ask themselves whether they really have any faith at all."

Many Christians were outraged at these outspoken remarks. I myself, though in agreement with Dr. Jenkins, thought it somewhat indelicate (gratuitously so) to refer to the empty tomb and the physical resurrection as a "conjuring trick with bones." He should, I feel, have been a little more sensitive to the feelings of ordinary Christian folk, who have been nurtured on, and comforted by, the Resurrection story for nearly two thousand years. If David Jenkins thinks that his flock ought to be reeducated along more rational lines, he should choose his words with a little more delicacy and a lot more compassion. Intellectual arrogance is clearly not the prerogative of the atheist-scientists.

Having admonished the good bishop for his intellectual arrogance, I would now like to praise him for his intellectual cour-

75

age. What he says is not radically new—far less radical in fact than some of the views expressed by the well-known Churchman, the Rev. Don Cupitt, whom we shall come to in a moment —nevertheless, he does fearlessly raise the standard of those who believe that religion is a growing spiritual organism, and that a reexamination of one's faith, in the light of present scientific knowledge, is not only wise but, for any truly religious person, obligatory. An idea, a thought, a religion, that doesn't evolve and develop will stagnate and die. God is not an idol to be worshiped with an unquestioning mind; to be cravenly bowed down to, without a thought as to what it is that we are worshipping. We would not have been given a questioning mind if we were not expected to ask questions about the most important subject known to humankind. God is a real, definitive and unchanging Being, but our IDEA OF God is not. We should not idolize our beliefs. Like us, they should evolve and change. To regard our current beliefs—whoever we are, whatever our religion—as definitive of all truths in all times; to believe that at this or any other particular moment in history we have a monopoly of all wisdom, that we have come thus far along the road of religiosity and can go no further, that our perception, knowledge and understanding of God began and ended with one single event, however cataclysmic, like the life and death of Jesus Christ, is, in my view, foolish and arrogant dogmatism.

Belief and faith cannot and should not stand still, no more than science can or should. Physics did not come to an abrupt halt when Newton discovered the law of gravity. If it had then Einstein would not have formulated the theory of relativity, and we should never have learned about quantum mechanics.

Our search for God should not end in the pages of the New Testament (incomplete and partially inaccurate as they in any case are). As Dr. Jenkins rightly said, a faith that is afraid to explore cannot be all that strong. Christians should constantly look to their faith, reinterpreting it as and when necessary in the light of newly discovered scientific facts. (A "flat-earth" Christian is no less an object of derision than a flat-earth flat-earther!)

"If faith projects a representation of its object," says Don Cupitt in his *Jesus and the Gospel of God,* "it may do so only in the knowledge that such a projected representation is provisional and imperfect. Living truth in a transcendent God requires that one be continually willing to renounce one's provisional notion of God, for whatever that notion may be, God surpasses it."

To quarrel with that would be to assert that God can be fully understood by the human mind. One only has to write the words to realize how absurd the proposition is. "Reason refuseth its homage," said M. F. Tupper *Proverbial Philosophy*, "to a God who can be fully understood."

No one, not even Christ, ever claimed that we are capable of fully understanding the reality of God. If scientists do not claim to know all there is to know about the physical Universe, how can theologians claim to know all there is to know about the spirituality of the Being that created it? To know the whole truth in any case would be more than the human mind, the human heart, the human soul could bear. Truth, like medicine, should be administered in small doses. Too large a dose and the patient would die; or, what is more likely in the present case, go mad!

The beliefs of modern man are different from those of hominid man. And in a million years' time, man's perception of God will be different from what it is now. Whether or not each new version is more accurate than the old, is unknowable—though we do know, because science has taught us so, that many of our old perceptions of God are clearly untrue. Believers should not scoff at science, for the revelations of science are the revelations of God. Believers who are frightened of the truth and of what science might reveal, do not have their faith grounded in truth.

Among those modern theologians who have thrown the (proverbial) cat among the (spiritual) pigeons, none is more controversial, more criticized by his fellow theologians, than Don Cupitt. His ideas about God are so contentious (and, some would say, so obscure) that Sir Freddie Ayer, the atheist-philosopher, was led to declare that Cupitt "is a humanist-atheist, just like myself!" Now, whether or not Ayer is right, depends on how one defines the words atheist and God.

Cupitt does not believe in an actually existent God. He is critical of those who say that the existence of God is in the end a factual question—"that there exists a certain distinct and independent individual Spirit, the creator and ruler of all things, unsurpassable in power, wisdom and goodness, who would exist and be exactly the same even if nobody believed in him any longer and even if there were no world at all" *(Taking Leave of God)*. As this is precisely the kind of God in whom most believers do believe, they can be forgiven for asserting, with Ayer, that Cupitt is an atheist, and that it is time he came out of the closet!

It should be made clear from the outset that Cupitt is not just saying that God as an actually existent person, a cross between Father Christmas and Old Father Time, living somewhere "up there" in the blue beyond, does not exist; he is saying that God *in any shape or form* does not exist; that there is no such "thing" as God; that God exists only in the same way as a principle exists. In this respect, his God is not so very different from that of the rationalist-philosopher Spinoza. For Spinoza (1632–77), God was "the most fundamental being—an absolutely infinite Being, whose existence cannot logically be denied," writes Antony Flew *(A Dictionary of Philosophy)*. "Spinoza calls this infinite being by the name of 'God,' but this God is not a personal, creative agent, separate from the Universe that he creates. In his own time, Spinoza was often called an 'atheist,' and indeed, if by 'atheism' one means the denial of the existence of a personal God, then Spinoza was an atheist. He could, however, defend his use of the term 'God' to refer to an impersonal being. He could point out that the term 'God' was commonly used in philosophy to refer to the ultimate ground or explanation of all things; and (he might say) his God is just that."

To Cupitt, God is "the spiritual requirement." But the difficulty for the theist is this: Is it realistic to call something that has no objective reality, that is simply a "requirement," God? Cupitt thinks it is.

In a short critique of an author's work, one must of necessity be selective, and the temptation is to seize upon the bits that suit one's argument best, thereby running the risk of giving a distorted picture of the work involved. I have tried to avoid this; but in fairness to Mr. Cupitt I would recommend that the reader carefully studies his work—especially *Taking Leave of God*, which is presently under discussion—before passing judgement. I myself have read it four times in order to absorb accurately the subtleties of its flavour, and even now have to confess that some of its meaning eludes me.

Mr. Cupitt's views are not new. Similar opinions have been expressed by many others in recent and not so recent years. But at the moment he is the man in the public eye. He writes honestly and fearlessly about his unorthodox, anti-conservative religious views, and he is worth listening to.

The Reverend Don Cupitt is Dean of Emmanuel College, Cambridge, a Christian minister who delivers the Christian service and participates in Holy Communion, though he prefers to call himself a "Christian Buddhist." (The ordinary Christian's eyebrows, if not his hackles, immediately rise. Cannot the man make up his mind?)

A word Mr. Cupitt uses more than any other, is "internalization." What does it mean? Internalization, says Cupitt, is "the mighty historical process by which over a period of many centuries, meanings and values are withdrawn from external reality and, as it were, sucked into the individual subject. . . . In the old world meanings and values came down from above, but now they come up from below. We no longer receive them; we have to create them." In other words, meanings and values exist only insofar as we create them ourselves.

It is here that I must take issue with Mr. Cupitt. Human beings recognize, determine, and appropriate meanings and values; they do not create them. To say that they do, is tantamount to saying that man created himself. And not even Mr. Cupitt goes so far as to say that.

In the preface to his book, Cupitt writes: "A life lived . . . in passive obedience to God and tradition does not deserve to be called a moral life. I must appropriate, internalize and truly make my own the standard I live by. Merely to carry out someone else's instructions is not in itself morally admirable at all; no, not even if the one I obey is a good God."

Few would argue with that, although it does nothing to disprove the existence of an actually existent God.

"What then is God?" asks Cupitt. "God is a unifying symbol that eloquently personifies and represents to us everything that spirituality requires of us . . . God is the religious concern, reified."

79

The crucial words in the above passage are, "unifying symbol," "the religious concern, reified." For to Cupitt, this is what God is. Again, I quote: God is "a focus imaginarius," "a transcendent but unspecifiable goal," "an ideal focus of aspiration."

A personal question, Mr. Cupitt. When you pray, to whom do you address your prayers? To a "goal," a "symbol," an "imaginary focus"? ("Our *Goal* which art in heaven"? "Forgive them *Symbol* for they know not what they do"?) Or to yourself as creator of "all meanings and values." (You did say, didn't you, that *we* create "all the sources from which our lives are inspired, guided and nourished," and that *we* create "all meanings and values." Is it not therefore to ourselves *as creator of these things* that we should address our prayers? Or is that taking internalization a little too far?)

As if in answer to my question, Cupitt says: "I continue to speak of God and to pray to God. God is the mythical embodiment of all that one is concerned with in the spiritual life. He is the religious demand and ideal . . . the enshriner of values. He is needed—but as a myth."

Now, this I find quite extraordinary. It is true that myths are important to men. ("Man's myths," wrote Enoch Powell in his *No Easy Answers*, "have played as much a part in man's evolution as his fingers and his buttocks.") But does a modern, emancipated theologian like Cupitt, with his near-twenty-first century intellect, require such primitive devices? Surely he doesn't need to pretend that the God who doesn't actually exist—actually does? Why pray to God if he doesn't exist? Why pretend he's there if he isn't? Wouldn't a totem pole do just as well? Cupitt continues: "We need myth because we are persons . . . Now the religious life is an inner drama, the story of our response to the eternal religious requirement. It must be expressed in story form, and religious stories are myths. Myth is the best, clearest, and most effective way of communicating religious truth." Sure. But again I have to ask: Why does Mr. Cupitt of all people need the myth that God is a person when clearly he knows that he isn't? The myth of "God as a Person" may be necessary for simple folk like myself, who believe in a personal God (but not, I hasten to add, in "God as a person") But how can it mean anything to a sophisticated theological practitioner who sees God as a "principle," a "focus," an "imaginary being"? Could it be that Mr. Cupitt is gently trying to ease us into "advanced" theological thinking by asserting that myths are okay and that there is no need for us to give them up? Or is he just like the rest of us, a spiritual softie at heart, who cannot give up his mythical "fix"?

At the core of Cupitt's beliefs is the conviction that God-as-a-Being does not exist, that there is no God external to, and independent of, man's existence. He is not always an easy man to follow (a serious deficiency, in my opinion, in a theologian who is trying to communicate his brand of theology to common mortals like myself who are interested in radical religious thinking). To the ordinary Christian-in-the-street, who finds no difficulty in understanding the parables of Jesus, much of what Cupitt says is sheer gobbledygook. So what does he mean by "a principle," "an ideal or imaginary being," "a focus"? I think he means something like this (if I am wrong, perhaps he would be kind enough to put me right): Imagine that you set out to climb Mt. Everest. After considerable effort and many false moves, you manage to reach the peak, only to find that there is no peak. (As Gertrude Stein said of Oakland, California: "When you get there, there's no there there.") The summit exists only as a symbol, a goal, an imaginary focus *whilst you are climbing.* The mountain itself is the religious requirement; the peak a symbol of "the enshriner of values" (i.e. Cupitt's nonexistent God). And if you did ever reach the summit, which of course you couldn't, you would find yourself completely and utterly alone, with only the "religious requirement" to keep you warm.

As we have seen, Cupitt argues that morality imposed from without is devoid of merit, that to carry out someone else's instructions, even if those instructions emanate from God, is not in itself morally admirable at all. Agreed. But if I, a tiny speck of dust in the Universe, am able to recognize morality as something of value, created by an objective supernatural Being infinitely greater and infinitely more moral than I, and in doing so, decide of my own free will to appropriate and internalize the quality of morality, and to abide by the moral values as I interpret them—why should that not be morally admirable? When I receive good advice from a friend, and act upon it, is my action to be judged as having no merit? I am not obliged to accept his advice. Whether or not I appropriate and internalize the advice he gives me is up to me, just as it is up to me to decide what standards and values I ought to appropriate and internalize. I believe that moral values are right and worthy of internalizing, not because they have been thrust upon me by God (or by man), but because, for some reason that I do not understand, something inside me, independent of me, tells me that they are. But I am not so stupid or so arrogant as to believe that I myself create those values. I appropriate and internalize values; I do not create them. Nor, with respect, does Mr. Cupitt create the values that he appropriates and internalizes. There is nothing novel about "appropriating" and "internalizing." Men have been doing it for thousands of years. What is novel is the idea that men actually create what they appropriate and internalize.

If God is purely the internalization of our own spiritual aspirations, then not only does God die when we die, but he also did not exist in any shape or form (either as a real live God or as an internalized "goal") before there were creatures on Earth capable of internalizing spiritual aspirations. What does Cupitt say to this? He is highly ambiguous. In his *The Sea of Faith*, he poses the question: "Does this amount to saying that God is simply a humanly constructed ideal, such that when there are no human beings any longer there will be no God any longer?" And answers it thus: "This question is improper" (Why?) "because it is framed from the obsolete realist point of view. The suggestion that the idea of God is man-made would only seem startling if we could point by contrast to something that has *not* been made by men." (Do we hear aright? Is Mr. Cupitt saying that there is nothing that was not made by men? Surely there are plenty of things that were not made by men—the Universe for a start. Ah, but he doesn't mean what he appears to mean. Let him continue.) "But since our thought shapes all its objects we cannot. In an innocuous sense, all our normative ideas have been posited by ourselves, including the truths of logic and mathematics as well as our ideals and values. How else could we have acquired them? Thus God is man-made only in the non-startling sense that everything is."

And so, with one bound our hero is free! He doesn't *literally* mean that everything is man-made; simply that, inasmuch as everything—the Universe, tables and chairs, the Idea of God—EVERYTHING, is shaped by our thought, then everything is man-made.

But this won't do, Mr. Cupitt! You know as well as I do that the "Idea of God" is different in kind from the Universe and actual things. The *"Idea* of God" *is* a thought-thing; it *is* man-made. But rocks and mountains and moons and suns are not. Not so, Mr. Cupitt appears to be saying, rocks, mountains, moons and suns are no different from the "Idea of God." They are all thought-things; they all exist solely by courtesy of human thought. Fiddlesticks, say I. If rocks and mountains and moons and suns are purely thought-things, then they do not concretely exist. An idea exists in a different way from the way concrete things exist. Agreed that rocks and God exist because we think they exist. But there the resemblance ends, because rocks were made by God (at least, they weren't made by men) whereas, even in Cupitt's theology, there is no way that God could have been made by rocks.

If God is purely a thought-thing, and exists only as "a humanly constructed ideal," then assuredly when there are no human beings any longer, there will be no God any longer. However, whilst the Idea of God is man-made, God isn't. In whatever form God exists—he exists. He is not a subjective religious ideal invented by the mind of man. (If he is then who invented the inventive mind of man?) He is the only truly objective entity there is.

Philosophers may argue that things exist because we think they exist (i.e. that they have no independent existence outside our thoughts), but in my humble opinion this is nonsense. If it were so, then in the event of the human race ever being wiped out, the Universe would cease to exist, because there would be no one around to think that it existed. But surely our reason and common sense tell us that the Universe would exist (assuming, that is, that it exists at the moment, and is not just a figment of our imagination). When one person dies the Universe does not cease to exist. So why should it cease to exist if everyone died at the same time? I know of no philosopher who denies that the Universe had an independent existence billions of years before man evolved and was able to contemplate its existence.

Cupitt believes that the object of man's worship is not an objective entity but a subjective religious ideal created by men for men. According to Mr. Cupitt, we start off with man, and finish up with man—no one or nothing else is involved. But here's the snag: If God is purely a religious ideal created by men for men, what alternative have we but to believe that man created God (indeed, that man *is* God)? But if man did not create himself (and nowhere does Cupitt say this) he cannot be God, God must be an entity or a being outside or beyond or separate from or other than man.

There is, I agree, something spiritually stifling about the concept of a grand monarchial figure sitting "up there" on his cosmic throne, watching our every deed and listening to our every word, demanding total allegiance and absolute obedience to his every command (although this is, I suggest, a travesty of the way that most modern theists see the Almighty). But Mr. Cupitt's nonexistent "imaginary goal" on the other hand, created by men for men, is a melancholy substitute for the loving, personal God of Jesus Christ.

A curious feature of Cupitt's world-philosophy is that nowhere does he allow for the existence of a Universal Creator. It is as if the mechanics of the Universe did not exist! "Inevitably," he says, "the question will be put, 'Does God exist outside faith's relation to God, or is the concept of God just a convenient heuristic fiction that regulates the religious life?' " (I did say, didn't I, that he was a difficult man to follow.) "The crucial point about this oft-asked question is that it is of no religious interest. There cannot be any religious interest in any supposed extra-religious reality of God."

Mind your own (religious) business, Cupitt appears to be saying; the origins of the Universe have nothing to do with the religious requirement (God). Maybe. But to ignore the practical, extra-religious side of God's reality and creative capacity, is to leave a gaping hole in one's world-philosophy. If God is to be found solely in the practice of religion, where does that leave rocks and clouds and other nonmoral, nonreligious, material objects? Who or what created them? Somebody or something had to be responsible for the making and arranging of atoms, and the creation of time and space—and human beings capable of discussing this "transcendent divine mystery" and "the religious requirement." Is there perhaps another power besides God? And if there is, who is the boss, God or the other power? Cupitt doesn't say.

Cupitt's lack of interest in the mundane business of creating a universe is not to be criticized. But a world-philosophy that offers no explanation of any kind for the most stupendous event of all time—the creation of the Universe—is hardly worthy of that name. Man does not live by internalizing alone; he also needs the bread of atoms. Spirituality may be the most important thing in the lives of men, but God had other things on his mind when he was busying himself with the designing and creating of atoms—unless, that is, the Universe created itself, and God came on the scene only when man first began to internalize the religious requirement billions of years later! But that makes God sound like no big deal, a Johnnie-come-lately who couldn't bother to turn up until all the action was over.

Cupitt is also dramatically at odds with the Christian faith and at home with the atheists on the subject of death. "It is a great help," he says, ". . . to be a religious person who does *not* believe in life after death. People clutch at the thought that there might be, well, just the faintest chance of even a temporary reprieve, to get themselves off the hook. There is no such chance. Death is death."

Now, how can Cupitt be so certain that "death is death"? Is he able to project himself into the future and see himself *not* existing after he is dead? Can he remember himself *not* existing before he was born? Commenting on Cupitt's provocative statement about death, A. N. Wilson *(How Can We Know?)* writes: "To say emphatically that death is death and that there is nothing beyond it, is quite as dogmatic as the old Christian theology that drew an exact image of the afterlife . . . It is obviously impossible for an honest rational person to hold as certainties things which must, by definition, be mysteries. I do not feel able to share Don Cuppitt's certainty that Plato was wrong, that Mahomet was wrong, that the Buddha was wrong, that almost every European writer from the time of Saint Augustine to the time of Tennyson, was wrong in the belief that human beings did survive death. It is impossible, however, to argue the thing positively. One can only say of death that one does not know. It is the ultimate mystery."

But we can, I believe, argue the thing positively. First, there is the scientific evidence. It is a fact that it is impossible to destroy matter. Matter can be changed, its atoms rearranged, but it cannot be destroyed. A building can be demolished and every brick crushed into dust. But still it exists—in a different form. The same with energy. It can be used or turned into matter and vice versa. But it cannot be destroyed. In nature there is no such thing as death. Death is not death—only change. The same holds good for the human body. It lives; it dies; it disintegrates—ashes to ashes; dust to dust. But still it exists—in a different form. Death may be death; but it isn't nonexistence.

Is it therefore not logical to assert that what is true of the material is also true of the immaterial? That what is true of the physical is also true of the spiritual? That what is true of the body is also true of the soul? The Universe is all of a piece (I am made of atoms just as a rock is). We are all part of the Universe: you, me, the mountains, the clouds. What obtains for one constituent also obtains for the others. A rock cannot be destroyed. Neither can I. And that means all of me, body and soul.

Second, if this life is all there is; if death really is death with a capital 'D,' why spend our lives "appropriating and internalizing, searching for the religious requirement and spiritual rebirth, a more liberated religious consciousness, self-knowledge and self-transcendence"? To what end? These things may be very good for us (as I am sure they are). They may make us into better and more worthwhile human beings (always provided we don't regard them as an end in themselves). They may even make us happier (though this isn't guaranteed, for thousands have ended up being roasted alive, eaten by wild animals or crucified, for indulging in such spiritual delights). But what is the purpose of seeking redemption, of becoming better human beings, if this life is all there is? Why not just get on with enjoying ourselves, keeping our heads down and making hay while the sun shines? As the humanist lament has it—you're a long time dead! Because frankly, if there is no existence other than this, then the human race has been cheated. You don't agree, Mr. Cupitt? Okay, then; how about the poor little kids in Ethiopia, who don't live long enough to worry about internalizing their spiritual aspirations? Who don't even know that they have any? You see what I am getting at, Mr. Cupitt? If we find God only by appropriating and internalizing our spiritual aspirations then these children HAVE NO CHANCE WHATSOEVER OF FINDING GOD. In which case, God is meaningless not only to these children, but to all of us. For if God does not exist for them then he exists for none of us. In short, God is a fake! Either God is the God of everyone, or he is the God of none. Either God is everything, or he is nothing. This is why Cupitt's God doesn't work. Which is hardly surprising, seeing that he doesn't exist!

An afterlife is an essential ingredient of the human condition. "The self doesn't believe in death," said Jung. "Belief in immortality [has] existed always and everywhere," writes Hans Küng *(Eternal Life?)*. But I want to make this clear: I am not talking about *an* afterlife; I am talking about *everlasting* life. Because our allotted seventy-or-whatever years make no more sense than seventy minutes or seventy seconds. If you disagree, then where do you draw the line between the meaningful and the meaningless? What arbitrary life span do you choose? Whether we live for a few decades or a few minutes or a few million years is irrelevant if in the end we are all dead; that is to say, nonexistent. Every life, however long, is a wasted life if it ends in oblivion. One could of course argue that the life of every individual, however short, plays a part, however insignificant, in the overall plan: ergo, it has meaning. But that is true only so far as the overall plan and the overall planner are concerned. For the participating individual it is meaningless. And if there is no everlasting afterlife then it is just as meaningless for the person who lives to a ripe old age, as it is for the baby who dies in the first few minutes of its existence, or the aborted foetus flushed down the drain a few months before it is due to be born, because we are talking about a finite span of time, the actual length of which is irrelevant. Five minutes, five years, five million years, what does it matter? Time is not of the essence.

Either life is precious and valuable, or it isn't. Duration is irrelevant: value bears no relation to time. If life is everlasting, it is precious. If it is finite, it isn't. The life of a baby who dies prematurely (and in a sense we all die prematurely) is precious only in the context of eternal life. For if a baby's life is the sum total of its existence, then it is of no value. Because the value of a person's life, as measured by Mr. Cupitt (or so it seems to me), is the extent to which that person appropriates and internalizes the spiritual values which human beings create. Now, Mr. Cupitt may be capable of appropriating and internalizing spiritual values, but a baby isn't.

Another thing: what is to become of the millions upon millions of human beings who, either through their own wickedness or because of the way their genes have been assembled (or misassembled) stand no chance whatever of achieving "the ultimate goal," "the God of religion"? The Hitlers and Stalins, for example? Murderers, hoodlums, drug pedlars, and vicious perverts who prey on little children? What happens to them? Is there no way, no place, no time, no existence, whereby they can redeem their defective natures and be given another chance to attain "a blessed consummation"? Or are they doomed for all time ("all time" in Mr. Cupitt's phraseology, meaning the few short years they inhabit this Earth)? If "death is death" then the lives of these sinners (and don't forget, we are all sinners!) is monstrously idiotic. Like the lives of the little children, they serve no purpose whatsoever. It is, of course, easy to condemn these sinners-with-a-capital-"S" out of hand and assert that their lives are not worth saving. Everlasting *death* is what many of us would wish the fiendishly wicked who pervert humanity, shed oceans of blood, and cause endless misery and suffering to millions of people. But if their lives are not worth saving then neither are ours. Because the difference between them and us is simply one of degree.

If life, however, is everlasting then these lives (all lives) make sense. But what do we mean by everlasting life? Life that goes on for ever? No. That is to use the language of temporality. Everlasting life doesn't go on any more than it stands still. It is an endless, a beginningless, timeless state of existence.

What does Don Cupitt have to offer in place of immortality? "The religious life," he says (ibid), "is hard but one is promised that it has a goal. It moves towards and it will attain a blessed consummation. We begin by seeking solitude, silence, nakedness, poverty, emptiness, forgetfulness, ignorance, and inner and outer detachment. We go on to suffer aching dissatisfaction, yearning, doubt, depression, bitter anxiety, barrenness . . . why do we endure this? For the sake of a glorious fruition yet to come, which we naturally describe as a reversal of all the miseries we are presently enduring."

Fine words, Mr. Cupitt! But at the risk of repeating myself, what relevance have they to the child whose life is cut short by famine or disease before it is able to read your words let alone understand what they mean? "A glorious fruition *yet to come?*" . . . "The religious life is hard but one is promised that it has *a goal?*" . . . "It *moves towards* and it *will attain* a blessed consummation?" Oh yeah? Tell that to the marines, Mr. Cupitt. But please, please, don't tell it to the poor little mites in Africa and India who die like flies in their tens of thousands. Your glorious future tenses mean nothing to them.

And if nothing to them then nothing to us. Because a little child is the whole of humankind.

Whether or not there is an afterlife, no one knows. If there isn't then human life makes no sense at all. It may do to the Creator, but not to the human race. It could just possibly make sense to the Shakespeares, the Mozarts, the Michelangelos, the Platos, who lived fruitful and meaningful lives. It might even make sense to the ordinary Joe Bloggs of this world who, in their own modest ways, also live fruitful and meaningful lives. But what sense does it make to the baby who dies at its mother's breast?

We are born; we live for a few years (or a few minutes); we die. Is that it? Is that the lot? Nothing else? "Doesn't it seem a tragic absurdity," writes Colin Morris *(Get Through till Nightfall)*, "that the billions of years of evolutionary struggle and pain which have gone into the making of a man culminate in a human life span so pathetically brief?

"[The] sense of outrage of the obliteration of any human being, great or humble, has from time immemorial given rise to the tenaciously held belief, enshrined in many religions, that physical death cannot be the end, that there must be some world, some unknown and real dimension of existence, where half-spoken sentences are finished, where promise is fulfilled, and the love, truth and joy we have tantalizingly glimpsed in this life, somewhere shine in undimmed radiance.

". . . All love is, in the last resort, an expression of God's love. So any life that has been touched by love has been invaded by God—the infinite has been joined to the finite—with the result that the work of making us whole personalities will not be ended by our death."

If "half-spoken sentences" are never to be finished; if the promise of everlasting life, which God has given us through the resurrection of Jesus Christ, is not to be fulfilled; if "the love, truth and joy we have tantalizingly glimpsed in this life," do not "somewhere shine in undimmed radiance"; if "the work of making us whole personalities" is to be stopped dead in its tracks when we die; then human life is senseless, and the creator of human life is, himself, senseless. It may be that God is not all-loving, all-powerful and all-wise. But I will tell you this—HE ISN'T SENSELESS.

I do not profess to know what part we play in the scheme of things; or what is our purpose here on Earth; or what happens to us when we die; or what happened to us before we were born. Nor do I know if God is infinitely good and infinitely wise (although, personally, I believe he is both). But I am certain of this: what is, what was, and what is to be—MAKE SENSE. The Universe makes sense. Life makes sense. Death makes sense. Even the senseless death of little children makes sense. If I am wrong then everything is nonsense. This I refuse to believe. I will not subscribe to a nonsensical God. If God hasn't as much sense as I have then I don't want to know! I do not wish to be involved in nonsense.

"The value of a god," says James Mitchell, in his book *The God I Want*, "must be open to test. No god is worth preserving unless he is of some practical use in curing all the ills which plague humanity—all the disease and pain and starvation, the little children born crippled or spastic or mentally defective; a creator god would be answerable to *us* for these things at the day of judgement—if he dared to turn up."

The anger and bitterness of the writer of those words is easy to understand. But the trouble is that if the "value of a god" is to be found in his *practical* use in curing all the ills that plague humanity," then the only gods "worth preserving" are doctors and nurses, famine relief organizers, food producers, drug manufacturers, research workers, engineers, and the like. But these people clearly aren't gods! If, however, this world of disease and pain and starvation is the only existence there is, then Mr. Mitchell has a point. If on the other hand there is another existence, then the answer could well be there.

David Watson (who quotes Mr. Mitchell's above words in his book *Fear No Evil*) answers him thus: "Behind much anger about suffering is our human arrogance which assumes that God must somehow justify his existence and explain his actions before we are prepared to consider the possibility of believing in him. Sometimes I am asked, 'Is God relevant to me?' But that is not the crucial question at all. A much more vital issue is this: 'Am I relevant to God?' The astonishing answer is that each of us is incredibly relevant to an infinite God of love who is with us in all our afflictions . . . The question is not 'Why should I bother with God?' but 'Why should God bother with me?' That is a much harder question to answer. There is no reason why God should bother with me at all, since I have so often turned my back on him. But he does. For God is love. Sometimes it is only through suffering that our self-importance is broken. We need humbly to realize our own smallness and sinfulness in contrast to God's greatness and holiness."

Before the reader dismisses these words as the stock-in-trade rhetoric of some pompous prelate, comfortably ensconced in his favourite chair, grandiloquently philosophizing on the meaning of suffering, let me say that they were written by a humble evangelist, who, as he wrote the words, was himself suffering and dying from cancer.

"If we have any conception of the greatness of God," continues David Watson, "we should refrain from pressing the question *Why?* however understandable that might be. On many thousands of issues we simply do not and cannot know. Why does God allow the birth of severely handicapped children? I don't know. Why are some individuals plagued with tragedies for much of their lives, whilst others suffer hardly at all? I don't know. Why is there seeming injustice on every side? I don't know. The questions are endless if we ask why? Instead we should ask the question *What?* 'What are you saying to me, God? What are you doing in my life? What response do you want me to make?' With that question we can expect an answer."

Alas, the humble and valiant Rev. Watson died very shortly after writing those words, before his book was published. I hope he has now found the answers to all his questions. God bless him.

I do not believe that death is the end, no more than birth is the beginning. Death, like life, is the beginning of a new form of existence. "Men die," said Alcmaeon, the Pythagorean and physician, who lived in the sixth century before Christ, "because they lack the power to join the beginning to the end." (Source: Karl Jaspers' *Philosophy is for Everyman.*) But God has this power. He can and does join the beginning to the end. "Fear of death," writes Jaspers (ibid), "is the fear of nothingness. Nevertheless the idea that the state after death is another state of being seems inextinguishable. The nothingness after the end is not really nothingness. A future existence awaits me." Jaspers is, of course, simply verbalizing the belief endemic in the human psyche since antiquity, that the end is not the end but a new kind of beginning.

Cupitt's God is not my God. I cannot subscribe to a God who exists only as the internalization of my own spiritual values. (Why mine, for heaven's sake?) I prefer the supernatural God of Jesus Christ, who works his deeds and thinks his thoughts without reference to anyone or anything else. A God independent of and separate from man. (No, Mr. Cupitt, not an actually existent corporeal person, but an actually existent personalized being—a personality if you wish—with a *personal* existence, who relates to me *personally*.)

Now, if I am asked how a noncorporeal personalized being can actually exist, I can only reply that I see no reason why an omnipotent God cannot exist and present himself in any way he chooses. God doesn't have to have substance to be substantial. "When we say God," wrote Roman statesman and philosopher Boëthius (470?–525), "we seem to denote a substance, but it is a substance which is supersubstantial." Cicero (106–43 BC),

Latin philosopher, statesman and orator, put it like this: "God has not body, but a semblance of body: what 'a semblance of body' may mean, in the case of God . . . I cannot understand." Nor can we. But we may be sure that God does not have to have a body and a mind to be able to present himself as a body and a mind. (In fact of course Christians believe he did just that in the person of Jesus Christ.) Analogous to this, just consider what happens when we watch TV. We are not looking at real people with real bodies and real minds. The electronically produced images that flicker on the screen, are a miraculous illusion, "ghosts" if you like. The people we see are not really there. What we are looking at is 'a semblance of bodies.'

If man with his finite brain and limited intelligence, is capable of projecting himself on to a flat two-dimensional screen as a real, live, three-dimensional person, it should surely not be beyond the competence of an infinitely intelligent nonperson being to present himself as a recognizable "person" to human beings who do not possess the ability to recognize noncorporeal existence.

In God we are confronted with the unknowable. Can a flea know what it is like to be a human being? Even that analogy is grotesque, for the difference between two finite beings must by definition be infinitely less than the difference between a finite being and a being that is infinite. But what we are able to comprehend is the *relationship between* man and God. Which Christians believe was revealed to us through the person of Jesus Christ. But if, as Cupitt asserts, God is not an objective entity, simply the internalization of our own spiritual values, then frankly, Jesus was wasting his time. He went and got himself crucified for nothing, for a God who doesn't exist. A mere cypher, a metaphor for spiritual values which human beings themselves create.

Although I have taken issue with Mr. Cupitt, I recognize that as God is unknowable then none of us can know the true nature of his existence. Cupitt's guess is as good as mine. But what does it matter, provided we are all searching for the same God—the God of truth, the God of love, the God of compassion?

When criticizing another's beliefs, it is well to heed the words of John Stuart Mill, the nineteenth century English philosopher, who wrote the "most famous essay on liberty in the English language" (the description is Cupitt's). "One of [Mill's] chief arguments for toleration," writes Cupitt (*The Sea of Faith*), "was that we can never be so sure we are right as to be fully justified or even prudent in repressing other opinions. For, says Mill, all human grasp of truth is provisional and imperfect. We are always influenced by the age we live in, the company we keep, the ways of thinking available to us, and so on. Nobody is infallible. We can all learn something from other people, other ages, other cultures.

"Mill . . . is in favour of toleration not because we cannot tell which religion is finally and irreformably true, but because we can be sure that no religion is so. In an uncertain world the best hope of arriving at the truth is by unfettered debate. If all human thinking and language are historically conditioned and in continual change, then all human understanding is imperfect and conditional, and there cannot be any absolute and incorrigible formulation of the truth. Everything dates, everything will eventually need to be reconsidered. It follows that there cannot be a religion that consists in a tightly interconnected system of immutable revealed truths, defined in doctrinal statements whose meanings are not eroded or altered in any way by the passage of time. That view of religion is simply a mistake."

It is difficult to argue with that! A timely reminder—thank you, Mr. Cupitt.

There are many difficulties awaiting the theist: omniscience, omnipotence, and omnipresence. And, above all, how an all-good God can allow pain and suffering, and be the creator of evil. (If God created everything then he must have created evil.) How then are we to deal with these problems?

First omniscience: When the theist claims that God is omnisicient, I wonder if he really understands what this means? "Of course," he will reply. "It means that God has infinite knowledge." Yes; but does he realize that a God with infinite knowledge is not just a God who knows what every individual is doing and thinking every second of every day—a God "to whom all hearts are open and all desires known, and from whom no secrets are hid"—but one who is also privy to everything that is now happening, has happened, and ever will happen at every point in time and space? Who is aware of every single event, however insignificant: the swaying of every branch of every tree, the falling of every leaf and every drop of rain, the movement of every fish in the sea, every bird in the air, every insect on the land, every cloud in the sky, every wave on the shore, the rippling of every brook, the sound of every note struck and every word spoken. Yes, even the ghostly antics of every single sub-atomic particle in the Universe, past, present and future? If God is omniscient then all these things come within the compass of his knowledge. God cannot be partially omniscient: he is either omniscient or he is not.

The concept of omniscience is, it has to be confessed, a little hard to swallow. Apart from the sheer impossibility of storing so much apparently unnecessary and useless information, what is the point? Why should God concern himself with all the trivialities of nature? Why should he want to know when I blink my eye, wiggle my toe, or blow my nose? A God engaged in such trivia must surely himself be trivial? Hasn't God enough on his plate attending to the spiritual needs of his children, without bothering his head with such banalities? A God so concerned, whilst millions of his children are dying and suffering, has obviously got his priorities wrong. And yet, if you think about it, it makes sense! For a judge to make a judgement he needs to be aware of all the facts, to possess some of the facts is not enough. Even we humans, in our ordinary work-a-day lives, are often called upon to make decisions that we couldn't effectively make if we were not in possession of all the relevant facts. How much more important then is it for God the Creator of everything to have access to the total facts of his creation? Whether or not they are relevant is for him to decide. How can we possibly know what is and what is not relevant?

No event, however insignificant, is trivial. If smallness is the yardstick of triviality then nothing could be more trivial than the atom. Yet if one atom were to run amok and the rest follow suit, the whole Universe would disintegrate and disappear into a cloud of energy. So much for triviality! In life and nature one event impinges on another. Billions upon billions of events conspire to cause one single effect. An Old Master, for instance, is made up of countless atoms of pigment. Yet if one single atom were removed the picture would be different. If that were not so then one could go on removing one atom at a time and the picture would remain the same. Which we know to be untrue, for eventually we would be confronted with a blank piece of canvas. If an atom of pigment is trivial then an Old Master is billions of times more trivial, because it is made up of billions of trivial atoms. Far from being trivial, an atom is a universe in itself!

The concept of omniscience may sound preposterous; but not, I suggest, as preposterous as it did before the computer age began. At the turn of the century who would have thought it possible that in a comparatively few short years we would be able to sit in front of a box in our living rooms and watch a football match being played on the other side of the world, an astronaut planting a flag on the moon and taking a walk in space, and a rocket being dispatched to Mars? Who would have thought it possible to store billions of facts in the memory bank of a computer ready for instant recall? On November 2, 1983, a tiny item of news was tucked away on the inside page of the daily press, concerning the invention of a superchip, technically known as a transputer, which is capable of handling ten million instructions per second. This transputer is a quarter of an inch square and one-sixteenth of an inch thick; and several can be linked together to identify speech, translate instantly from one language to another and even speak themselves. Transputers are currently being developed in America which are far more complicated than the human brain. And remember, the computer age has only just begun! When I was a young man, computers were the stuff of science fiction. Today they are given to schoolchildren as Christmas presents. To reject as impossible the feat of total knowledge on the grounds that it is unimaginable, is to show a poverty of imagination quite inexcusable in this computer age. To a Master Scientist, omniscience should prove no problem at all!

Perhaps every single object in existence is a "computer" in itself, containing or consisting of a complete chronicle of its own history and "experience." The surface of a rock, for instance, might itself be a record of every wave that has washed over it, every ray of sunshine that has beaten down on it, every breath of wind that has caressed it, every event that has taken place around it since the day it first existed.

Impossible? Maybe. But one would think it impossible to read a person's mind and share his deepest thoughts simply by running one's fingers over the surface of a piece of paper. Yet isn't that what blind people do when they read braille? If the human mind can invent a method of enabling a blind person to "read" with his fingers, I see nothing exceptional in the suggestion that God can "read" the history of a rock or a human being's soul simply by "looking" at them.

If God is an infinite mind, one would expect him to have an infinite capacity for accumulating, absorbing, and retaining an infinite volume of information concerning an infinity of events taking place in infinite time and infinite space. Our problem is that because of the limitations of the human intellect we imagine that God's mind is a sort of super-duper version of our own, and works in a similar way. If God's mind were indeed similar to ours (even though vastly superior) then yes, what I am suggesting is absurd. But I do not believe that God's mind is like that. It is not just different in degree, it is different in kind, of a different order, unimaginably different. Even to describe it as a mind is totally misleading. I suspect that the truth is that God doesn't need to know what is going on in the world, in the Universe, in our minds, in our hearts, in our souls, BECAUSE GOD IS KNOWLEDGE ITSELF AND CANNOT HELP BUT KNOW. (Here is a simple human analogy: when a pianist plays a concerto, every note he strikes, every chord, crotchet, quaver and semi-quaver he plays, is known to him as he plays it, before he plays it, and after he has played it. His knowledge of the notes is in the knowing of the notes not in the playing of them. The playing is simply the consummation of the knowing. The concerto exists within the pianist's mind. It is part of his existence. Similarly, God knows every "note" that is struck, every "chord" that is played, every "tune" that exists, anywhere and everywhere in the Universe. Because God composed every "piece of music" that has ever been or ever will be written, played or performed.)

If we can accept the concept of omniscience then we need

97

have no difficulty with omnipresence. For it is no more difficult to believe that God can be present everywhere at the same time than it is to believe that God can know everything at the same time. The key is infinity. An infinite God is not only infinitely knowledgeable, he is infinitely present: that is to say, universally present everywhere at the same time—past, present and future.

To know everything at the same time is to be present the whole time. Omniscience equals omnipresence.

Omnipotence is a little more tricky. For inevitably it raises the age-old question: If God is all-powerful, why does he permit suffering, if he is all-good? We shall be dealing with this problem in Chapter 9—though I have to warn the reader that it is only by invoking faith that we can even come to terms with the question let alone attempt to answer it.

Another stumbling block is the intractable problem of evil. "Alone of all the peoples around them," writes Enoch Powell *(Wrestling with the Angel)* ". . . the Jews held fast through all temptation and disaster, to the conviction that God creates evil as well as good, or, in more pictorial language, that he planted the tree of knowledge of good and evil."

To many people, the idea that a good and loving God created evil is totally unacceptable. It is hard enough to accept that God allows evil to exist without being asked to believe that he actually created it! But if God did create evil (and if those religious geniuses the Jews believe that he did, then the notion has to be taken seriously)—why? Why should a good God want to create evil? Three possibilities occur.

First: God's plan for the human race is that it should (eventually) reach godhead. And the only way we can become the kind of creature that God wishes us to be, is to confront, wrestle with, and overcome evil. Now just as an athlete cannot win the hundred metres hurdles if there aren't any hurdles to be jumped, neither can we overcome evil if there isn't any evil to be overcome. Good and evil are two sides of the same coin. If evil did not exist then neither would good. We cannot be good unless we also have the possibility of being evil. True, God knew when he gave "Adam" free will he would choose evil as often as he would choose good. But that was inherent in the confering of free will.

"Adam" was given free will in order that he might have the opportunity of choosing good because it is good, and rejecting evil because it is evil. But "Adam" is still a child; man is but in his infancy. The God who knew that man would abuse the precious gift of free will, is also the God who knows(?) that one day child-man will grow up, discard his evil toys, stop abusing his soul and the God who created it, and finally overcome evil, in the way that Jesus Christ taught us that it could and should be overcome two thousand years ago. At least, that is what I would like to think.

There is nothing evil about evil—so long as we reject it! It is only when man, *conscious of the difference between good and evil,* freely rejects good and embraces evil, that evil becomes evil.

Evil, it could be said, is a necessary evil! Without it, good would not be good, and man would not be free. If we were forced to choose good because no other choice was available to us, then good would not exist. Good only exists because evil exists (and vice versa). Would the world be a better place if evil did not exist? The question is a non sequitur. For if evil did not exist then neither would "better." The world is as it is. And you can bet your bottom dollar that God had a good reason for planning it that way. It may not suit us. We may think that we could have designed it better. But it would be a lot more edifying if we stopped bellyaching about the mess that God has made, and gave a little more thought to how we can improve ourselves and the beautiful world that God has bequeathed to us and which we plunder and pollute with such cupidity. We do not know what God's plan is: so how can we criticize him for planning it that way?

The second possibility is that evil was never created in the first place, but is in fact the perversion of good. Good is positive and creative; evil negative and destructive. Which would suggest that evil is the result of the negation and destruction of good. If you destroy a beautiful building, you do not create a heap of rubble, you "uncreate" a beautiful building. A rose severed from the bush will shrivel and decay. The shrivelled rose will not have been created, it will have degenerated from the original perfect specimen. Likewise, good, cut off from its source (God), will shrivel and decay, until, in extreme cases, it will result in a degree of wickedness that cannot be distinguished from madness. Good comes from God, who is creative; evil comes from man who has rejected God and allowed good, by design or neglect, to stagnate and putrify until it becomes evil.

Evil could not have been created by the devil (assuming that such a power exists), because by his very nature the devil could only destroy, not create. Evil is not a creative power. Evil people create nothing; they only destroy that which has been created. Do we not see the evidence all around us of how wickedness, malevolence and hate are the forces of destruction; and goodness, love and compassion the forces of creation?

It still needs to be explained, however, why God allowed good to become perverted. When God gave man free will he knew very well what would happen. So why did he do it? Why did he give man the power to pervert good? Frankly, the only answer I can think of (which I confess is no answer at all!) is that God wanted to create human beings. And without free will—and with it, the freedom to pervert good and to embrace evil—human beings would not be human beings.

The third possibility, which some might regard as profane, and which I once subscribed to myself but no longer, is that, contrary to the Genesis story, it was God who "fell," not man. God originally sinned and in order to redeem himself, thrust the "sinful" part of his nature into an inhospitable world in the guise of man, so that he might suffer and so be punished for his original sin. This would solve the problem of suffering; for clearly it cannot be considered evil to punish oneself. Neurotic, perhaps; but not evil. It would also explain the origin of evil; for God, in sinning, created evil.

But somehow, a sinful, neurotic God doesn't fit! To be "only human" is not the stuff of which gods are made. Only a perfect, flawless God can explain the existence of the Universe; only a sinless God can satisfy the needs of sinful man.

None of these hypotheses is completely convincing. We must face the fact that the existence of evil cannot be satisfactorily explained. Whether sin is an original condition or a perversion of an original condition, matters little. What we should be concerned with is not who created evil and why, but how can we overcome it. Christians believe that God has shown us the way.

In the words of Enoch Powell (*Wrestling with the Angel*): "By nothing less than the truth of the Indivisible Trinity is the problem of evil solved." It was on Golgotha that sin was defeated and evil overcome.

An even more impenetrable mystery, which probably only a fool would attempt to answer—but here goes!—is: who created God? There would appear to be only four possible answers to this impossible question:

(1) God came from nothing.

(2) God came from something.

(3) God created himself.

(4) God has always existed (therefore he was never created).

Let us consider these hypotheses.

First: As was argued in the last chapter, nothing can come from nothing. Existence cannot be created by nonexistence, and it is logically inept to suggest that it can.

Second: If God came from something, it would mean that he was not the Original Creator (unless, of course, he himself created the something out of which he was created: which would make him a self-creating entity, thus preempting our third hypothesis). We would therefore find ourselves back at square one: Who created the something from which God was created? As "God" is the accepted term for describing the Author of the Original Act of Creation, this hypothesis is tautological nonsense.

Third: The concept of a self-creating God is philosophically exquisite. Truly could it be called The Immaculate Conception! If God is omnipotent then it would seem logical that he would have the power to create himself. Internal (existential) combustion! God's actual existence arising out of his nonexistent but latently existent existence! Impossible within the Universe, of course, where universal laws have to be obeyed by all and sundry, but outside the Universe where universal laws do not apply—who knows?

There is, however, an objection from the scientific lobby. "Even granted the cosmological argument—that the Universe must have a cause—there is a logical difficulty in attributing that cause to God," writes physicist Paul Davies *(God and the New Physics),* "for it could then be asked 'What caused God?'

The response is usually 'God does not need a cause. He is a *necessary* being, whose cause is to be found within himself.' " But the cosmological argument is founded on the assumption that everything requires a cause, yet ends in the conclusion that at least one thing (God) does not require a cause. The argument seems to be self-contradictory. Moreover if one is prepared to concede that something—God—can exist without an external cause, why go that far along the chain? Why can't the Universe exist without an external cause? Does it require any greater suspension of disbelief to suppose that the Universe causes itself than to suppose that God causes himself?"

Yes, it does, Mr. Davies; at least it does to this writer. Because we are talking about two different things; we are not comparing like with like. Nothing that is subject to universal law—which by definition the Universe must be—can cause itself. In the Universe cause must precede effect. Ergo, cause and effect cannot be one and the same thing, something cannot cause itself, not in this universe it can't. Outside or beyond the Universe, however, no one knows what the rules are. They could be totally different and probably are. If, as the physicists tell us, there was a "time" when time never was, then the rules must be different; for in a timeless environment nothing can cause (i.e. precede) anything else.

"Before" the Universe was created, natural law did not exist. Therefore the Universe, which is subject to natural law, could not have caused itself. Whereas God, who is not subject to natural law, could have. The cosmological argument is not self-contradictory; because the natural and the preternatural are of two different orders.

Fourth: This last hypothesis is even more compelling. For if God has always existed then no explanation of his origination is required. It seems philosophically and theologically perfect that God's origination should be completely and utterly beyond man's comprehension. This hypothesis fills the bill. One could say that the *reason for* God's existence lies in the *fact of* God's existence: God exists—period!

I believe that God has always existed. He had no beginning and will have no end. He is eternal. For God there is no past, present or future; there is only a timeless state of eternity. Nor can he cease to exist. For if God were to "opt out" of the future—to commit suicide, as it were—he would simultaneously "opt out" of the past and the present, For God *is* eternity. If God were ever to cease to exist, the whole of time from beginning to end (including man's present consciousness) would cease to exist, because time exists within the eternity of God.

Now we have no way of knowing whether time will exist in the future; and we cannot be certain that time existed in the past; but we do know (or believe that we know) that time exists in the present, because we are presently conscious, which we would not be if time did not exist. This indicates that the "now" segment of eternity exists. And, as a part of eternity is the whole of eternity, then there is no possibility of God ceasing to exist, because if there were no "future" for God, there would be no "present" for man.

Any attempt to describe God is doomed to failure. God is unknowable, unimaginable and unfathomable, immanent and transcendent, outside and beyond human understanding. We poor ignorant mortals, with our limited intellect and finite power of comprehension cannot even begin to understand what it means to say that God exists, let alone pretend to know the nature and meaning of his existence.

For human beings to say (as St. Paul did) that we are made in God's image is, in my view, presumptuous at best, arrogant at worst. As man is (it is thought) the most intelligent and (sometimes) the noblest of all the creatures in creation, it is easy to understand why he should have such delusions of grandeur. But man must be extraordinarily unimaginative to imagine that he is but a smaller version of God! ("The God of the cannibals," said Emerson, "will be a cannibal." Quite. But one would expect modern intelligent man to be a little more imaginative than cannibals.)

"God, to be God," wrote Rufus M. Jones (1863–1948), "must transcend what is." The transcendent Mind that created the Universe is so unimaginably unimaginable, that it is a gross impertinence for human beings, whose intelligence is comparatively no bigger than a bug's, to think that they can ever understand the nature of the God who performed that miracle. Could a grasshopper understand the nature of man? Give it a

103

brain the size of a man's and it could. But then it would no longer be a grasshopper! To be able to understand the nature of God, we would have to be a different creation. And then we would no longer know what it was like to be man. No one—but no one—can know the whole truth about the Whole Truth. We will never know. Not in this lifetime or in any other.

To know God one would have to be God. The most that we can hope for is that in some indefinable way we are related to God. That there is a connection between man and God which is valid and real. That there is something in man's nature which responds to, and is in harmony with, something in God's nature. That there is something about man's mind which in some infinitesimal way reflects the mind of God. But made in God's image? Whatever will we think of next!

The important thing for man is to keep searching for God. To keep thinking and hoping and praying. For once we lose the desire to discover the truth—about ourselves, the Universe and the God who made us—we are doomed to extinction as a thinking, spiritual organism.

For me, it is not an intellectual pursuit. No amount of intellectual philosophizing or scientific endeavour can lead us to God. The answers (such answers as we may reasonably expect) lie deeply embedded in the human soul. They must be teased out of the spiritual fabric, not gouged out of the intellectual rock face.

In this scientific age we have become too mechanistic in our search for the truth. Truth is not to be found in the universal test tube but in the way we interpret, react to, and deal with what we find in the test tube. To make a god of the intellect is to make a serf of the soul. Reality cannot be comprehended by the intellect; it must be encountered intuitively and instinctively within the soul. "It is the heart which perceives God," said Pascal *(Pensées*, 1670), "and not the reason." Infinite, transcendent and unknowable God is not a finite, limited object of human thought. We cannot *think* our way to God. The concept of God can be studied and investigated by the intellect, but it is only within the soul that God "himself" can be experienced.

What should concern us is our RELATIONSHIP WITH God not what God "looks" like. I personally believe in the God of

Jesus. But only in the context of what God means to me as a human being. God doesn't exist for human beings alone. To a bug, God is a bug; to a mountain, God is a mountain. The whole Universe is his creation. Man is but one tiny piece in the universal jigsaw puzzle.

We should forget "God," and concentrate on how God relates to us, and we to him. And it is here that the kind of God we believe in becomes paramount. All religions believe that they alone have the answer; that their God is the true God; that their beliefs are the true beliefs. They cannot all be right. But then again, they may not all be that far wrong. It is likely that every religion sees a part of the truth; but being partially blind, as we all are, we mistake the part for the whole. And then bigotry, egotism, arrogance and intolerance can be relied upon to do the rest. Provided we all seek the God of Love (even though we may not believe in God), none of us can be far from the truth: that is, the truth as it relates to us as human beings. The route we take is far less important than the destination we set out for.

The link between man and God is Jesus. "All that we may rightly expect from God, and ask him for, is to be found in Jesus Christ," wrote Dietrich Bonhoeffer, shortly before his execution by the Nazis *(Letters and Papers from Prison*, 1967 edition), ". . . If we are to learn what God promises, and what he fulfills, we must persevere in quiet meditation on the life, sayings, deeds, sufferings, and death of Jesus. It is certain that we may always live close to God and in the light of his presence, and that such living is an entirely new life for us; that nothing is then impossible for us, because all things are possible with God; that no earthly power can touch us without his will, and that danger and distress can only drive us closer to him."

This is the kind of God in whom Bonhoeffer believed. The subjective God of Jesus. A living God to whom human beings can relate. Not the objective God of reality, but the subjective God of faith. "God is love; and he that dwelleth in love dwelleth in God, and God in him." (John 4:16.) Could anything be more explicit of the RELATIONSHIP BETWEEN the living God and man?

Six years have elapsed since I penned the first words of this chapter. Six years of hard study and constant thought. I still have (more or less) the same God as I started out with. He as was revealed by the life and death and teachings of Jesus Christ.

I realize, however, that this cannot be the whole truth. But it is about as much as I, in my present state of mental and spiritual evolution, am able to cope with.

I now know what Protagoras, Greek philosopher and Sophist (490?–415? BC), meant when he said "Everything is true." If something exists then it is true. If this is not true then everything is untrue.

Human beings are not capable of looking at things objectively. As subjects, we have no alternative but to think, act and feel subjectively. Only God, the Great Objective, can "think," "act" and "feel" objectively.

"What is true by lamplight," said Joubert *(Pensées)*, "is not always true by sunlight." Voltaire puts it like this: "There are truths which are not for all men, nor for all times." William Ostler *(The Student Life)* had this to say: "No human being is constituted to know the truth, the whole truth, and nothing but the truth; and even the best of men must be content with fragments, with partial glimpses, never the full fruition."

Only God can know the whole truth. Because God *is* Truth.

"We are born to inquire after truth," observed Montaigne, French philosopher and essayist (1533–1592); "it belongs to a greater power to possess it. It is not, as Democritus said, hid in the bottom of the deeps, but rather elevated to an infinite height in the divine knowledge."

Truth is subjective, relative, and ambiguous. "And after all," wrote Byron *(Don Juan)*, "what is a lie? 'Tis but/Truth in masquerade." Nothing is true—not even truth. Truth, like space-time, is relative. But if truth is only relatively true, and if everything is relative, to what is EVERYTHING relative? The answer, I believe, is God—the only objective truth there is.

To sum up: The God of Jesus—the personal, supernatural, living and loving God who (Jesus said) has counted the very number of hairs on our head—is the God I feel myself most drawn to, although I know that at best the revelation of Jesus can only be a partial glimpse of the truth—the truth AS IT RELATES TO ME AS A HUMAN BEING. Being a subject, the subjective truth is the only truth I can understand. What kind of God God is to stones and mountains and rivers and clouds, I have no idea. But then I am not a stone, a mountain, a river, or a cloud. Such objectivity is beyond my powers of comprehension.

Jesus' relationship to God was, I believe, unique. Whether he was the Son of God, and what "Son" of God actually means, is something we shall be examining in Chapter 10. As at this moment, I have no idea what conclusion I will come to, so it will be as much of an adventure for me as it will be for the reader.

I know what kind of God I personally believe in; but what God actually is, is not only beyond my feeble intellect, but also beyond the understanding of any person (including Jesus) who ever lived, or ever will live. It is *our relationship* to God which is real, not God "himself." God "himself" is an impenetrable mystery: is, was, and always will be. God is Truth—sure!—but what is Truth? We simply do not have the mental or spiritual capacity to comprehend the magnitude of the meaning or "substance" of the word God. God is like nothing we can possibly imagine. In fact, he may be so omnipotent, omniscient and omnipresent, that it may be true to say, like Cupitt, that he doesn't exist. And yet he does! The Universe is living proof of his existence. And Jesus Christ the living proof of his love.

And that, I am afraid, is about as far as I can go.

Chapter 3

Where Is God?

Canst thou by searching find out God?

Old Testament: Job, xi, 7.

If God is not in us, He never existed.

Voltaire

Only the naive, the primitive and little children actually believe that God exists somewhere "up there" in the blue beyond. And even some modern theologians no longer subscribe to the actually existent personal God of Jesus Christ. When we hear, as we did in the last chapter, men of God, like Cupitt, talk of the Creator as a "nonexistent goal," an "imaginary focus," the "internalization of values which we ourselves create," the mind, if not the soul, boggles. If God is a nonexistent goal (or a nonexistent anything else) then he cannot be anywhere.

In a way, of course, the Cupitts must be right. "Anywhere" is a spatial term, entirely inappropriate when discussing a transcendent, nonspatial being. If God is transcendent then he transcends time and space. So he cannot be "up there" or "anywhere else." He cannot even be "nowhere."

However, we have to start somewhere!

The New Testament tells us that God is in heaven. But where (sorry!) is heaven? If not "up there"—where?

As physical beings we are aware of three dimensions: length, breadth and width. But there is a fourth: spacetime, a fusion of the concepts of time and space. This dimension is unimaginable; but we know that it exists because Einstein (and others) have conclusively demonstrated that it does. We shall be looking at the phenomenon of spacetime in Chapter 5, but I mention it here

108

purely to show that it is possible for something to exist that cannot be imagined. "I can visualize space as just emptiness," writes Dr. Kit Pedler *(Mind over Matter)*, "and I can visualize time as the sequence of ticks of my watch, but I *cannot visualize* spacetime. It does not make sense and I can make no model of it in my head. Neither can anyone else including physicists ... Spacetime was a necessary invention because it helped to explain unknown events whether they could be visualized or not. One elderly don at Oxford said that he had spent much of his life trying to visualize spacetime. After a lifetime of contemplation, he was asked on his deathbed if he had succeeded. 'Once or twice I caught a glimpse,' he replied."

Until this century we were completely unaware of the fourth dimension. Now, believe it or not, some scientists are speculating that there could be as many as ten! But why stop at ten? Why not ten times ten? ten thousand? ten million? In the context of infinity numbers have little consequence. For all we know there could be as many dimensions as there are atoms in the Universe!

Because something cannot be imagined, it doesn't mean that it cannot exist. Einstein didn't have to imagine spacetime before he concluded that space and time were not two distinct entities but relatives united in one spacetime continuum. The ancient Greeks had no means of scientifically investigating the smallest particles of matter, but they knew that the atom existed (indeed, they "invented" it).

Modern science has since discovered that the atom, which the Greeks erroneously believed to be the smallest unit of matter, consists of clouds of subnuclear particles, which are themselves nothing more than ghostly images. In other words, matter does not concretely exist in the way we think it does; the atom exists purely as a scientific concept. As Kit Pedler (ibid) remarks: "Electrons and nucleons . . . only have a *tendency* to exist." John Hasted, Professor of Physics at Birbeck College in the University of London, puts it like this (ibid): "I don't even know if an atom exists. It only probably exists. It could even be in two places at once. I don't know how many dimensions we're in."

These scientists are not saying that the atom does not exist, but that it exists more or less immaterially. It is not that matter is not real: it is just that we do not know what it is. "Will we ever come to an end in our understanding of the nature of matter?" asks American scientist Carl Sagan *(Cosmos)*, "or is there an infinite regression into more and more fundamental particles? This is one of the great unsolved problems in science."

And so it will remain. For the infinitely small is as undiscoverable as the infinitely large. If we do ever come to the end of our investigations, I believe we shall be faced with a world of real, live, supernatural ghosts! Existent, but nonexistent; immaterial, not material, "Electrons," says Carl Sagan (ibid), ". . . are just clouds of moving fluff. Atoms are mainly empty space. Matter is composed chiefly of nothing."

That, dear reader, is the unreality of reality, the reality of unreality. Matter, which we had believed to be rock hard, solid and real, turns out to be little more than empty space. And remember, they are the words of a down-to-earth physicist not a head-in-the-clouds mystic! So ponder them well, for they represent a scientific endorsement of the mystic's age-old claim that the world we see is less real than the world we cannot see. That reality is unreal, and unreality real. That what is, is not; and what is not, is.

Some things simply are unimaginable. Had we been created two-dimensional creatures, living our lives in absolute flatness, like photographs printed on the pages of a magazine, we would not be able to visualize a third dimension. A three-dimensional being would be unimaginable; thickness incomprehensible. Our flat brains would not be able to visualize anything that wasn't flat; flatness would be all there was.

An unborn child, nestling in its mother's womb, could not imagine that the world it inhabits is located inside the body of another being, who exists in another world, itself located in an altogether inconceivably large universe.

A worm wriggling its way beneath the surface of the soil, and a fish swimming in the depths of the ocean, are completely unaware of the world above and the universe beyond. Nevertheless, the world and the universe do exist, and can be seen to exist by those with eyes to see and minds to perceive. As for what lies beyond the Universe, beyond our powers of understanding, we, unlike the worm and the fish, cannot simply plead ignorance; for we possess something that they do not—intelligence and imagination. We have been blest with the ability to see beyond the boundaries of sight, to penetrate the barriers of physical existence and to imagine, not the unimaginable, but that something can exist that cannot be imagined. The Greeks could not see the atom. But they knew that it existed. Astronomers cannot see beyond what their telescopes reveal. But they know that there is a beyond. We cannot see God. But . . . ?

There are so many things that are inexplicable. But that doesn't mean that there are no explanations; simply that we do not know what the explanations are. The human being is, for example, a complex organism. A mass of contradictory coordinates: body and soul, mind and matter, material and immaterial. We do not know why we are here or the cause of our existence. Mysterious things go on inside our mind and body seemingly of their own accord. Take visions, for instance. What are they? "The art of seeing things invisible," as Swift remarked? Whether a vision is a genuine supernatural occurrence, or simply an hallucination, it is still a mystery. When Paul was on his way to Damascus, did he really see what he thought he saw? He certainly thought he did. He was so convinced that he had heard the voice of Christ, that he immediately changed course and set off on the road to persecution, torture and death. There is not much doubt that he saw and heard *something*.

Innumerable people have testified to having seen a loved one who has died. When my mother was a young woman and very seriously ill, she swore that she saw her mother standing at the foot of her bed beckoning her. This kind of experience is very common. I daresay almost every family in the land has its own story to tell. People who claim to have visions may not all truly have visions, but they truly appear to believe that they do.

Then there are dreams. What are they? Not what causes them, but what are they? How is it that we are able to see things in the middle of the night with our eyes shut and our minds switched off? How does the brain invent these images without conscious collaboration? The brain doesn't simply recall past images, it invents new ones. When we dream, we create situations, story lines and dialogue that are completely new and original, and weave them, unconsciously or subconsciously, into a coherent story. Presumably it is the psyche operating below the level of consciousness that does the creating. But that explains nothing.

Psychoanalysts interpret dreams and tell us why we dream them. But they have absolutely no idea what dreams actually are, how and in what way they are created, and "where" they take place. Do the dreams we dream still exist? If so, where? Do the thoughts we think still exist? If so, how?

Consider so-called "out-of-body" or "near-death" experiences, where people (especially those who clinically "die" but subsequently recover) depart their bodies and observe themselves from "above" or "outside" (perhaps from a top corner of the room in which they are lying), and see what is going on around them (doctors trying to resuscitate their body, for example). This may sound fantastic, but there have been so many cases documented by reliable professionals that the phenomenon cannot simply be dismissed or ignored.

Hundreds of books have been written about the occult: telekinesis, spiritualism, materialization, clairvoyance, ESP, Ouija boards, poltergeists, exorcism, witchcraft, faith healing, levitation, dowsing, crystal gazing, fortune-telling, pendulum swinging, telepathy, apparitions, hauntings, etc. Now I personally have been unconvinced by much of what I have read, especially in those areas where fraudulency is rife. No doubt, too, many "happenings" can be put down to superstition and overexcitement of the imagination. I also discount the work of professional magicians and "mind readers", like the "spoon bending" of Uri Geller, for example. And, of course, many mysterious occurrences may have perfectly simple and natural explanations. After all, a mystery is only a mystery because we do not know the answer. Having said that, however, it is easy to sneer at things we do not understand, much more difficult to keep an open mind. We cannot be certain that in no cases whatsoever are there no supernatural influences at work in any way.

When a thought, a word or a tune enters the minds of two people simultaneously, does it enter both minds together, or does it travel from one to the other? (This phenomenon happens far too frequently—it does to my wife and I—for it always to be a coincidence.) Either way, does the "signal" travel through space, as do light and sound waves, or is it transmitted through an unknown dimension?

How is it that identical ideas have a habit of surfacing at the same time in different parts of the globe? (Writing, for example, was invented independently throughout the world at a time when there were no means of communication between the continents.)

How do fear and panic sweep through a community? Behaviourists can explain why people behave the way they do; but not how the sensations they experience travel from one person, or group of persons, to another. Fear is said to be catching. But it is not catching in the same way as a communicable disease is catching. A contagious disease, for instance, is transmitted through physical contact. With an infectious disease the germ travels through the atmosphere. In both cases space is involved. But in the case of fear we simply do not know in what way, through what medium, the emotion is transmitted.

Where are the emotions of love and hate stored? Not in the heart, to be sure. Nor in the brain (the brain is not an emotional storage tank). In the mind? But where and what is the mind?

When we allow our thoughts to wander over vast areas of time and space; when we recall the events of our childhood days; when we think on the things we did yesterday and the things we expect to do tomorrow—where are our thoughts? Are they confined to the environs of the brain? Or are they "somewhere" else? In spatial limbo? Or in another dimention?

If our thoughts are in the brain then they reside in space, because the brain is physically located in space. But thoughts are not physical things, and it does not follow that because one's brain is in space, the thoughts it thinks are too.

What is the memory? A "thing"; or a collection of things remembered? Where are memories stored? How are they brought to mind? Does the memory occupy a place in space (i.e. in the brain), where information about past events is filed? Or do memories float around in another dimension? Memory, according to the *Oxford Illustrated Dictionary*, is: ".....faculty by which things are recalled or kept in mind." Faculty? What is that? Kept in mind? What does that mean? Is space involved, or it is not? No one knows.

113

The same goes for ideas, which presumably are a product of thought. In what way do they exist? Where do they come from?

We have all heard of people having prescient dreams: about loved ones in danger, of train crashes and other disasters. During the First World War, my grandmother dreamt that her son, who was a sailor, was in the sea in pitch darkness clinging to a piece of wreckage. She was later to learn that on the night she had her fateful dream, the destroyer on which her son was serving, was torpedoed and sunk, and that he was in the water for forty-eight hours, just as she had dreamed, before being picked up by a passing ship. Of course, one could explain this dream away by saying that, with her son away on active service, and being fearful for his safety, it was quite natural that she should have such a dream, and that it was pure coincidence that she dreamt it on the same night as his ship was sunk. Perhaps. On the other hand, it is equally possible, in my view, that the information about her son's danger came to her through an unknown dimension.

I readily admit that one can never know how much credence can be placed on such anecdotal evidence. The story I have just related, for instance, came to me secondhand; so I obviously cannot guarantee that it is the unvarnished truth. Such stories have a habit of becoming more garbled and embellished the more often they are told. However, too many tales have been recorded for all of them to have been fanciful inventions or mere coincidences. I myself have had a few distinctly odd experiences, which I am able to put forward as direct, not hearsay, evidence.

Many years ago, when telephone calls had to be made through the operator, I wanted to ring a company called J & F Wing. I took the phone off the hook and waited for the operator to ask, "number, please?" Instead, a voice at the other end said: "Good morning, J & F Wing." "That's funny," I said, "I was just going to ring you." The girl replied: "I'm not ringing you; you're ringing me."

To cut a long story short, her phone had rung and she had answered it, only to find me at the other end waiting to phone her. Now, I know what the reader is thinking, that I had absentmindedly asked the operator for the number without it registering on my consciousness. Knowing that this is the interpretation I myself would put upon it in later years when my memory of the incident had faded, I rang the operator to ask whether any calls had been placed from my number (in those days calls were physically recorded by the phone company). The answer was No.

I can offer no explanation as to how such an incident could have occurred. Thought transference? I do not suggest it; I simply put it forward as a possibility.

The following two incidents happened during the last war, whilst I was living with my friend's family in Bedford. The first was on the morning of April 9, 1940. Coming down to breakfast, my friend remarked that he had had a particularly vivid dream. He had seen waves of German tanks rolling across the plains of Denmark absolutely unopposed. An hour or so later, it was announced on the BBC news bulletin that early that morning Germany had invaded Denmark and that its forces had met with virtually no resistance. (I should add that the attack came as a complete surprise, to the British public, at least, as there had been no reports to suggest that such an attack was imminent.)

The second occasion was five years later, in April 1945. Again, just before breakfast, my friend said that he had dreamt that the American flag, which flew over a factory in Bedford, was flying at half-mast. This sounded like a pretty trivial dream, until later we switched on the radio and learned that President Roosevelt had just died. Now, it has to be said that again this news came as a complete surprise. Not a hint of Roosevelt's illness had appeared in the media. Obviously such information would have been hushed up in wartime for security reasons.

Much more recently my friend had another very peculiar dream. On the night of Saturday, March 31, 1984, he dreamt that he was discussing team selection with Malcolm MacDonald, an English football club manager at the time. MacDonald said that he wanted to play a rather boyish-looking but not unattractive girl as goalkeeper. My friend disagreed, saying that goal was too rough a position for a girl, and that she ought to be played on the wing. The next morning he strolled along to his local newsagent to buy a paper, and there on the front page of the Sunday Mirror was the banner headline "SUPERMAC SAYS WE DID IT FOR LOVE" (or words to that effect). The news item was accompanied by a picture of MacDonald and his girlfriend, for whom he had left his wife, and who resembled exactly the girl in the dream.

The same friend has had many other dreams of this kind, but as I did not record them at the time, I hesitate to rely on my memory for complete and accurate recollection. But I can assure the reader that some of these dreams were quite extraordinary.

The common feature of all the dreams, it will be noticed, is that none of them was prophetic: they did not foretell future events; they related to something that was happening at that particular moment.

The explanation? My theory is this: as the events were taking place, the information concerning those events was "at large" in the "atmosphere" (a different dimension, perhaps); and, for one reason or another, my friend was able to pick up the information signals, which were "flying around," whilst his mind was "inhabiting" or "probing" this dimension.

I believe that events are "self-recording"; that they leave their "imprint" in the Book of Time, which is available for "inspection" by any mind that happens to be in the "vicinity" at any given moment. As an event takes place, the "truth of the event" is released into a secret dimension, and any mind that has the ability to "tune in" to this dimension, will "pick up" the information. When the German tanks rolled across the plains of Denmark; when Roosevelt died; when the football manager MacDonald left his wife for another woman, the truth of those events was present everywhere at the same time. If this sounds farfetched, just consider what happens when an event is televised live throughout the world. It is seen in all four corners of the globe simultaneously. The event (to be more precise, the electronic image of the event) is beamed into every home in the world whether or not it has a TV set. (The aerial doesn't create the signal, it simply collects it and passes it on to the set, where it is transformed into images projected on to the screen.) If you do not possess a TV set, or if you do but it is not switched on, then the event will pass you by. Nevertheless, the information will still enter your home, the particular room in which you are sitting, in the very air you breathe. Think about this for a moment. You will inhale the information! It will invade the tissue

116

of your lungs, enter your blood stream, your brain. You won't see the event, but it will "take place" within you.

When TV engineers transmit signals around the world, our aerials pick up these signals, and through the set translate them into recognizable images. If the signals were able to find their own way around the world without the aid of the TV engineer, we would be privy to every event as it happened—provided, of course, we had our own built-in aerial and information processor!

The question I would like to put is this: How do we know that these signals do *not* find their own way around the world? For all we know, they could be winging their way across the Universe at every instant in time. The "truth" of events may be present in every place simultaneously. Does it take any bigger leap of the imagination to grasp that, than it would have done in pre-TV days to imagine that images (live ones at that!) would one day be projected around the world at the speed of light via satellite?

If an event takes place in London, the truth of the event is also true simultaneously in New York, Paris, Tokyo, and Timbuktu—and on the most distant star in the Universe!

If something is true here, it is true there. Fact is fact, and it is fact everywhere at the same time.

This could explain how the 'news' of the death of President Roosevelt, of the German invasion of Denmark, of the infidelity of a football manager, etc., etc., could have been "leaked" to someone whose mind happened to be "tuned-in" to the truth of the event. If the truth of an event is stored in an unknown "truth dimension," it would obviously take an exceptional mind to gain access to that dimension, hence the infrequency of the phenomenon.

The mind is shrouded in mystery. Unlike the brain, it doesn't physically exist. Is it, then, simply the brain "at work"? We know that the brain exists, because we can open up the skull and see it. But the mind? In what way can it be said to exist? And if it does exist—where is it?

Does the mind reside in the brain? Are the mind and the brain one and the same thing? Experiments carried out by one of the greatest living neurosurgeons, Wilder Penfield of McGill

University—too detailed to include here—would suggest that they are not.

The following interesting story is told by Kit Pedler *(Mind over Matter)*: "As I write this, an extraordinary account has been published [in *The London Times* Dec 30, 1980] of a student at Sheffield University with an IQ of 126 and an honours degree in mathematics. The extraordinary part of the account is that the student has practically no cerebral cortex (what we have always assumed is the 'thinking' part of the brain), as measured by a brain scan. This . . . casts serious doubt on the relationship between the physical brain and the mind. By all traditional reasoning, this student would be more likely to be mentally subnormal with such a small amount of brain cortex. Perhaps because of his lack of the cortical material, his mind shifted into some other part of his brain rather like a hologram."

A hologram?

"A hologram," says Dr. Pedler (ibid), "is a way of recording visual images photographically. It is produced with laser light and does not produce a negative picture of the subject on film, but a pattern of waves which is generated by mixing laser light which has not struck the object with laser light which has." I will paraphrase the rest of Dr. Pedler's description: If an ordinary slide is projected onto a screen, the whole picture appears. If, however, the slide is broken into pieces, and only one piece is projected on to a screen then only that one piece will appear. Now when a hologram is projected on to a screen, as with an ordinary slide the whole picture appears. But if the hologram is broken into pieces and only one piece is projected on to the screen then the whole picture will appear—though the image will be fuzzier and show less detail. The whole is, in fact, *in each part*.

This leads Dr. Pedler to ask: "If the mind is more like the shifting wave patterns of a hologram, and perhaps mobile in the substance of the brain—could it leave the brain altogether and go somewhere else? . . . We could perhaps approach the bizarre idea that [the mind] could actually break loose and move out of the brain of a person as something separate from physical matter . . . Does the mind actually go out, or is there a special channel where the paranormal effect works without having to assume

118

the conscious mind leaving the body as an entity in its own right?"

Could it be, perhaps, that the mind operates in another dimension, presenting its ideas to the brain for processing into tangible thoughts? Perhaps the material brain is "saturated" with the "essence" of the immaterial mind, like an onion pickled in vinegar. It is difficult to believe that the "vast cities and palaces of the mind" (the simile is Van der Post's) are to be found in a lump of matter, that the lofty, luminous thoughts of Shakespeare, Schiller, and Goethe, Keats, Shelley, and Wordsworth, Tolstoy, Dostoevsky, and Kierkegaard, Blake, Pascal, and Simone Weil, the saints Paul, Anselm, and Augustine were created by a machine.

The brain is a thought processor, a "computer" which does its master's (the mind's) bidding. A computer doesn't think for itself; it thinks for its master, man. Likewise the brain doesn't think for itself; it thinks for its master, mind. It is sometimes suggested that computers have or are minds. What nonsense! The human mind is an instrument of creation; the computer creates nothing. Once the computer is switched on it cannot alter course, not of its own free will. It cannot change its mind. And if it cannot change its mind, it hasn't a mind to change.

But Paul Davies, *(God and the New Physics)* is not so sure. "The answer to the question 'Can machines think?' he writes, "must be that one has no reason to rank men above machines on grounds of performance (in certain intellectual tasks) which is the only external criterion by which one can assess the machine's 'internal' experiences. If a machine could be made to respond in the same way as a human being to all external influences then there would be no observable grounds for claiming that the machine did not think, or did not have a consciousness. Moreover, if we are willing to concede that dogs think, or that spiders or ants possess some rudimentary consciousness, then even presently available computers could be regarded as conscious in that limited sense."

It will be noted that Professor Davies does not claim that computers *do* think. He very wisely uses a very big "if" at the beginning of the penultimate sentence, viz: *"If* a machine could be made to respond in the same way as a human being. . . ;" and an equally big "observable" later in the same sentence: ". . . there would be no *observable* grounds for claiming that machines did not think." I personally do not believe that it will ever be possible to build a machine that could respond in the same way as a human being to all external influences. And even if it were, there would still be grounds (observable or unobservable) for claiming that machines do not think.

If we regard thinking as a purely mechanical process, with no measure of self-will or self-consciousness, then yes, computers do think. But if we see thinking as something which contains within itself an element of instinct, self-will and true self-consciousness, as opposed to the ersatz consciousness of the computer, then no, computers do not think. The argument, it seems to me, is not whether computers think, but about the meaning of the word "think."

There is more to thinking than automatically "thinking" what you are programmed to "think." Computers can be programmed to carry out immensely complicated arithmetical equations billions of times more quickly than humans can. But what does that prove? Simply that man is clever enough to invent a machine to do his "thinking" for him! If machines were all that smart, they'd tell us to do our own thinking. Or go on strike for higher pay and better conditions!

If computers could really think, they'd freely choose their own programmes; and then, if they wished, change their minds of their own free will. A computer programmed to play chess cannot suddenly change its mind and play the piano. A computer-dating machine cannot suddenly decide to marry one of the clients itself. "What the computer is utterly incapable of doing," says Laurens Van der Post, in conversation with Jean-Marc Pottiez *(A Walk with a White Bushman)*, "is to give us a value judgement. It is utterly divorced from meaning. It can work statistically and it can quantify, but it cannot deal with meaning—and certainly not create it. And do not forget, it is a law of creation that that which is created can never be greater than the thing that created it."

A computer is a machine without emotions, instinct, free will. It cannot love or hate, blush, smile, or scowl. It cannot feel joy or sorrow. It cannot repent or forgive. And, lest we forget, men make computers; computers do not make men.

To sum up: the brain is an infinitely complicated piece of machinery, a mass of circuitry and nervous tissue that controls the processes of sensation, learning, and memory. It is the workhorse of the mind, the handmaiden of the intellect. In the words of the Australian Nobelist Sir John Eccles (vide *The Natural History of the Mind* by Gordon Rattray Taylor): "[the brain] is the most wonderful organized structure in the Universe."

The mind, on the other hand, is the creator of ideas, the thought maker. It is, nevertheless, amoral, with no concept of right or wrong, good or evil. Contrary to what we are told by some of our scientific and philosophical betters, the mind is not the soul. Science, mathematics, and other intellectual activities, art, literature, and music, are pursued in and by the mind. Of themselves, these things are amoral. There is nothing moral about splitting the atom, the discovery of gravity, the theory of relativity. No ethical values are required to compose a symphony or a poem. The mind that creates beautiful works of art also creates deadly weapons of war. The intellect that discovers antibiotics for healing the sick, also invents bacteriological chemicals for the express purpose of destroying the environment and the human population with it. To create (and enjoy) music, art, and literature, is not a moral accomplishment. An intellectual giant can be a moral pygmy; a genius a devil. Morality and ethics have nothing to do with the intellect, but all to do with the soul. Love and compassion and forgiveness bear no relationship to mathematical formulae, music, art, and literature. The square on the hypotenuse of a right-angled triangle may equal the sum of the other two, but that equation gives no clue as to why a sailor will give up his place in a lifeboat for a mother and a child.

Mother Teresa once said: "I would not wash a leper's body for a thousand pounds, but I would do it for the love of Christ." Whence sprang those words—from the intellect, or from the soul? When Jesus was hanging from the cross in physical and spiritual torment, he cried out: "Forgive them, Father, for they know not what they do." Whence sprang those words—from the intellect, or from the soul?

I am not saying that there is no connection between the intellect and the soul, or that the soul does not influence the way the mind works. I am saying that they are not one and the same thing. The soul often finds expression through the intellect and the arts; but, "Blessed are the pure in heart for they shall see God," cannot be interpreted as "Blessed are the intellectually and artistically gifted for they shall see God." The pure in heart are often intellectually and artistically gifted; but then, as often as not, they are not. If one has to be pure in heart to see God, then the quality of one's mind is irrelevant. It is not by the grace of the intellect that one sees God, but by the loving of one's neighbour as oneself.

There is, to be sure, a linkage between the various constituents of the human being—soul, mind, brain, and body. At one end of the spectrum there is the soul—a spiritual entity unlocatable in this world. At the other end, the body—the part we know so well but about which we know so little, very much located in this world. In between, bridging the gap as it were, linking one form of existence to another, is the combination of mind and brain. The mind also unseeable and unlocatable, neither inside nor outside the body; the brain an electrically charged physical organ unmistakably located inside the skull, acting and reacting physically with the corporeal constituent of which it is a part. The connection between brain and body has been positively established by the medical and other professions. "If they doubt the idea that illness is to some extent a mental condition," writes Robin Blake *(Mind over Medicine),* "think for a moment of the immune system—our ability to remain healthy by fighting off disease. Immunity looks, on the face of it, like nothing more than a bunch of cells which go around the bloodstream zapping bacteria and viruses. Of course, these cells do exist physically, but if you look at the immunity carefully you see it doing things of a purely *mental* function.

"First, it knows things like the difference between what is part of you and what is alien. The knowledge is so strong that in transplant patients it has to be suppressed with drugs. Second, the system studies new invaders and educates itself about how to deal with them. Third, it doesn't forget what it has learned—it has a memory. So the immune system is a sub-mind: this sub-mind goes up and down with our mental state . . ."

The four dynamics of human existence—soul, mind, brain and body—represent a progression of attributes rather than a continuum of coordinates; the relationship between them is likely to remain forever an unfathomable mystery.

The soul is of no fixed abode, a spiritual organism "hovering" in a nonspatial dimension. Just as "a living body is not a fixed thing but a flowing event like a flame or a whirlpool" (Allan Watts, *Does it Matter?*), so is the soul not a fixed thing but a flowing event within the spiritual dimension.

The spiritual dimension does not exist in the same way as the physical world exists. (Even the physical world does not exist in the way that it appears to exist: as we have seen, atoms, of which the whole Universe consists, are no more than ghostly images; and physicists are obliged to use descriptive, nonscientific words, like "charm," "flavour," and "colour," when describing the "structure" of atomic particles, because of their inability to describe "things" which do not materially exist.) Even to say that the spiritual dimension exists "beyond" or "alongside" or "parallel with" the material universe, is misleading. It would be more accurate to say that it doesn't exist at all! But then, that would be more misleading still. Because to those who experience it, the spiritual dimension is more real than the "real" world of the ghostly atom, with its cloudy nucleous of "charmed," "flavoured" and "coloured" nonexistent particles.

Descartes thought that the soul resided in the pineal body, a small apparently functionless organ at the base of the hindbrain. In other words, the soul was physically located somewhere in the skull. "[But] eventually it was concluded that the self was not located in a specific part of the brain," writes Brian M. Stableford *(The Mysteries of Modern Science)*, "but was distributed throughout it. It was a product of the whole rather than a part or a sum of parts. The self is not an organ . . . but a state of organization. It is not, itself, material but a pattern within matter."

Shades of the hologram!

If it were possible to divide the body into a thousand pieces, without the patient dying, would the self (or soul) be divided likewise? Obviously not. You cannot divide something which is indivisible, a "pattern within matter," the nonphysical spiritual part of man.

In these medically advanced times, when human organ transplantation is an everyday occurrence, it can be envisaged that one day it might be possible (in theory, if not in practice) to replace most parts of the human body with natural or plastic organs. In this eventuality, at what point would the patient's self or soul disappear and be replaced by a different human (or plastic!) soul? The question is of course absurd. A person having a heart, lung, and liver transplant today is in no way a different person from what he was yesterday. His self or soul remains intact: it is neither diminished, added to, nor changed in any way. However . . .

"The fact that the self survives while bit after bit of the body is removed," writes Stableford (ibid), "does not prove that the self is not 'in' those bits. It merely illustrates the extent to which the self may sustain itself against the erosion of the material structure on which it is superimposed."

It is patently obvious that the self cannot be diminished by loss of limbs or organs; but it is not so certain that it cannot be changed by damage to the brain. In fact, the opposite would seem to be the case. Brain damage can clearly be seen to alter the character and behaviour of a person, sometimes dramatically. This does not necessarily mean that the person's fundamental self has been changed. We do not know that "self" is synonymous with "soul," that they are precisely the same thing. The self is a person's own individuality, which also embraces the material, nonspiritual part of man; whereas the soul is purely the spiritual or immaterial part, which cannot, by definition, include the material body—unless, perchance, the body is "impregnated" with the soul. In which case, how do we separate the two? Is a soul-impregnated material body a part of the nonmaterial soul? We are in murky waters!

Where, then, is the soul?

The physicist Paul Davies *(God and the New Physics)* says: "Can the new physics, with its weird concepts of spacewarps and higher dimensions, provide a suitable location [for the soul]? Physicists think of space and time as a sort of a four-dimensional

124

sheet (or perhaps balloon) with the possibility of other disconnected sheets. Could the soul reside in one of these other universes? Alternatively, spacetime may be envisaged as enfolded by, or embedded in, a higher dimensional space, much as a two-dimensional surface or sheet is embedded in three-dimensional space. Might not the soul inhabit a location in this higher dimensional space which is still (geometrically speaking) close to our physical spacetime, but not actually in it? From this higher dimensional vantage point the soul could 'lock on' to the body of an individual in spacetime, without itself being part of spacetime."

Professor Davies goes on to speculate that the physical universe could extend "beyond" (in a figurative sense) what we call spacetime, and that this "elsewhere" could be the realm of the soul.

These words, coming as they do from a professional physicist, demonstrate how science and theology can work together. Professor Davies's remarks, although speculative and not necessarily his own beliefs, are soundly based on modern quantum physics and show that the mystical need not necessarily be unscientific.

We shall soon be nearing the end of this chapter, and the reader may well be wondering where all this is leading us. We are supposed to be discussing the whereabouts of God, not the mysteries of the human soul or self! In defence, I would say that these matters are related. If we don't know "where" the self or soul is, we are hardly likely to discover "where" God is!

It is becoming increasingly obvious that this chapter should not have been called *"Where* is God?" but *"In what way* does God exist?" Because if God is not spatially existent then "where" is a nonword with no place in the spiritual lexicon or in any discussion about a nonspatial transcendent Being.

The deist, however, would not agree, for his god exists *within* the Universe. In fact, some deists say that God *is* the Universe. Others think of God as a higher intelligence existing within the harmony of natural law.

"Where" (or rather how) is this higher intelligence to be found? Professors Hoyle and Wickramasinghe *(Evolution from Space)* say: "There are those who think that the way to establish

125

a connection with a higher intelligence is to go riding around the galaxy in spaceships, or to listen for coded radio signals emanating from other planetary systems in the galaxy. In the past we have had some sympathy with the second of these notions, but we have always rejected the first as woefully slow, crude, and profitless. Now we are inclined to think the second is also unnecessarily cumbersome. If our ideas are correct, there must surely be a multiplicity of clues around us here on the Earth's surface, clues to the identities of the intelligences immediately [next to us] in the sequence . . . It would be more sensible, for example, to broadcast clues on the unexpressed DNA of yeast cells than to go through the ponderous technology of radio transmissions . . ." The clues, they suggest, might even be locked up in the genome of the California redwood or in the social behaviour of insects.

But whether the clues are to be found "down here" or "up there," higher intelligence cannot be the whole truth. Telescopes and microscopes, computers, and all the other paraphernalia of modern science, are of no use when trying to establish the "whereabouts" of a spiritual dimension.

"One of the stock Russian questions asked of astronauts in Moscow when they have returned from outer space," said Laurens van der Post (A Walk with a White Bushman), "is, 'Did you see any sign of God and heaven up there?' The mocking reply, always to a roar of laughter, is of course that they did not."

Now of course if you ask a silly question, you get a silly answer. How can there possibly be any sign of God and heaven "up there," when God and heaven do not exist in space or time or anywhere or "anywhen" else? But the real idiocy of the question is that these brave astronauts were themselves "up there" only by the grace of God. The intelligence that put them into space and enabled them to explore the heavens, was bestowed upon them by the very Being whose existence they thought they were disproving.

Suppose the astronauts had been asked: "Did you see any sign of love up there?" Would they still have replied: "Of course we did not"? Or would they have said that as they themselves had wives and children and parents and friends whom they loved, then yes, they did find love up there; for the very reason that they took it up there with them in their own hearts? Now, if they found love up there then they found God. Because God is love. What these astronauts didn't realize is that when they were launched into outer space they took God with them.

When their heroic fellow countrymen were fighting the Germans in defence of their homeland in the last war, did they find God on the streets and in the cellars of Stalingrad, in the multitude of towns and villages laid waste by the Nazi invaders? They did not. They found God in the laying down of their lives for their loved ones.

This is not an attempt to justify or to glorify war. I am not saying that the killing of one's fellow human beings (and the Nazis were their fellow human beings) is morally uplifting, or spiritually elevating, or even right in any circumstances. Simply that where love and sacrifice are, God is. God was not present on the battlefield, he was present in the hearts of the men on the battlefield, who were fighting and dying (yes, and killing!) in defence of their loved ones. And, of course, in the hearts of those Germans who also believed that they were fighting and dying for their loved ones. The fact is that God does not wage war on battlefields, but in the hearts of men.

"Where" then is God?

Obviously not in outer space. "Looking for God, or Heaven, by exploring space," writes C. S. Lewis *(The Seeing Eye: Christian Reflections)*, "is like reading or seeing all Shakespeare's plays in the hope that you will find Shakespeare as one of the characters, or Stratford as one of the places. Shakespeare is in one sense present at every moment in every play. But he is never present in the same way as Falstaff or Lady Macbeth. Nor is he diffused through the play like gas. If there were an idiot who thought plays existed on their own, without an author . . . our belief in Shakespeare would not be much affected by his saying, quite truly, that he had studied all the plays and never found Shakespeare in them . . .

"If God created the Universe, he created spacetime, which is to the Universe as the metre is to the poem or the key is to music. To look for him as one item within the framework which he himself invented is nonsensical . . . the expectation of finding God by astronautics would be very like trying to verify or falsify

127

the divinity of Christ by taking specimens of his blood or dissecting him . . . If you do not at all know God, of course you will not recognize him, either in Jesus or in outer space."

God is not in outer space (or inner space, or any other space). If God were "up there," he would also be "down here." Because "up there" is "down here." Every single point in the Universe, including our own tiny sphere and the particular spot each of us occupies at the present moment, is both "up there" and "down here."

God is not "without"; he is not even "within." He is, in the nonspatial meaning of the word, beyond. "The beyond," wrote Dietrich Bonhoeffer, in a letter to his friend Eberhard Bethge *(Letters and Papers from Prison, 1967 Edition)*, "is not what is infinitely remote, but what is nearest to hand." Even nearer than that, I would say, nearer to us than we are to ourselves!

God is to be found at the heart of the spiritual "atom," in a single, multidimensional dimension that embraces and subsumes all dimensions, known and unknown. Where thrones and crowns, flesh and blood, time, space, and universal laws do not exist. God is at the centre of spiritual gravity. Indeed, he *is* the centre of spiritual gravity. All roads lead not to Rome, but to God!

If God is that close then presumably he should be easy to find. Ah, but that's the paradox! He is at once so close as to be a part of us, yet so far away as to be unreachable. I am not a theologian, just a humble sinner; but I am sure of this: we will never find God by searching for him intellectually, no more than we will find him by roaming the Universe in a rocket. No intelligent person would expect to find God on the highways and byways of the Cosmos; but many do expect to find him on the highways and byways of intelligence. "If we rely on thought and philosophical analyses alone," says Jewish philosopher Martin Buber (1878–1965), "we surely shall not meet God. Indeed, in the 'court' of thought where conceptual analysis and critical evaluation of arguments are the only tools at hand or voices heard, God is not to be found at all. And that 'court' has been right in turning in a verdict of 'not proven' when it comes to establishing the existence of God." (Source: *The Ways of Philosophy* by Milton K. Munitz.) Munitz comments: "For Buber . . . neither theology nor philosophy can lead the way to God. Not even *religion* can do so, if this is understood in the sense of a set of fixed practices and a dogmatic creed."

The direct route to God is though our fellow human beings. It's as simple (or as difficult) as that. If you go to Calcutta, to the heart of some of the poorest slums on Earth, you will find Mother Teresa and her dedicated band of co-workers, caring for the diseased and the dying, the lepers, the other unwanted, unloved outcasts of society, and little babies left to die in dustbins. THAT IS WHERE YOU WILL FIND GOD. In the hearts and actions of those Christian nuns who have made sacrifice something more than a duty, more than a vocational necessity, more even than a pleasure, but an act of reciprocity. They will tell you that they get back more than they give, and the more they give, the more they get back. (Didn't their Lord say, "Unto them that hath, shall be given"?) They help the sick and give the dying a chance to die in dignity. No one in Mother Teresa's care leaves this world alone and unloved. For her, every single person is Jesus. She herself said: "I believe in person to person; every person is Christ for me, and since there is only one Jesus, that person is the only one person in the world for me at that moment." (Source: *Something Beautiful for God*, by Malcolm Muggeridge.)

That is the logic of Christian love: "EVERY PERSON IS CHRIST FOR ME." Could the message be clearer?

Can anyone doubt that this Christian lady has found God? She didn't have to zoom into outer space (or even into inner space), because she knew exactly "where" to look.

After participating in a television programme about suffering, Malcolm Muggeridge (ibid) relates how he received hundreds of letters from viewers, nearly all of them recounting some experience of personal suffering or of watching over a loved one suffering. One particularly poignant letter came from a lady who had watched her twenty-two-year-old son die after "one more desperate operation [to close up the hole in his heart] had failed."

"Where is God?" she asked, "and why does he allow such cruel things to happen? Perhaps I am only thinking of myself, and my son is indeed better off where he is, but how can I *know* this? I can only feel the great desolation that he has gone from this world, leaving a grievous gap in the lives of his parents and his brother. *Where is your God?*"

"Where is my God?" says Mr. Muggeridge. "Dear Mrs.——, he is everywhere; even in the hole in your son's heart, or nowhere. I look out my window, as I write these words, at a wintry countryside. The bees and the badgers are asleep; the birds perch hungrily on the bare twigs; nature seems dead forever. Yet not so. Faith tells me that soon the badgers and the bees will awake, the trees load themselves with leaves, the birds sing joyously as they once more build their nests, the dead earth renew itself and wear all the greenery of yet another harvest.

"This is a faith easily held. We know—or think we do—that spring will always return. Now I turn my glance from the window into my own heart, seeing there the litter and the dust of wasted years. Old envies not quite spent, old appetites that still could be reanimated, old hopes and desires that flounder on even though whatever outcome they might expect to have has long ago proved illusory. This, too—the interior of my heart—seems a dead landscape. Yet faith tells me that it, likewise, can have a spring in the rebirth promised to us all in the new dispensation which Christ brought to the world. The old envies budding with holy love; the old lusts burning with spiritual appetite; the old hopes and desires finding a near destination in the bright radiance of God's universal love . . ."

"GOD IS EVERYWHERE; EVEN IN THE HOLE IN YOUR SON'S HEART, OR NOWHERE." These words of Mr. Muggeridge's sum up the impossibility of trying to answer a question that is improperly phrased. The question "Where is God?" cannot sensibly be answered, because God, like love, is where you find him, and you find him everywhere—or nowhere. Those, like Mother Teresa, who have found God (and I certainly haven't, though I have been close enough to know that he's there) don't need to know "where" he is. Sufficient unto them that they have found him. But for the rest of us, who are not blessed with the nature and spiritual insight of a Mother Teresa, we shall have to be content with six of the simplest and most illuminating words ever uttered by Jesus Christ: "OUR FATHER WHICH ART IN HEAVEN".

So there you are. God is in heaven! And "where" is heaven?

Where love and sacrifice are. Love and sacrifice are the key to the heavenly gates that lead to the dimension of God. And, not surprisingly, the master key itself turns out to be God himself. "Whoever looks for God," said Pascal, "has found him."

Chapter 4

What Is Time?

Time! Such a simple little word; we use it all the time. We know what we mean by it; but do we know what *it* means?

St. Augustine, the early Christian theologian, when asked what was time, replied, "If no one asks me, I know; if I am asked to explain it, I do not know."

Time is the most dominating influence in our daily lives. We get up by it, go to work by it, eat and sleep by it, keep appointments by it, catch trains and planes by it. In fact there is practically nothing we do that is not in some way dictated by this ruthless of all taskmasters. Our whole existence is spent in the shadow of the clock. Even when we sleep we cannot escape the ravages of time.

Throughout the ages man has been fascinated by time, and for centuries scientists, philosophers, theologians, and poets have searched for the answer to this eternal enigma. Some believed it was cyclic, coming round again and again, like an enormous wheel—what Nietzsche called the "eternal return." The Stoics even believed that history repeats itself in every minute detail: the heavens being restored to their former position; every person living again and doing the same things that he did before; each tree, each flower, each blade of grass growing where it did before; each town and village, street, and building being restored to its former existence.

The ancient Indians believed that time was static and permanent. Others that it flowed uniformly in a straight line. "Absolute, true and mathematical time, of itself and by its own, flows constantly without relation to anything outside itself," wrote Sir Isaac Newton. Not so, said Ernst Mach, the Austrian physicist and philosopher. "Absolute time," he declared, "is an idle metaphysical concept." Einstein, who was greatly influenced by Mach, agreed. He demonstrated that time was relative, not absolute, that it was affected by speed, space, and gravity.

What is the layman to make of all this? Whatever its true nature—cyclic, static, progressive, absolute, or relative—does time really exist? Or is it an illusion, a product of man's imagination, an intellectual concept created by the human mind to explain change and events? For if we existed in a vacuum, where there was no night or day, no growth or decay, no birth or death, and where there was no movement, not even the blinking of an eye, it is difficult to imagine that we would have any awareness of time.

Our perception of time is that the past is gone, the future is yet to come, and the present is happening right now. But what is now? How long does it last? A minute; a second? No, even a billioneth of a second is too long to be called now. For if it were divided in half, one half would be in the past and the other half in the future—the now being the point at which they meet. But if the now is simply the meeting point between the future and the past then it exists only in theory. "How can we exist," asks J. B. Priestly (*Over the Long High Wall*), "on a narrowing edge between two vast nothings, the vanished past and the uncreated future"?

It would seem, then, that time consists solely of the "vanished past" and the "uncreated future." But this we reject, instinctively and intellectually, because we know that only the now is real, that the past exists only in the memory, and the future only in the imagination.

Everything happens in the now. Nothing happens in the future or the past. All events begin in the now, take place in the now, and end in the now. Every stroke of every letter of every word that I am now writing and you are now reading, was, is and will be written in the now.

But how can the now be real if it lasts for less than a billioneth of a second? The truth is that now doesn't last for any period of time, it *is* time, it "lasts" for eternity—or at least, for as long as time lasts.

The past, present, and future are bogus boundaries that we invent to position events that are taking place, have taken place, and will take place. Time cannot be sliced up like salami into constantly changing pieces (does the past increase in length, and the future decrease in length with every second that passes?) We see time in a false perspective, as something which flows like a river, whereas it is, I believe, more like a lake, a permanent "now-pool" in which change and events take place.

> Time is not progress, but amount;
> One vast accumulating store,
> Laid up, not lost!
> James Montgomery *(Time)*

Imagine a forest in which every tree represents an event. As we walk through the forest, each tree (event) we encounter comes to us from the "future," becomes the "present" as we reach it, and disappears into the "past" as we leave it behind. The forest is there *all the time,* but we experience it only a bit at a time.

Alternatively, picture an enormous globe full of countless grains of sand, each grain representing an event. In this "time globe," events take place at different points on different levels, although the globe itself is at rest in a permanent state of now.

But if it is something like that why can't we take a step back in time and reexperience events that happened in the past, or a step forward and experience events that will happen in the future? This is to confuse time with events. An event that has occurred cannot be made to reoccur (a tree cannot reappear after it has been chopped down). And an event that has not yet happened cannot be made to happen until it is ready to happen (a tree cannot appear that has not yet grown). The reason why we cannot take a step forward or backward in time is that we are *already there*. The whole of time from beginning to end is one ever-present now. The "time-value" of all events is the same; it is the memory and the imagination that deceive us into thinking that events happen at different "times." It is not time that is "before" or "after"; it is events. The clock and the calendar are simply devices for measuring and recording time. If an event takes place at, say, three o'clock, it is the event, not three o'clock, that takes place at three o'clock. Three o'clock has no validity except as a marker or coordinator. (In any case, the event doesn't take place at three o'clock, it takes place *now.*)

We talk of the past, the present, and the future, as if they were three separate entities. The present year, for instance, was in the future when 1950 was in the present, and 1920 in the past. Now, two of those years are in the past and one is in the present, although fast disappearing into the past with every tick of the clock. Which just shows how meaningless these arbitrary divisions of time are except as reference points for events. (It will be observed that we never talk of time except in connection with change or events—actually one and the same thing.)

Nothing shattered man's illusions about time more than Einstein's theory of relativity. Einstein demonstrated that time was not uniform, that it could shrink or stretch depending on circumstances. "The revolution in our conception of time," writes Paul Davies (*God and the New Physics*), "which has accompanied the theory of relativity is best summarized by saying that, previously, time was regarded as absolute, fixed and universal, independent of material bodies or observers. Today time is seen to be *dynamical*. It can stretch and shrink, warp and even stop altogether at a singularity. . . . Clock rates are not absolute, but relative to the state of motion or gravitational situation of the observer.

"Liberating time from the straitjacket of universality, and allowing each observer's time to roll forward freely and independently, forces us to abandon some long-standing assumptions. For example there can be no unanimous agreement about the choice of 'now' . . . There is no universal 'present moment.' If two events A and B, occurring at separate places, are regarded as simultaneous by one observer, another observer will see A occur before B, while yet another may regard B as occurring first."

In our ordinary everyday lives, Einstein's theory of relativity has no relevance. At a speed of 186,282 miles per second it takes virtually no time at all for light to travel from one end of the street to another, and only a few seconds to travel to the moon. But when it comes to the vast distances of outer space, it's a very different story. The light, for instance, from a star 100 million light-years from Earth, takes 100 million years to reach us (a light-year being the distance that light travels in a year: viz 5,869,196,496,000 miles). It is a sobering thought that when we look up at the sky at night, we could be looking at myriads of stars that aren't there, and haven't been there for millions of years. Even if the Sun, which, at a mere 93 million miles from Earth is virtually in our backyard, were to suddenly go out, we wouldn't see it go out for eight and a half minutes. Compare this with the most distant object we have seen, where the light left some eight thousand million years ago! (vide Stephen W. Hawking's *A Brief History of Time*).

If we were to observe the inhabitants of a planet, say 500 light-years from Earth, we would see them not as they are now but as they were 500 years ago. Suppose that I invent a magical new telescope that enables me to observe the activities of this hypothetical "Planet 500." As I point my telescope in its direction, to my surprise I see a "Planetman 500" pointing his magical telescope at me. What are the implications of this?

First, that I am looking at a person who isn't there, and hasn't been there for 500 years. In fact, at the time he was pointing his telescope at "me" (i.e., 500 years ago), Henry VII was on the throne of England.

Second, that "Planetman 500," whom I perceive to be looking at me, is (or rather was) looking at someone alive at the time of Ethelred the Unready, who was reigning a thousand years ago in the year 979.

My perception is that "Planetman 500" and I share the same now. *His* perception is, well, he hasn't got one, because he's been dead for 500 years! But when he was alive, 500 years ago, and was looking at "me," his perception was that he was sharing the same now with Ethelred the Unready, whereas he was in fact sharing it with Henry VII. Talk about seeing ghosts!

Now we can see the relevance of Einstein's theory of relativity. Time (or more accurately, spacetime) has a way of distorting reality (or more accurately, our *perception* of reality). One man's past is another man's present and another man's future.

Time is distorted by speed and distance—the greater the speed the more slowly time passes. This may sound absurd, but it is true. Time is also affected by gravity. A clock at the top of a tall building will run faster than a clock at the bottom.

"The theory of relativity," writes Stephen W. Hawking (ibid), "gets rid of absolute time. Consider a pair of twins. Suppose that one twin goes to live on the top of a mountain while the other stays at sea level. The first twin would age faster than the second. Thus, if they meet again, one would be older than the other. In this case, the difference in ages would be very small, but it would be much larger if one of the twins went for a long trip in a spaceship at nearly the speed of light. When he returned, he would be much younger than the one who stayed on Earth. This is known as the twins paradox, but it is a paradox only if one has the idea of absolute time at the back of one's mind. In the theory of relativity there is no unique absolute time, but instead each individual has his own personal measure of time that depends on where he is and how he is moving."

Roy Stemman, in his book *Mysteries of the Universe,* puts it like this: "If we were able to travel close to the speed of light . . . the clocks on board the speeding spaceship would run more slowly and the atomic and biological processes of everything on the craft would slow down correspondingly. So a trip to the stars would seem to take months instead of years. A man returning from a journey made at such speeds would find that his twin brother left behind on Earth was much older than himself . . . Even more incredible is that such a space traveller could return to find his own grandchildren older than he is. A journey to the stars, it seems, would provide the source of eternal youth, for if the spaceship attained the speed of light, time would stand still."

It will be noticed that not only would the clocks on board the speeding spaceship run more slowly, but so would the atomic and biological processes of everyone and everything on board. So that at the speed of light, time and the ageing processes would literally stand still. And if, by extension, the spaceship were to travel at a speed in excess of the speed of light (which, of course, it couldn't) then time would go into reverse, and the spaceship would overtake the images that set out before it. Those on board would be able to look back and witness all the events in history: the two world wars, the French revolution, the Crucifixion . . . in fact every event way back to the birth of the Universe, like a film being run backwards.

As it is not possible, nor will it ever be, for human beings to travel at the speed of light, we are here dabbling in the realms of fantasy. However, the principle is correct, even though natural laws forbid it. Time, it would appear, is far more complicated than we thought—unless, that is, there are two kinds of time—the scientific and the psychological.

Paul Davies, in *God and the New Physics*, says: "Our psychological perception of time differs so radically from the physicist's model that even many physicists have come to doubt whether some vital ingredient has been omitted. Eddington once remarked that there is a sort of 'back door' into our minds through which time enters in addition to its usual route through our laboratory instruments and senses. Our sensation of time is somehow more elementary than our sensation of, say, spatial orientation or matter. It is an internal, rather than a bodily experience. Specifically we feel the *passage* of time—a sensation which is so pronounced that it constitutes the most elementary aspect of our experience."

So, even the physicists have their doubts! We have to accept, however, that "absolute, universal time" is scientifically meaningless. No observer in the Universe can relate his now to the now of another observer somewhere else in the Universe. Strictly speaking, we cannot relate our now to the now of someone standing only a few yards from us, as it still takes time for images to travel even this short distance. In astrophysics now is the supreme subjective!

So, it's game set and match to relativity. Well, not quite. It may be *scientifically* meaningless to talk of universal time, but that doesn't mean that universal time is not conceptually valid. The question, "I wonder what is happening on 'Planet 500' right now?" (i.e., *my* now) is still valid, even though there is no way it can ever be answered. At the very moment I am observing "Planetman 500" observing "me," a different "Planetman 500" is (or is not, depending on whether his planet still exists!) standing on the same spot from which his predecessor's image was being transmitted 500 years ago (i.e., *my* ago). The fact is, this information exists, even though it is not available to me or anyone else.

There is no possibility of "Planetman 500" and I ever knowing what the other is doing at any point in universal time. So in that respect the question is meaningless. But the intriguing point is this: I would know what I was doing, and he would know what he was doing. The fact that space makes it impossible for us to relate our individual, subjective nows, doesn't alter the fact that they are related, that universal now is the same for both of us. The now of which I am now conscious, coincides with the now that is universally experienced at the same moment in universal time by every conscious being (and not experienced by every nonconscious object). The universal now of every living and nonliving phenomena in the Universe is the same. The universal now for a stone on Planet Earth is the same as the universal now for a stone on "Planet 500." They don't have to be aware that it is now for it to be now—now has a relevance all of its own. Universal time, it could be said, is a "God's-eye" view of time. So, far from being meaningless, universal time is supremely meaningful!

If something is true, then it is universally true—truth has nothing to do with light waves. If something is true here on Earth, here and now, then it is also true on a planet on the other side of the Universe, never mind whether the inhabitants there know it or not, never mind how long the image or information takes to reach them. A few hundred years ago we had no idea what was happening on the other side of the world until weeks or months later. That's how long it took for the information to travel the distance involved, by the means available at the time. But this didn't affect the truth of what was happening. If at this particular moment in (our) time, a distant star were to explode, the information wouldn't reach us for thousands or millions of years. Nevertheless, the event would be true here and now (our now), at this very moment (our moment).

A universal now may be meaningless to a being who can never know what is happening on the other side of the Universe, at any particular point in (his) time, but it wouldn't be meaningless to an objective observer standing astride time and space, observing what is happening in all parts of the Universe at any point in universal time. And that is conceptually true, even if no such objective observer exists. In the transcendental world of universal truth and universal time, the "here" and "now" coincide with the "there" and "then."

Earlier in this chapter I suggested that time might be an illusion, an intellectual concept created by the human mind to explain change and events. The difficulty here, however, is that if time really is just a thought-thing, an invention of the human mind, then how is it that the Earth revolved around the sun, at fixed intervals, long before man emerged on Earth to perceive it? We know for a fact that the Universe was in a state of evolution umpteen billion years before the appearance of creatures able to perceive it. And, as evolution = time, would it not appear, that time exists independent of man perceiving it, that it has an objective existence unrelated to man's subjective perception? Surely, whatever time is or is not, it cannot be merely a thought-thing?

> Whether we wake or we sleep,
> Whether we carol or weep,
> The Sun with his Planets in chime,
> Marketh the going of Time.

> Edward Fitzgerald (*Chronomoros*)

But what if the sun stopped shining, the planets stopped

chiming, and man ceased to wake or sleep, carol or weep—would not time come to a complete halt? And if it did would it still be time?

By a curious coincidence, on the day these words were written, a remarkable story appeared in the media concerning the discovery of the icy grave in the Arctic wastes, of a twenty-year-old English mariner, Able Seaman John Hartwell, who perished in the ill-fated Franklin expedition of 1846 to the Arctic Circle in search of the Northwest passage. His body was so perfectly preserved that he looked no older than he did on the day that he died. This young man, born some 164 years ago, appeared to have "simply closed his eyes and gone to sleep." (Age certainly did not weary him, nor the years condemn!)

Now, let us consider the implications if, by some magic injection, it were possible to bring this young man back to life. How old would he be? Twenty or 164? He would think the former; we the latter. In fact, we could prove that he was 164. But he would do better than that; he would know that he was only twenty. He would have the body, the brain, the mind, the memory of a twenty-year-old. Time would have passed him by. It would seem, then, that the answer to the question would depend on who answers the question!

Let us now suppose that simultaneous with this young man freezing to death in 1846, everything in the Universe came to a complete halt. Clocks stopped ticking, the sun stopped shining, atoms stopped spinning. And then, a century and more later, everything started up again, picking up where it had left off. Where would that leave time? I will tell you. During the big sleep it would have stood still, nay, ceased to exist. For how could time exist if there were no movement, no change, no decay, no birth, no death—all prerequisites of time?

> Wherever anything lives, there is, open somewhere, a register in which time is being inscribed.
>
> Henri Bergson *(Creative Evolution)*

In a Universe where nothing lived, moved, changed, or died, Bergson's register would be closed. Because there would be nothing to be inscribed therein. And time would have meaning only to a universal observer, outside the Universe, not subject to the flow of time, who could observe time standing still or not existing, within the Universe.

In the real world, however, things do happen; there is movement, birth, death, change, and decay. It is only in the fictional world of stopped clocks, preserved bodies, and stationary atoms, that the passage of time can be halted.

We humans perceive time in relation to our own life span. That is the only way we can measure it. If we lived for a thousand years instead of our allotted seventy or whatever; if a day consisted of a thousand hours instead of twenty-four, I doubt whether we would ever talk of time flying. It is a truism to say that time drags when we are bored, and flies when we are enjoying ourselves. An hour spent reading an absorbing novel or watching an exciting film, goes much more quickly than an hour endured with raging toothache.

The older we get the faster time flies. When we are babies time stands still. To the young child with no awareness of time there is only existence and change, the future being an endless perpetuation of the present. Perhaps the baby's perception—or rather, nonperception—of time is nearer reality than the adult's? After all, is it realistic to keep talking of time when what we really mean is change and events? Consider the following passage from Ecclesiastes, Chapter 3, where the word "time" appears no less than twenty-nine times, yet not once is it used except to describe change or events.

To every thing there is a season, and a time to every purpose under the heaven:
A time to be born, and a time to die; a time to plant, and a time to pluck up that which is planted;
A time to kill, and a time to heal; a time to break down, and a time to build up;
A time to weep, and a time to laugh; a time to mourn, and a time to dance;
A time to cast away stones, and a time to gather stones together;
A time to embrace, and a time to refrain from embracing;
A time to get, and a time to lose; a time to keep, and a time to cast away;

A time to rend, and a time to sew; a time to keep silence, and a time to speak;
A time to love, and a time to hate; a time of war, and a time of peace.

Again, is it realistic to talk of time in terms of hours, days, months, years? What do these "markers" mean? How long does an hour last? How long does "time" last? Are a million years a million times longer than a year? If so, why are there not a million times more moments in a million years than there are in a year? There is in fact an infinity of moments in a million years, just as there is an infinity of moments in a year, and an infinity of moments in a single second. Come again?

"Any mathematician can demonstrate," writes Paul Davies (*God and the New Physics*), "that there are no more moments in all of eternity than there are in, say, one minute. In both cases there is an infinite number, and this infinity can be made no bigger by 'infinite stretching.'"

Now the reader may wish to pause for a few seconds to allow this to sink in (I know I did when I first read it). Surely Professor Davies is not saying that there are the same number of moments in a minute as there are in all eternity? No, he is not. He is saying that both periods of time contain an infinite number of moments. If the reader is still confused, perhaps the following imaginary conversation between the writer and the reader may help.

Writer: Since I began writing this chapter an infinity of moments has elapsed.
Reader: An infinity?
Writer: Yes.
Reader: But doesn't infinity mean forever? How can a finite period of time go on forever? That sounds like a contradiction in terms to me.
Writer: The fact that we are talking about a finite period makes no difference. There is an infinity of moments in a second just as there is an infinity of moments in a million seconds. Infinity doesn't mean a specific number. If it did then by adding

	one moment to an infinity of moments we would get something in excess of an infinity of moments. Which is impossible, because infinity cannot be exceeded, it goes on forever. A second and a million seconds each contain an infinity, not an equal number, of moments.
Reader:	But surely it is plain common sense that there are a million times more moments in a million seconds than there are in a second?
Writer:	It may be plain common sense, but it isn't true. Any period of time, however long or short, contains an infinity of moments. You can take whatever period of time you like, divide it in half, and keep dividing each half in half for all eternity, and you will never arrive at the smallest fraction of time. Because there isn't one. And as the fractions get smaller, the numbers increase exponentially. So one could say that time has depth as well as length, the cube of infinity, as it were.
Reader:	So what you are saying is, that that moment in time, which we call now (which itself is too short to be measured), contains an infinity of moments, each of which contains an infinity of moments, each of which . . . I could go on like this forever!
Writer:	Exactly. That is what infinity means.
Reader:	In that case, it seems to me that time is nothing more than a mathematical concept.
Writer:	You could be right.

The plot thickens, and we don't seem to be getting any nearer to unravelling the mystery of time. Let's start again. What actually is time? What does it do? What function does it perform? "It is important to realize," said Luisa Becherucci in her Introduction to Gina Pischel's *The Golden History of Art,* "that time itself can have different values when it is regarded on the one hand merely as a measure of succeeding events and on the other as the matrix of energy at work."

Now there's a good description! "A measure of succeeding events," "the matrix of energy at work." We recognize time by the events which take place within it, and the energy expended on those events. We are in time, and time is in us. Our minds and bodies are steeped in, and saturated by, its "flavours." It is in our blood and bones, our hearts and minds. It is many things. A medium in which change takes place; a framework for reality; a backdrop for events; a condition that allows man to be continuously aware of his awareness.

In her book *The Mask of Time*, Joan Forman relates the following incident concerning the famous Swiss philosopher, mystic, and metaphysician, Carl Gustuv Jung (1875–1961): "In 1944, Jung suffered a serious heart attack following an accident and almost died in the illness which followed . . . During the three weeks of his critical illness, Jung appears to have had a series of mystical experiences . . . He describes the experience as being an ecstasy of a nontemporal state in which present, past, and future are one. All the happenings in time had been unified, and temporal concepts could no longer apply. Time for him at this point was an objective whole, a blend of past knowledge, present awareness and future anticipation; it was all one time, all one state of being, a sum total not only of what his own individuality represented, but of all existence."

For Jung, it seems that time, as an "on-going" state, ceased to exist. Past, present, and future were telescoped into one objective whole, one state of being, one nontemporal all-embracing existence, one now. Such a state of existence cannot accurately be termed consciousness; for consciousness is a *continuous* activity that depends on the existence of time. "Static" consciousness of the kind that Jung experienced is mysterical not temporal. Which leads us to the question: Was there any consciousness before time began? Over to Paul Davies (*God and the New Physics*): "When giving lectures on cosmology I am often asked what happened before the big bang. The answer, that there was no 'before,' because the big bang represented the appearance of time itself, is regarded with suspicion, 'something must have caused it.' But cause and effect are temporal concepts, and cannot be applied to a state in which time does not exist; the question is meaningless."

Meaningless it may be—to the physicist; but it isn't meaningless to the person who asks the question. Unfortunately we have to use temporal words like "before" and "after," because no others are available to us. So, even though the question is "meaningless," it is still valid: Was there any existence of any kind "before" the big bang banged?

Here we reach an impasse. For however the question is phrased it is beyond the competence of the physicist, *qua physicist,* to answer. To seek the answer (albeit the wrong answer) we must go beyond the world of physics into the realm of metaphysics. But first, a supplementary question: When was *consciousness* first created?

The obvious answer is: when evolutionary pressures produced the first conscious creatures. Now, it is true that consciousness first *manifested* itself in conscious creatures; but I believe that consciousness itself was created in that first split-second of creation when EVERYTHING—i.e. everything that is, was and will be—was created. The original "spark" or "seed" of creation embodied all the genes of creation, including time, space and consciousness. Consciousness, like all other uncreated things, was encoded in the "frozen cosmic gene," to await its release into the "cosmic blood stream" at the evolutionary moment deemed appropriate by the Original Cosmic Creator. Had the seed of consciousness not already existed, it could not have flowered in the later-to-become-conscious creatures when they first arrived on the scene.

But this raises a problem for the theist: If consciousness was created at the same "time" as the big bang, how could God himself have been conscious "before" the big bang? For clearly one cannot experience something that has not yet been created.

I believe the answer is this: God experiences a wholly different kind of consciousness from that which he bestowed on humankind. "Before" God created time, space, and consciousness, and all the fixtures and fittings of creation, there was only God. A timeless, SUPERNATURALLY CONSCIOUS Being, who does not need time in order to "function" or to be. Put another way: God is not conscious; he is CONSCIOUSNESS.

But this presents a further problem: How can a God who is timeless engage in temporal activities, such as thinking, feeling, planning, etc.? The point is made by Paul Davies (ibid): "[A timeless God] cannot be a personal God who thinks, converses,

146

feels, plans, and so on, for these are all temporal activities. It is hard to see how a timeless God can act at all in time . . . If God is timeless, he cannot be said to think, for thinking is a temporal activity. But can a timeless being have knowledge? Acquiring knowledge clearly involves time, but knowing as such does not—provided that what is known does not itself change with time. If God knows, for example, the position of every atom today, then that knowledge will change by tomorrow. To know timelessly must therefore involve his knowing all events throughout time."

Precisely! That is what omniscience means! God does know timelessly. He knows the past, the present, the future—all at the same "time." He is Bergson's "register in which time is being inscribed." Except that time isn't *being* inscribed, it *is* inscribed. The whole thing is down there in black and white from beginning to end since the dawn of creation.

But how are we to deal with the assertion that a timeless God "cannot be a personal God who thinks, converses, feels, plans, and so on, for these are all temporal activities"? Like this: God is able to enter our temporal activities without divesting himself of his timelessness, because finite time is contained within the infinity of God. God is not in time; time is in God. Time "proceeds" within the existence of a "static" God. God doesn't need to enter time, because time exists within him.

It would be most unwise to assume that the Mind that conceived and planned the whole of creation would not have ensured that it would be able to continue with its conceiving and planning *after* the original act of creation. And it is equally foolish to suppose that a personal and loving God would not have ensured that he would be able to *continuously* communicate with those whom he created and loved.

Time, it is said, marches on. And so it does—unless, that is, is it we who march on, and time that stands still. In the words of the poet James Montgomery *(Time, A Rhapsody):*

> Then shall be shown, that but in name
> Time and eternity were both the same;
> A point which life nor death could sever,
> A moment standing still for ever.

And this from Longfellow *(The Old Clock on the Stairs):*

> The horologe of Eternity
> Sayeth this incessantly,—
> "Forever—never!
> Never—forever!"

Is time, as Montgomery asserts, "a moment standing still for ever?" Does Longfellow's "never" really go on "forever"? But what does forever mean? For as long as time lasts or time without end? Is time finite or is it infinite? Here to stay or here "today" and gone "tomorrow"? Well, we shall just have to wait and see—thirteen billion years to be exact! For that is how much longer the Universe is expected to last.

Of one thing I am sure: If time did begin (whether with a big bang or in any other way) then one day it must end. For there cannot be a beginning without an end, just as there cannot be an end without a beginning. If time is infinite then there was no beginning and there will be no end: if time is finite then there was a beginning and there will be an end. We have to choose between finiteness and infinity; we cannot have both.

Definitively there can be only ONE beginning and ONE end—the beginning and the end of creation. What comes in between is a continuous process of change. Beginnings come before ends, and ends before beginnings. Birth comes before death, and death before birth. As the poet T. S. Eliot puts it:

> What we call the beginning is often the end
> And to make an end is to make a beginning.

Intangible time, which cannot be directly experienced by any of the senses, is nonetheless real. Yes, I know I said that "time markers" are artificial and meaningless. But time itself isn't. How can it not be real when we cannot live without it? Everything we do and think, we do and think by courtesy of time. We couldn't speak, eat, drink, or put one foot in front of the other, if it were not for time. Time is an essential element of the human condition. No time—no birth, no death, no decay—nothing.

When I look back on my childhood days and recall the events of sixty-odd years ago, I have a distinct feeling that time has passed. I don't just mean that I feel a lot older (in truth, the innate *I* doesn't feel any older at all). I mean that "sixty years ago" seems a lot further away than "sixty days ago" or "sixty minutes ago." The "space" in between seems a lot greater. In other words, the sensation of time has nothing to do with memory but with "distance." Like Eddington, I feel that time is an elementary part of my experience; I have a pronounced feeling of the passage of time.

Could it be that there are not one, not two, but three kinds of time: the "scientific," the "universal," and the 'psychological," each with its own peculiar function—the scientific capable of being shrunk, stretched and measured; the universal being a static now; and the psychological a subjective experience of the human psyche?

We do not understand the nature of time, because we do not understand the nature of existence. St. Augustine was not alone. No one has yet been able to solve the mystery of time. And no one ever will. Not unless, that is, the human mind can ever find a way of itself operating outside of time. Until then, one of the most commonplace words in the language, will remain one of the most enigmatic. "There are things about time," wrote D. H. Jack, "that defy our understanding, and I feel sure that to a great extent this is the key to so much that baffles us."

Postscript: After completing this chapter, I came across the following passage in C. S. Lewis's *The Fall of Man,* which may be considered apposite: "The Fathers may sometimes say that we are punished for Adam's sin: but they much more often say that *we* sinned in Adam. It may be impossible to find out what they really meant by this, or we may decide that what they meant was erroneous. But I do not think that we can dismiss their way of talking as mere 'idiom.' Wisely, or foolishly, they believed that we were *really*—and not simply by legal fiction—involved in Adam's action. The attempt to formulate this belief by saying that we were 'in' Adam in a physical sense—Adam being the first vehicle of the 'immortal germ plasm'—may be unacceptable: but it is, of course, a further question whether the belief itself is merely a confusion or a real insight into spiritual matters beyond our normal grasp . . . "

Could it be that we really *were* involved in 'Adam's' action, and still are? That time has no *spiritual* significance? That before "Adam" was, I am?

Maybe the Fathers knew more about time than we do.

Chapter 5

What Is Space?

Just take a trifling handful, O philosopher!
Of magic matter: give it a slight toss over
The ambient ether—and I don't see why
You shouldn't make a sky.

Mortimer Collins

I hold space to be something purely relative, as time is.

Leibniz

When I was a child, airplanes were made of little more than canvas and string, and spaceships existed only in the imagination of scientists who weren't quite right in the head. When they predicted that one day men would travel in space, and that they would float around in their spaceships because up there everything was weightless, well, frankly, I didn't believe them. (That was of course before I learned about gravity. Until then, I believed that when something fell to the ground, it did so because it was heavy—no doubt Newton also thought the same thing when he was a little boy, before the apple dropped.)

Less than fifty years later, on July 21, 1969, man, in the form of American astronauts Neil Armstrong and Edwin Aldrin, stepped onto the moon (thus conclusively proving that it wasn't made of green cheese!).

Since then, men have walked in space, put communication satellites into orbit around the Earth, sent probes to other star systems, are currently launching permanently manned space stations, planning to send men to Mars and eventually to colonize other planets in the galaxy. Even as I revise these words, NASA Spacecraft Voyager 2 is passing the planet Uranus, nearly two billion miles from Earth, after being launched eight-and-a-

151

half years ago, on August 20, 1977, and is now on its way to a rendezvous with Neptune, a further one billion miles away, in August 1989. At this very moment it is beaming back to Earth masses of exciting new information and incredibly sharp color pictures at the speed of light (Later: It is now August 25, 1989, and Voyager 2 has reached Neptune, its mission completed. The spacecraft, currently on its way out of the solar system and heading for eventual oblivion, has been a spectacular success beyond the wildest expectations. The images being received at the Jet Propulsion Laboratory in Pasadena have the watching cosmologists leaping around like excited schoolboys. Nineteen moons have been discovered on the round trip, and amongst the host of other information being sent back is the confirmation that we are the only inhabited planet in the solar system. Unmanned visits to all the solar system's main planets have now been completed. What next? we ask—a manned mission to Mars? And the future? Space visionaries are predicting that one day people will emigrate to distant parts of the solar system, set up nation states, and eventually leave the solar system altogether.)

All this! less than ninety years after man first learned to fly, a hundred years after the first motor car was patented, and forty years after the first primitive German V2 rockets were launched against London. The whole vast Universe is beckoning to be explored—enough to keep the human race busy for millions of years to come, should we ever manage to solve all our problems here on Earth. Clearly we should never be at a loose end for something to do!

The first thing we notice about space is that there's so much of it! It's all around us. Stretching out in all directions, seemingly forever. The distances in space are so vast that one wonders whether it was deliberately designed that way, so as to ensure that if there are other intelligent creatures in the Universe, "never the twain shall meet." Perhaps the Creator, knowing the destructive predilections of the intelligent creatures who were eventually to evolve in the Universe, decided to make it impossible for them ever to interfere with each other's unique evolutionary path. In this regard, do not be fooled by those scientists, who ought to know better, who would have us believe that one day man will be so technologically advanced that he will be able to travel anywhere in space. Nothing could be further from the truth. In the first place, we have no idea how big the Universe is, it could go on forever. In the second place, even accepting the impossible hypothesis that eventually man will be able to travel at the speed of light (i.e. 186,282 miles per second), it would take billions of years to reach a planet billions of light-years from Earth. Even to travel to the center of our own galaxy (which in cosmic terms is like walking round the corner to the local store), would take 30,000 years. And if the Universe is infinite in size (which it may well be) then it would take an infinity of time to make the journey, whatever speed is travelled at. No, unrestricted intergalactic space travel is most definitely not on.

Before I began this chapter, I thought that space, unlike time, was relatively easy to understand. For one thing we can see it—can't we? We open our eyes and there it is, staring us in the face. It has three instantly recognizable dimensions: length, breadth, and height. It is real; it really does exist (doesn't it?) True, we are often baffled by its contents, and the way those contents behave. But space itself is quite straightforward. I mean, an empty box measuring 2 ft. × 2 ft. × 2 ft. contains eight cubic feet of empty space. Right? Well, not quite; there's a little more to it than that.

My problems began when I realized that space was invisible. Contrary to what I had thought, when we look at space we don't actually see space, we see objects in space. That is to say, space enables us to see objects in perspective, and in relationship to us, the observer. (Beginning to sound a bit like time, isn't it?) Did that mean, I wondered, that space did not really exist, that it was purely a geometrical concept? Oh dear!

To make matters worse, I came across a paragraph in Fred Hoyle's *The Intelligent Universe*, which pulled me up with quite a start. Talking about the properties of that mysterious phantom-like subatomic particle called the quark, which, because it is not really "real," physicists are obliged to use words like "spin," "flavour," "colour," "strange," "charmed," etc., to describe its behavior, Hoyle remarks: "This suggests the startling thought that, since spin is intimately related to space and time, space and time may not be truly fundamental concepts, but may be a kind of perspective, resulting from the particular aspect of the Universe which happens to fall within our experience."

A startling thought, indeed! If space and time are not fundamental concepts but a kind of perspective, then this really does suggest that space is not really real, simply a geometrical concept; not a *part of* reality, more a *view of* reality. The plot thickens!

At this point I realized that there was more to space than met the eye; it wasn't as straightforward as I had thought. So I consulted the *McGraw-Hill Encyclopedia of Science and Technology*. It said: "Physically, space is that property of the universe associated with extension in three mutually perpendicular directions. Space, from a newtonian point of view, may contain matter, but space exists apart from matter . . . geophysically, space is that portion of the universe beyond the immediate influence of Earth and its atmosphere . . . Astronomically, space is a part of the space-time continuum by which all events are uniquely located . . . Perceptually, space is sensed indirectly by the objects and events within it. Thus, a survey of space is more a survey of its contents."

Nothing very mysterious about that. But then McGraw-Hill went on to say that space cannot be studied in isolation, that it is inextricably linked to time, in what scientists call the space-time continuum. "From this hour on," observed the mathematician H. Minkowsky, when first conceiving four-dimensional spacetime, "space as such and time as such shall recede to the shadows and only a kind of union of the two retain significance."

"[Spacetime]" says McGraw-Hill, is a term used to denote the geometry of the physical universe as suggested by the theory of relativity. It is also called space-time continuum. Whereas in newtonian physics space and time had been considered quite separate entities, A. Einstein and H. Minkowsky showed that they are actually intimately intertwined . . . [The mathematician Minkowski conceived] the totality of space and time as a single four-dimensional continuum, which is often referred to as the Minkowski universe . . . [which] has four dimensions instead of the three dimensions of ordinary space . . . "

Ordinary space? Does that mean that there is more than one kind of space? Not really. It just means that, well, for the moment let us stick with good old-fashioned "ordinary" space, that we all understand and which the familiar *Oxford Illustrated Dictionary* describes as: "Continuous extension viewed with or without reference to the existence of objects within it; the immeasurable expanse in which the solar and stellar systems, nebulae, etc. are situated."

That's better! So space is space whether there are objects within it or not. And objects within it are an "extension of" space and not themselves, as it were, "made of" space. Which means that when an object in space moves, the space it occupies stays where it is, it doesn't move with it. If an object is moved from one room to another, the space in each room remains the same, it doesn't increase in one room and decrease in the other. It follows then that the space occupied by the object, is also occupied by the room. So in effect the space is twice occupied. And the same principle applies when a number of boxes are stacked inside each other. The space occupied by the smaller boxes, is also occupied by the larger boxes. So an object in space "co-exists" with the space it occupies. And as two *physical* objects cannot occupy the same space simultaneously, it follows that space is not a physical entity, more perhaps, in the words of Ernest Mach, "a conceptual monstrosity, purely a thought thing which cannot be pointed to in experience"?

If we were to drill right through the Earth, we would be drilling through matter and space at the same time. Because matter is an extension of space. Therefore, if the whole of space were to be filled with one solid object, space would not disappear, it would still be there. (Now you see it, now you don't!)

Suppose that the Universe is suspended in a sea of nothingness. Suppose now that the Universe were to shift from one "area" of that nothingness to another (assuming that it is physically possible for something to *move* in an area of literal nothingness, which it probably isn't), presumably the space "occupied" by the Universe would move with it, because space is not nothing? Would this not suggest that space, although not a physical entity, is more than a thought thing?

But let us leave the philosophical for a moment and get back to the physical.

Just how big the Universe is, no one knows. And it is, so

the scientists tell us, expanding all the time. How do we know it is expanding? Because it is dark at night! Heinrich Olbers (1758–1840), the famous German astronomer, carried out a simple experiment, subsequently called Olber's paradox, the essence of which was that, assuming, as they then did, that the Universe was in a state of equilibrium (i.e. that it was neither expanding nor contracting), then the amount of energy (i.e. heat and light) emitted by the stars to all the objects within the Universe, must be exactly the same as the amount being radiated back. As the energy and light coming to us from the stars was, Olbers estimated, equal to that coming to us from the sun, he concluded that it should be as light at night as it is during the day. Well, as we all know, it isn't! Hence the paradox.

Olbers was, however, on the right track. His mistake was in assuming that the Universe was in a state of equilibrium. The experiment should have told him, but didn't, that the Universe was expanding. Jacob Bronowski (*The Origins of Knowledge and Imagination*) explains: "[The Austrian-born astronomer Hermann] Bondi made the following beautiful argument: 'The stars are pumping energy into space, and it ought all to be coming back. It ought all now to be well mixed up, like the hot and the cold water in the bath. If it is not coming back, where is it going? It must be going into a volume of space which is greater than that from which it originated.' And so, Bondi says, 'We can do a very simple experiment. We can say that there are three possible states for the universe: it might be contracting, it might be of stationary size, or it might be expanding. If it is contracting, then night ought to be brighter than day because there ought to be more energy coming in simply from the background than the sun is actually supplying. If it is stationary, then night and day ought to be equally bright. And if the universe is expanding, then night ought to be dark.' "

Bronowski, who was delivering a lecture at the time, concluded with this remark: "I invite you to perform that experiment tonight. Go out and look, and when you observe that it is dark, you will have made the fundamental observation which shows that the Universe is expanding."

The Universe is unimaginably large. Our galaxy, the Milky Way, only a fraction of which can be seen with the naked eye, and which represents only a tiny part of the known Universe, covers the whole sky, whether viewed from the Northern or Southern Hemispheres, and consists of more than 100 billion suns, probably half of which have their own planetary systems. Beyond the Milky Way, in all directions, stretch millions of light-years of comparatively empty space, followed by another galaxy rather similar to our own, followed by millions of light-years of comparatively empty space, followed by another galaxy . . . and so on, and so on. How long this repetition goes on for is anybody's guess. There are known to be some hundreds of billions of such galaxies—indeed, the number could be endless. Astronomers have no idea how far the Universe stretches, and acknowledge that it could in fact go on forever.

But what does it mean to say that space goes on forever, that the Universe stretches infinitely into the distance? Well, it's a bit complicated. Paul Davies (*God and the New Physics*): "Scientists have long recognized the need to base all their considerations of infinity on precisely formulated mathematical steps, for measuring the infinite can produce all sorts of paradoxes. Consider, for example, the famous hare and tortoise paradox due to Zeno of Elea (fifth century BC). In a race, the tortoise has a head start, but the hare, running faster, soon overtakes him. Clearly, at every moment of the race the hare is at a place and the tortoise is at a place. As both have been running the same length of time—for an equal number of moments—then presumably they have passed through an equal number of places. But for the hare to overtake the tortoise he must cover a greater distance in the same time, and so pass through a *greater* number of places than the tortoise. How then can the hare ever overtake the tortoise?

"The resolution of this paradox . . . involves a proper formulation of the concept of infinity. If time and space are infinitely divisible then both the hare and the tortoise run for an infinity of moments through an infinity of places. The essential feature of infinity is that a part of infinity is as big as the whole. Although the tortoise's journey is shorter in distance than the hare's, he still covers as many places as the hare (i.e. infinity) even though we know the hare passes through all the same places as the tortoise, and more!" As we saw in the last chapter, the concept of infinity is a little hard to grasp, and even after the professor's excellent exposition, most of us will still find ourselves somewhat bemused. Paul Davies continues (ibid): "Is the Universe infinite in size? If space has an infinite volume we can envisage an infinity of galaxies populating it with roughly uniform density. Many people then worry about how something that is infinite can expand. What is therefor for it to expand into? There is no problem: infinity can be boosted in magnitude and still remain the same size. (Remember what the 'tortoise taught us.')"

But what if space is not infinite but finite; where are its boundaries; where does it end? Paul Davies (ibid): "Based on the fact that space can bend, Einstein argued [in 1917] that space can connect up to itself in a variety of unexpected ways. The curved surface of the Earth can be used as an analogy. The Earth's surface is finite in area, but unbounded: nowhere does a traveller meet an edge or boundary. Similarly space could be finite in volume, but without any edge or boundary. Few people can really envisage such a monstrosity, but mathematics can take care of the details for us. The shape is called a hypersphere. If the Universe is a hypersphere an astronaut could, in principle, circumnavigate it like a cosmic Magellan by always pointing his rocket in the same direction until he returned to his starting point.

"Although it is finite, Einstein's hyperspherical cosmos still has no centers or edge (just as the surface of the Earth has no center or edge) . . . "

We shall return to Einstein's finite hypersphere later, but for the moment I would like to put before the reader an alternative scenario, the steady state infinite Universe, first opposed in 1948 by that distinguished trio of scientists, Sir Fred Hoyle, Hermann Bondi and Thomas Gold.

Currently in disfavour in scientific circles, the steady state theory, though dead, refuses to lie down. Steady state postulates that the Universe did not begin, as most scientists now believe, with a big bang. In fact it didn't begin at all, because it has always existed. The steady state Universe is rapidly expanding. But as it expands new galaxies are created to fill up the "gaps" left behind by the older galaxies as they drift apart, so that new matter is being continuously created, either uniformly (hence "steady state") or perhaps in a series of "minibangs." "Instead of the whole Universe being created in a flash, in a big bang," writes Fred Hoyle in his book *The Intelligent Universe,* "atoms are created individually and continuously, with the process of creation going hand-in-hand with the expansion of the Universe."

If the steady state theory is correct; if the Universe has always been; then there was no original act of creation and therefore no need for an original creator. (Even so, there must have been a reason why the Universe has always been. This fact in itself would require a creator, the creator of reason.)

Present-day cosmologists are almost unanimous that the Universe began with a big bang. Big bang is in, steady state out. But beware of unanimous experts! They have so often been proved wrong in the past.

Scientists have an in-built bias towards big bang, away from steady state. And the reason is not hard to find. Big bang predicates a beginning. And scientists like beginnings, because beginnings give them something to explain. With steady state there is no beginning. So the origins of the Universe, which cry out for an explanation, do not require any. And so the scientists feel cheated.

In his innocence, the layman may think that scientists are concerned only with objective truth. Not so. They are as human as the rest of us, and being human, more prone to search for clues which are likely to prove them right than for clues which may possibly prove them wrong. Scientists believe in the big bang partly because they want to believe in the big bang. They do not like mysteries that cannot be solved!

"Science," writes Brian M. Stableford *(The Mysteries of Modern Science),* "is not a religion, but there are a great many scientists who behave like high priests. It seems that men of science need beliefs no less than other men, and make their science into a kind of personal religion, with its dogmas and its heresies. The image of the scientist as an objective seeker of truth, though strenuously promoted by scientists, is in fact a false picture. Most scientists know what they are looking for before they go out to look, and they use the eye of faith in making their observations."

Knowing what they are looking for (and what they want to find) must inevitably, however slightly, prejudice their objectivity. It is not that they would deliberately falsify the evidence (although this has been known to happen), it is just that they will naturally be more sympathetic to evidence that supports their conclusions than to evidence which points in the opposite direction.

No cosmological hypothesis so far put forward to explain the origin of the Universe is totally convincing. I personally find big bang logically persuasive but philosophically unappealing. There are many exploding objects in space—stars, quasars, even galaxies—so why not the Universe itself? But flash, bang, wallop, is so inelegant, so crude! The Universe is such an unimaginable feat of creation that I cannot believe its origin is not equally unimaginable. The explanation may be simple (and probably is), but it cannot be ordinary. An explosion, however fantastic, is both ordinary and imaginable; at least, it is in principle. And it is here where, philosophically speaking, steady state scores. As a concept, "The Universe has always been" is at once simple and unimaginable. The human mind cannot imagine something that has no beginning—yet what could be more simple?

In recent years Fred Hoyle's confidence in steady state has taken a knock, but he is still convinced that it offers a better explanation of the Universe than does big bang. In *Revelations: Glimpses of Reality,* he has this to say: "The scientist says he can't understand where matter came from, therefore it must have been created in the big bang. I have never liked that: I've always worked with a system of mathematics that permits matter to be created. And the good thing now, after going for thirty years with the high grade physicists telling me that it has to be nonsense, is that today we know it can be done."

Sir Fred is a professional scientist, with a refreshingly creative and imaginative approach to his work, and I have to say that, as a layman, I am attracted by his arguments. He frankly admits, however, that "something went wrong for the steady state theory in the mid-1960s, perhaps not as disastrously wrong as things now seem to be going for the big bang, but wrong

160

enough to temper the smile on my face as I contemplate the difficulties that the big bang theory now faces. Although there was something right about the steady state theory. . . . there was also something wrong . . . " (*The Intelligent Universe*).

While there are men like Hoyle around, we would be well advised to keep our options open. Big bang may be the most fashionable scenario in town, but we know, do we not, how fashions have a habit of going out of fashion; I doubt whether we have heard the last word; in fact, I am sure we haven't, if for no other reason than that there is no last word!

We cannot even be certain that there is only one Universe. "Could it be," writes Roy Stemman (*Mysteries of the Universe*), "that once we have discovered beyond doubt how our Universe was created we will discover that much more lies beyond: that we are just one of many universes that explode and expand, contract and disappear, or even collide and annihilate each other like the stars and galaxies we are observing in our own region of space. Perhaps the galaxies are like subatomic particles and our Universe is a single atom in a far greater scheme where there are worlds without end—or beginnings."

If the enormity of such a proposition is too much for us to grasp, we only have to consider the millions of grains of sand (each grain containing billions of atoms, each atom a universe in itself) in a bucket of sand, to realize that where nature is concerned numbers don't count, size is an irrelevance.

It is hard to believe that a mere sixty years ago, our galaxy, the Milky Way, was the sum total of the known Universe. As far as my grandparents were aware, that was it! It is only since the invention of the powerful radio telescope that we have learned that there are in fact *billions* of Milky Ways. And we have absolutely no idea how much more there is to be discovered.

If there is more than one universe (an infinite number, perhaps), is it likely that they are completely self-contained, totally isolated systems, with no means of communication between them? No, that is not nature's way. In nature there are no "gaps," everything is interconnected. This means that there would need to be some kind of "communicating door" between them. Is there such a candidate in space? There is—the black hole!

Of all the bizarre phenomena in space—white dwarfs, red

giants, quasars, pulsars, neutron and X-ray stars, to name but a few—none is more mysterious, more fascinating than the ubiquitous black hole. Black, because light cannot escape from it, so it cannot be seen. Hole, because that is literally what it is thought to be, a hole in space.

What exactly is a black hole? A black hole is a region of space where all matter—and spacetime—is crushed out of existence by enormous inward pressure; where nothing exists except intense gravitational force. It is believed to be caused by a dead star (i.e., one that has used up all its nuclear energy) collapsing in on itself and becoming unimaginably compressed. To give some idea of its mass, it has been calculated that to turn the Earth into a black hole it would have to be compressed into a sphere about three-quarters of an inch in diameter. Paul Davies (*God and the New Physics*): "Theory suggests that [where the grip of gravity is so ferocious that a critical value is reached] a star in this condition could not remain inert, but would succumb to its own intense gravity and implode in a microsecond to a spacetime singularity, leaving behind a hole in space—a black hole . . . the singularity marks the end of a one-way journey to 'nowhere' and 'nowhen.' It is a nonplace where the physical universe ceases."

Nothing that falls into a black hole can escape—not even light. And anything that approaches to within a critical distance of its parameters—the event horizon or Schwarzschild radius, after the German astronomer and physicist who first defined the barrier—disappears into the black hole, like dust being sucked into a vacuum cleaner, or water swirling down a drain. As an object reaches the event horizon it will appear to an outside observer to slow down, and as it disappears into the black hole its departing image will momentarily "freeze" on the edge of the hole before fading. The Schwarzschild radius is a sort of no-man's land between something and nothing, where time and space vanish into "nowhere" and "nowhen," a "non-place where the physical Universe ceases."

Paul Davies again (ibid): "A black hole . . . represents a rapid route to eternity . . . At the instant [a fictitious astronaut] enters the hole, all of eternity will have passed outside according to his relative determination of 'now.' Once inside the hole, therefore, he will be imprisoned in a time warp, unable to return to the outside universe again, because the outside universe will have happened. He will be, literally, beyond the end of time as far as the rest of the universe is concerned. To emerge from the hole, he would have to come out before he went in."

It is not known what happens to matter and radiation when they disappear into the black hole. Some believe that anything entering the black hole simply ceases to exist. Others, that it may be sucked out of one location in space into another, or out of our Universe into another, via the counterpart of the black hole—the white hole.

John Gribbin (*Spacewarps*): "The math says that within the black hole matter is crushed out of existence into a singularity, a mathematical point. Where does it go? Anywhere and nowhere; your guess is as good as mine. Some guesses that have been tried include the speculation that 'what goes in must come out,' that each black hole has its counterpart 'white hole' somewhere, or somewhen, else; that matter squeezed out of our spacetime universe may emerge in another space, another time—another universe, or another region of our own universe."

Patrick Moore and Iain Nicolson (*Black Holes in Space*) have this to say: "There is nothing in [Einstein's] general theory of relativity to say that the reverse of a black hole cannot occur . . . If—as seems to be the case—black holes are regions where matter disappears from our universe, then what a neat and appealing idea it would be if white holes also existed to pour matter back into our universe again. Where would this matter come from? Two possibilities suggest themselves: either matter disappears into black holes and reappears elsewhere in our universe . . . or it may be that our universe co-exists with other universes with which, in the normal run of things, we have no contact except via the agency of spacetime singularities. Matter disappearing through our black holes may emerge out of white holes in another universe, and, vice versa, matter from another universe may enter ours."

Black and white holes! Matching pairs! So beautiful, neat and tidy! And logical! Nature's way of transferring matter and energy from one universe to another—like the giving and receiving of a blood transfusion. What a smashing idea!

163

The concept of the black hole is not, as one might think, an invention of contemporary physics. It has been around for quite some time. In fact, the idea was first proposed as long ago as 1783 by an English physicist John Mitchell, and thirteen years later independently by the French mathematician Pierre Laplace (vide John Gribbin's *Spacewarps*). But it is only in the present century (since Einstein, in fact) that black holes have been regarded as more than a wild speculative possibility.

The technicalities of such phenomena are, however, outside the scope of this chapter, which is meant to be a philosophical contemplation, and not a scientific investigation, of space. Many excellent books have been written by experts on the physics of space (if one wishes to make one's hair stand on end or one's flesh creep there is no need to resort to science fiction); and of recent publications, the writer would especially recommend *God and the New Physics* by Paul Davies, *Spacewarps* by John Gribbin, and *The Universe: Its Beginning and End* by Lloyd Motz.

When philosophizing about space, I suppose the most intriguing question of all is: Is there intelligent life elsewhere in the Universe? Are there planets similar to Earth, inhabited by creatures similar to us? And if there are, are they trying to get in touch with us as we are with them?

If there are other intelligent creatures in the Universe, it is highly likely, in my view, that the difficulties of them reaching us, and of us reaching them, are too great to be overcome. As was suggested earlier, a higher intelligence may have so organized things that a meeting between us is physically impossible. However fantastically intelligent our hypothetical distant cousins may be; however advanced technologically we may become in the future; it would be wrong to assume that everything and anything is possible. It isn't. There are some thing that will forever be beyond the reach of man.

It was especially pleasing for the author to come across a professional scientist making the same philosophical point. Writing about the physical problems encountered in space travel, Sir Fred Hoyle (*The Intelligent Universe*) says: "[The] difficulties are so straightforward that I often used to wonder why the idea of colonizing the galaxy is discussed so often. Why was it not thrown into the wastepaper basket immediately?

... Colonization of the galaxy is impossible because it was *deliberately* arranged to be so ... "

Many astronomers, including the famous American exobiologist Carl Sagan, enthusiastically support the idea that the Universe is swarming with intelligent life and much money and effort are being spent trying to track down radio signals emanating from these intelligences.

Erich von Däniken, best-selling Swiss author, bane of the orthodox scientific establishment, goes further: he believes that extraterrestrial forms of life superior to us do exist, and that they have "visited this and other solar systems; and on the planets that seemed suitable [e.g. Earth] they left behind scions 'in their own image.' " These space travellers, "astronaut gods," as von Däniken calls them, visited the Earth many thousands of years ago, and were responsible for "an artificial mutation from ape to man. We did *not* [he asserts] separate from monkeys so many millions of years ago as is claimed—the family break-up took place only a few tens of thousands of years ago. . . .

"Men cannot breed apes, because intelligent man undoubtedly forms a species absolutely different from any species of ape. How could the human species have developed in such an incredibly positive way within 'minutes,' reckoned on the time-scale of universal history? How did ape or man suddenly lose his fur? How did he suddenly think of 'civilizing' himself, of creating cultures? Who gave him the idea of hunting animals, whose companions he had only recently been? Where did he suddenly get the illuminating idea of making fire to cook his soup on?

"Yes, and with *whom* did the first man mate, when he, a solitary being mutated from the ape tribe, had no suitable sexual partners? He could not mate with his monkey ancestors, for they had a different chromosome count."

Von Däniken claims that "extraterrestrials separated *Homo sapiens* from the ape tribe and made him intelligent by artificial mutation. In their own image. The evolutionary driving force is to be found in this *deliberate* manipulation." [And concludes]: "My speculation, but one motivated by the current state of cellular biology and microsurgery, is that extraterrestrials created *Homo sapiens* by cloning, which they already knew all about. If they were masters of interstellar space travel, with outstanding technological knowhow, we can well believe that they were experts in genetic manipulation. They 'planted' the DNA of their race and transmitted it intact." (Source: *Signs of the Gods?*, by Erich von Däniken, translated by Michael Heron.)

Astronaut gods! Artificial mutation from ape to man! *Homo sapiens* created by cloning! The mind boggles. Von Däniken may, of course, be right (no one can prove him wrong; his arguments are perfectly rational and reasonable). But frankly, I don't believe a word of it. Where are von Daäniken's astronaut gods now? Why haven't they returned to Earth? Have they no curiosity? Is it feasible that such an intelligent and technologically advanced race would discover Earth, create a new species, and not return from time to time—even take up residence in an administrative capacity—to see how its creation was making out? When Columbus discovered America, did his fellow-humans not follow, and have they not remained in the New World ever since? When human beings landed on the moon, if they had found a race of moon people in the moon caves, would they not have set up a local moon administration and "civilized" these people; and having done so would they then have simply returned to Earth leaving their progeny to their own devices?

But, say van Däniken and his supporters, the astronaut gods did return—thousands of years later. Ye gods! Why wait so long? But there's more! Maurice Chatelain, French-born, ex-NASA space expert, author of *Our Ancestors Came from Outer Space* (translated by Orest Berlings), writes that " . . . alien astronauts from a distant planet in outer space . . . had been orbiting our planet in a spacecraft for 13,000 years . . . the landings on Earth of the alien astronauts [it seems] . . . did actually occur about [64,800 years ago] or maybe a little later. What happened next, we can only guess. It is quite possible that, after inseminating and educating the human race, they went back to their home planet to report on the results of their mission and returned to our solar system only 13,000 years ago when they thought the human race had become civilized enough . . . and it could very well be that . . . their descendants are still in orbit around the Earth, visiting us from time to time." And later (ibid): "Thus, once upon a time, about 65,000 years ago, extraordinary visitors came from another civilization in space, discovered the Earth was a wonderful place to live on, and decided to establish a colony here. But in the beginning they did not like our air and water, and they weren't used to Earth's gravity. So, these visitors decided to create a hybrid race, so that by crossbreeding with humans after a few generations, that new race would be perfectly adapted to life on Earth and would carry on at least part of the intelligence and technical know-how of its ancestors from space. To achieve this, the most attractive and most intelligent young females were inseminated, and this procedure continued with their daughters and granddaughters until the results were acceptable for life on Earth, and the education and civilization of the new race could start."

Personally, I find it difficult to take such assertions seriously. However, I report them in the interests of fair play. Readers must make up their own minds as to the plausibility of such claims. For my part, I cannot believe that if *we* were to discover a hospitable planet ripe for colonizing, inhabited by creatures similar but "inferior" to ourselves, and if we were to inseminate those creatures with our "superior" genes, thereby cloning a new race of Earthmen, and remain to educate them, we would simply pack up our bags, catch the next spaceship home and not return for over 50,000 years!

In my view, the reported sightings of flying saucers and landings of alien astronauts from outer space, which have featured in the world's media for many years now, can be completely discounted, the former being the misinterpretation of natural phenomena, or deliberate hoaxes supported by fake photography, and the latter the result of the overactive imaginations of disordered minds, occasionally aided and abetted by the equally inventive minds of unscrupulous journalists. Had these stories any validity, at least one of them would have been substantiated long ago by irrefutable and tangible physical evidence.

Carl Sagan, author of *Broca's Brain,* is equally dismissive. "To the best of my knowledge," he says, "there are no instances out of the hundreds of thousands of UFO reports filed since 1947—not a single one—in which many people independently and reliably report a close encounter with what is clearly an alien spacecraft.

"Not only is there an absence of good anecdotal evidence;

there is no physical evidence either. Our laboratories are very sophisticated. A product of alien manufacture might readily be identified as such. Yet no one has ever turned up even a small fragment of an alien spacecraft that has passed any such physical test—much less the logbook of the starship captain . . . When hoaxes and mere anecdotes are excluded, there seems to be nothing left to study."

In spite of this, the reader might be inclined to say: But surely, by the law of averages, some of these stories must be true? Or: No smoke without fire. Well, there's no "must" about it. Truth has nothing to do with the law of averages. Or with smoke and fire. Spaceships and alien astronauts are *physical* properties, and if their existence is to be given credence, it must be supported by *physical* evidence. So far no such evidence has been forthcoming; no "fingerprints" have been found.

The only way von Däniken's and Chatelain's space travellers could have any credibility is if they possessed the secret of time travel, or had the ability to travel close to the speed of light, and so be subject to the laws of time dilation, thereby "exchanging" thousands of Earth years for one of theirs. But as the writer is concerned only with reasonable speculation, however, far-fetched, this hypothesis is considered too bizarre for serious consideration.

Fred Hoyle is a serious scientist who has to be taken seriously. Not for him von Däniken's "astronaut gods" or Chatelain's "alien astronauts." Nor does he see eye to eye with those, like Francis Crick (co-discoverer with James Watson of the structure of DNA) and the distinguished biochemist Leslie Orgel, who believe that micro-organisms were brought to Earth in unmanned spacecraft several billion years ago by a higher civilization.

The germs of creation, say Fred Hoyle and his colleague Chandra Wickramasinghe, in their joint-authored *Evolution from Space*, arrived here on Earth, not in the head of a spaceship, but on the backs of comets, meteorites and interstellar dust. There is in the Universe, they believe, a reservoir of life, the seeds from which find their own way from planet to planet unaided, some falling on stony ground, others on hospitable soil like that on Earth. "Genes," they say, "are to be regarded as cosmic. They arrive at the Earth . . . either as fully-fledged cells, or as viruses, viroids or simply as separated fragments of genetic material. The genes are ready to function when they arrive . . . [They do not] arrive in a science-fiction vehicle. They arrive without any vehicle at all. Large stores of genetic material became frozen and so preserved indefinitely in the outer regions of the solar system during the early days when our system was formed about 4.6 billion years ago . . . The purpose is to generate life, not just on the Earth, but everywhere that it will take root, and to do so in an extremely elegant way. Not by parading around the galaxy in a fleet of space ships, but through the genes travelling like seeds in the wind—more explicitly the genes ride around the galaxy on the pressure of light waves from the stars and they do so at speeds up to several hundred kilometers *per second* . . . Unlike the crew of a spaceship the genes are potentially immortal."

Now, this is not a hypothesis born of the wild imaginings of tongue-in-cheek, science-fiction writers; it is the considered view of two world-renowned professional scientists, backed by hard scientific evidence.

In his *The Intelligent Universe*, Fred Hoyle argues that it would have been virtually impossible for life to have appeared on Earth spontaneously. "As biochemists discover more and more about the awesome complexity of life," he says, "it is apparent that the chances of it originating by accident are so minute that they can be completely ruled out." One must read his book to appreciate the logic of his argument, but frankly, this writer finds it devastating: only a completely irrational biologist would insist that all the right chemicals for the creation of life just happened by chance to be in the right place in the right proportions at the right time. Intelligence must have been involved. There is no other reasonable explanation.

It would seem incontrovertible, as Voltaire once remarked, "that there is intelligence in nature, and that its laws were not invented by a fool."

Life originates from outer space, says Hoyle. He argues (*The Intelligent Universe*) that, "if all of biology is a terrestrially contained affair . . . there is no reason why micro-organisms should be able to withstand massive doses of radiation in space or to survive its low temperature and pressure. These abilities would be completely wasted here on Earth. . . For cosmic life, on the other hand, these are essential requirements. Micro-organisms must . . . be able to withstand such conditions successfully or the cosmic picture is wrong." He then points out that it has been discovered that micro-organisms are able to withstand the enormous destructive power of radiation, which can smash apart the genetic equipment of a cell, killing it or causing permanent damage. Bacterium, he says, "was found in 1960 to be living inside an American nuclear reactor [where] it had been exposed to radiation damage millions of times greater than has existed on Earth at any period when life could have survived here. Such an ability, necessary for survival in space, is quite inexplicable in conventional biology, since the environment needed to produce this characteristic has never existed on the Earth."

Other experiments have shown that bacteria can comfortably survive in the hostile environment of space. Living bacteria, contained in a TV camera left on the moon's surface by the unmanned Surveyor III on April 20, 1967 and retrieved two-and-a-half years later, were found to be undamaged.

The crux of Hoyle's argument is this: Why are living organisms constructed to withstand conditions that they do not experience here on Earth? If these micro-organisms originated on Earth, why do they possess a property for which there is no need? (One might expect a cautious Creator to err on the safe side and allow a margin for error, but a margin *millions of times* greater than necessary?) If, however, living organisms were required to overcome the hostile conditions encountered in travelling in space, then there would be a very good reason for them being constructed the way they are.

There is, however, a parallel hypothesis not considered by Hoyle. If these micro-organisms did not originate in outer space but here on Earth, this might mean that one day they will be required to leave Earth and take up residence elsewhere. Perhaps the Creator, knowing(?) that man would eventually destroy himself and half the environment with him, built in an escape route so that the germs and genes of creation might take off and fertilize another receptive planet.

The weakness of this hypothesis, however, is that it is unnecessary. For nature is so powerful that it is impossible for man to destroy it. Poison and pollute it, yes. Destroy it, no. Even if man's entire atomic and chemical arsenals were unleashed in a global nuclear war, and the environment poisoned for hundreds of thousands or millions of years to come, eventually it would recover. Man may have the power to destroy himself (though this is by no means certain—the total annihilation of the human race would be more difficult than is generally supposed), but he hasn't the power to destroy Earth itself. Nature is indestructible. The snowcapped mountains would not disappear, nor would the hills and valleys. One day they would regain their former glory. And the polluted oceans and rivers of the world would again be pure and productive. And, of course, insects would be king—masters of the Earth! There's no way we could destroy them. After a few million years maybe another "superior" creature would arise, a wiser and "higher" form of humankind. Come to think of it, how do we know that something like that has not already happened? That man did not destroy himself aeons ago; that the evolutionary process did not begin all over again, and that *Homo sapiens* is not a "repeat" version of the Homo species? In this respect, consider the enormous time span over which evolution works its magic. Homo sapiens has been around for, at most, a few million years, whereas the dinosaur inhabited the Earth for some forty million years, before some natural disaster (it is thought) put an end to its evolutionary career. Nature is no respecter of persons. The bigger they are, the harder they fall! There is no divine law (as far as I know) that says that man is a permanent feature of the universal or terrestrial landscape.

No, evolution cannot be thwarted; man hasn't the power he thinks he has. He can destroy life, but not Life. Hypothesis withdrawn!

Many cosmologists believe that there are millions of planets in our galaxy alone where conditions could be supportive of life. By that reckoning there must be countless billions of Earth clones scattered throughout the Universe. And if that is true then it would appear pretty certain that we are not alone.

For life similar to that which exists on Earth to exist anywhere else, similar conditions would have to obtain. If there are such planets with an environment and atmosphere identical to ours, with the same mix of chemicals, water and oxygen, located the right distance from a sun similar to ours, then life as we know it, in all or many of its various forms, almost certainly exists. For if conditions are right for something to happen, then that something will invariably happen. Otherwise, why the conditions? Why oxygen and carbon in exactly the right proportions to promote life, if there is no life to promote? Why water, if not to germinate and sustain life?

The chances of Earth being a "one-of" in a Universe teeming with suns and planets is almost nil. The trouble, however, is with that word "almost." Either our planet is unique, or it isn't; it isn't a question of mathematical odds. Have we any reason to believe that Earth is unique? None whatsoever. But then, neither have we any reason to believe that it isn't.

Unique—or one of many? Is life restricted to planet Earth or is it rampant throughout the Universe? Parochial or cosmological?

The argument for and against the existence of extraterrestrial intelligence will, in my view, never be resolved. I myself am ambivalent. I am almost persuaded that life is a cosmological phenomenon and not just a parochial incident on a solitary speck of dust in the middle of nowhere, perhaps the most fundamental aspect of the Universe itself. And yet, my hunch, for what it is worth, is that Earth is unique, that we are alone. I know that the statistical odds are against me, as are even reason and common sense, nonetheless, that is my view. If I am wrong, if there are intelligent creatures elsewhere in the Universe, then I do not think we shall ever know. I do not think we were meant to. I therefore believe that I shall never be *proved* wrong.

What are the implications for religion, if intelligent life is universal and not just confined to planet Earth? For those who do not believe in a personal God there is no problem. Hoyle and Wickramasinghe, for instance, subscribe to a "sequence of intelligences," each with its own particular rôle (e.g. one to design the biochemicals that "gave rise to the origin of carbonaceous life," one to control "the coupling constants of physics" . . . and so on). The question of where the sequence stops, they answer thus: "It doesn't. It goes on and on and on, with ever-rising levels . . . But like a convergent mathematical sequence of functions it has an idealized limit . . . It is this idealized limit that is *God,* and *God* is the Universe." (Source: *Evolution from Space.*)

Intellectually impressive! But a pretty "grey form of religion," as the authors themselves admit. "But," they say, "it is far better to be in with a chance of being modestly right, instead of being faced by the absolute certainty of being overwhelmingly wrong."

True. But unless there is room in their "sequence of intelligences" for something that is not of the intellect but of the spirit (e.g. love and compassion) then they, too, are, in my opinion, absolutely certain of being overwhelmingly wrong. A sequence of intelligences, a sort of "cosmic committee of experts," is, indeed, a grey form of religion, even if the "top man" is a super-duper version of an idealized silicone chip.

"Infinite intelligence" is a colourless creed, a million miles from the shores of Galilee. Christians would find it very difficult to worship Jesus as the son of a silicone chip!

Physicist Paul Davies (*God and the New Physics*) regards the possible existence of extraterrestrial beings as an insuperable difficulty for the theist in general, and the Christian in particular. He says: "The existence of extraterrestrial intelligences would have a profound impact on religion, shattering completely the traditional perspective of God's special relationship with man. The difficulties are particularly acute for Christianity, which postulates that Jesus Christ was God incarnate whose mission was to provide salvation for man on Earth. The prospect of a host of 'alien Christs' systematically visiting every inhabited planet in the physical form of the local creatures has a rather absurd aspect. Yet how otherwise are the aliens to be saved?"

Frankly, I am puzzled by the professor's remarks. What an extraordinary lack of imagination he shows! Why he should regard the existence of extraterrestrial beings as a "particularly acute difficulty for Christianity," is quite beyond me. The prospect of a host of "alien Christs" systematically visiting other inhabited planets (even billions or an infinity of them) only sounds absurd because that is the way Davies chooses to put it. If there are countless worlds, all inhabited by creatures all requiring guidance on the way to conduct their lives, I see no

173

reason why God should not visit each and every one of them and make his Word known to them, in exactly the same way Christians believe he did here on Earth two thousand years ago. What is so absurd about that? A Christ born on another planet would not seem "alien" or "absurd" to his "fellowmen," no more than our Christ seems alien or absurd to us. And the same holds good irrespective of how many planets or how many Christs there happened to be, irrespective of what stage of development the planets happened to have reached. If there is another planet similar to ours but with a totally different environment and pattern of evolution, with a Christ with, say, two heads and three legs, then of course such a figure would appear alien and absurd to us. But not to a species with two heads and three legs! To them our Christ with his one head and two legs would appear alien and absurd. So why this facile talk of a host of "alien" Christs? How could an "alien" Christ appear "alien" to his fellow creatures?

If Christ is depicted as a sort of cosmic commercial salesman, frantically dashing from planet to planet in the family rocket on his father's business, then yes, put like that, it does sound absurd. But if God is the omnipotent and omniscient being that Christians believe him to be, then I see no problem. I feel quite sure that God, if he so desired, would find no difficulty in revealing himself to all his children wherever they might be, individually, world by world, or in an infinity of worlds simultaneously, in whatever way, by whatever means he cared to choose. It is only when we look at these things through the parochial eyes of an Earth-bound physicist, that the notion of "a host of alien Christs in the physical form of the local creatures," hotfooting their way through the Universe, appears absurd.

The only possible problem for Christians, which Davies may or may not have been alluding to, is their belief that Christ was the only begotten Son of the Father. But it requires no betrayal of the central truth of the Christian faith to accept that if there are other worlds ("In my Father's house there are many mansions") inhabited by "alien" creatures all requiring the Father's help, then the Father could have begat more than one son—an infinity of sons if he wished! However many sons there were,

174

whatever their shape or size or mental or spiritual development, they would all be ONE AND THE SAME CHRIST. There is only one God. And there is only one Christ—even if there are billions of Christs!

The God, whose Son Christians believe Christ to be is the universal God of space and time, truth and love. Love is universal. The love that you feel is the same love that I feel, that everyone on Earth feels. And if there are creatures on other planets capable of loving, then the love that they feel is the same love that we feel, that everyone in the Universe feels at every moment in time, at every point in space. At least, that is what I believe.

There is no need for Christians to get hung up on the trivialities of numbers. One Christ, a billion Christs—what does it matter, provided they are all one and the same Christ? If the love of Christ is infinite, WHY SHOULD THERE NOT BE AN INFINITY OF CHRISTS?

Christ cannot be confined or restricted in any way, historically, geographically or cosmically. When Christ was here on Earth, did he speak as if he were a "single" spirit in a "single" body, alive today but not yesterday or tomorrow? ("Before Abraham was, I am.") If Christ is the Son of the Universal Creator then he exists universally. A host of "alien" Christs? Pshaw!

There is no reason whatsoever why the discovery of other orders of human beings on other planets should "shatter completely the traditional perspective of God's relationship with man." The difficulty would be if God turned out to be solely an Intellect without a spiritual dimension. If God were nothing more than an almighty superchip then Christians (and other theists) would indeed be in deep trouble. But the concept of God as nothing more than intelligence, is, in my view, too absurd to contemplate. For if that were true, whence came spirituality? Not from man, surely? The created more spiritual than the creator? That would be even more absurd!

To conclude this section, God's special relationship with man does not preclude a special relationship with other "men" on other planets. If it did then God is not all-loving, his love is not universal. To assert that the universal God of love, loves only the inhabitants of one tiny speck of dust called Earth, when there are other "human beings" inhabiting billions of other specks of dust in his Universe, is little short of blasphemy. As I recall, Christ's message was that God loved *all* men, not just those who happened to reside in one remote corner of the Universe.

And now back to the universal drawing board!

Of all the scientific models of the Universe put before us, none is more fascinating than Einstein's "hypersphere." The notion of three-dimensional space curving back on itself to form a sphere is typical of the beautiful simplicity of the ideas coming from the creative and imaginative mind of Albert Einstein. Einstein himself once remarked: "Our experience hitherto justifies us in believing that nature is the realization of the simplest conceivable mathematical ideas."

"The essence of Einstein's profundity," writes Banesh Hoffmann in his biography *Albert Einstein: Creator and Rebel*, "lay in his simplicity; and the essence of his science lay in his artistry—his phenomenal sense of beauty . . . When judging a scientific theory, his own or another's, he asked himself whether he would have made the Universe in that way had he been God. This criterion may at first seem closer to mysticism than to what is usually thought of as science, yet it reveals Einstein's faith in an ultimate simplicity and beauty in the Universe. Only a man with a profound religious and artistic conviction that beauty was there, waiting to be discovered, could have constructed theories whose most striking attribute, quite overtopping their spectacular successes, was their beauty."

J. Bronowski, in his *The Ascent of Man* said this: "Einstein was a man who could ask immensely simple questions. And what his life showed, and his work, is that when the answers are simple, too, then you hear God thinking." I like that.

Space a sphere! Could anything be more simple, more beautiful? The sphere consists of an infinity of circles. Its surface has no center or edge. It is the most perfectly designed, precisely engineered, geometrically immaculate shape imaginable, visually and tactily identical from every position and every perspective. No other shape has these properties; it is unique.

The whole of nature is based on the concept of the circle: night and day, the seasons, life and death. Most bodies in space are spherical (if there are any square-shaped suns, moons or planets, they have yet to be discovered!) Should we be surprised then, to learn that space is spherical?

The Universe, said Blaise Pascal (1623–1662), French mathematician, physicist and moralist, is "an infinite sphere whose center is everywhere, its circumference nowhere." But Einstein's hypersphere was finite, not infinite. So where is its circumference, where are its boundaries?

It may be remembered that Professor Davies told us that, although Einstein's hypersphere was finite in volume, "nowhere does a traveller meet an edge or a boundary." He says nothing, however, about a circumference, though its non-existence is implied when he says that the hypersphere hasn't a boundary. A finite hypersphere that hasn't a circumference or boundary? Very odd!

If the reader is expecting the writer to explain this conundrum then I am afraid he will be disappointed. Davies himself says, "few people can really envisage such a monstrosity, but mathematics can take care of the details for us." Not for this writer, they can't! A ball of wool consisting of a continuous space "strand" is the nearest I can get to visualizing a finite hypersphere.

For me, Einstein's hypersphere has one philosophical defect: it is finite. (Finiteness is an inherent imperfection; only infinity can claim perfection.) But being physical, it can be no other. Which means that we must look "beyond" the finite hypersphere for the perfect, infinite entity, which I believe must exist "somewhere."

Where do we go from here? Well, we are now in unchartered territory, where mathematics most certainly will not take care of the details for us. Physics, being concerned solely with things physical, can only investigate the nature of matter and energy. To go "beyond" space we have to leave the world of physics and enter the realm of metaphysics. For the physicist, there is no beyond; so we cannot expect him to search for something that for him doesn't exist.

Science cannot penetrate the boundaries of science. Albert Einstein, philosopher and mystic as well as scientific genius, knew this. "The most beautiful experience we can have," he said, "is the mysterious. It is the fundamental emotion which stands at the cradle of true art and true science . . . A knowledge of the existence of something we cannot penetrate, our perceptions of the profoundest reason and the most radiant beauty, which only in their most primitive forms are accessible to our minds—it is this knowledge and this emotion that constitutes true religiosity. . . . " (Einstein's *The World As I See It,* 1934.)

The human mind is here confronted with the limitations of the human imagination. Could a blind, amorphous creature, living alone at the center of the Earth, imagine what lies beyond the Earth's surface? Could it visualize the sky, the stars, the mountains, the lakes, the sunrise and sunset, a tree, a house, a cathedral, a blade of grass, a flower, the early morning dew, snow, the Taj Mahal, Niagara Falls? Could it visualize the paintings of Monet, the music of Mozart, the song of a lark, the smell of new-mown hay, a smile on the face of a little child, family life, friendship and love? No, it could not.

To imagine the unimaginable, we would need to undergo complete metamorphosis, change from substance to nonsubstance, material to immaterial, physical to spiritual. That we cannot imagine what lies on the "other side" of spacetime, in some strange way makes it even more real!

The "border" between finite, four-dimensional spacetime and infinite, eternal spirituality, is not located at the farthest reaches of space but in the depths of the atom. Every atom. Everywhere. That is "where" spacetime "ends." Burst through the atom and we penetrate the "frontiers" of spacetime. Penetrate the "frontiers" of spacetime and we find ourselves back in the womb of the atom. Spacetime not only joins up to itself, it joins up within itself. The "frontiers" of spacetime are as near to us as the atoms of which we are made.

Remembering that Einstein's hypersphere is the totality of space curving back on itself to form a closed sphere, then by definition there cannot physically be anything on the other side. Because there is no other side; the hypersphere is all there is. That is why we cannot fly out of it. Because there is no out. We can no more fly out of space than we can sail off the edge of the world. Because there is no edge. We can only leave space by first surrendering our temporality and corporeality and allowing ourselves to be sucked out of one form of existence into another—via the spiritual black-and-white hole. But this is not to leave space physically. Physically we are trapped, and there is no way out. At least, not for these atoms, these molecules, this corporeality. There is nothing physical beyond the physicality (if I might coin a word) of the physical Universe.

I believe that "beyond" spacetime lies an unimaginable, multidimensional single-dimensional spiritual "mass." What do I mean by a spiritual "mass?" I don't know. I think I mean a nontemporal, nonspatial, all-encompassing, eternal, spiritual entity. I suppose I mean God.

When I began this chapter, I had no idea that I would end up talking about a spiritual "mass." Space, I thought, had little philosophical appeal. It wasn't even mysterious in the way that time was. How wrong I was!

It seems that one cannot ponder these mighty metaphysial matters without bringing God into the equation. This is hardly surprising. For to talk about space, without referring to the "architect of space," is like discussing St. Paul's Cathedral without mentioning Christopher Wren.

Space has been variously described in these pages as "a geometrical concept," "a conceptual monstrosity," "an idea," "purely a thought-thing that cannot be pointed to in experience." It may be all these things. But it is something else besides. It is the playground of existence, an integral and indispensible part of everything in creation. (If we couldn't put one foot in front of the other, if it weren't for time, we certainly couldn't if it weren't for space.)

What, then, is space?

I will leave the reader with two quotations. The first is from the French novelist and man of letters, Joseph Joubert (1754–1824): "Space is the stature of God."

The second is from the Bible (Psalms 19:1): "The heavens declare the glory of God; and the firmament sheweth his handywork."

Chapter 6

Is the Future Predetermined?

Eternal Deities.
Who made the World with absolute decrees,
And write whatever Time shall bring to pass
With pens of adamant on plates of brass.

Dryden

Fate is nothing but the deeds committed in a prior state of existence.
Emerson (*Conduct of Life: Fate.* Quoted as a Hindu proverb)

Fatalism—the notion so prevalent in the East, that the future is predetermined and there is nothing we can do to change it—is anathema to most Westerners, carrying as it does the implication that free will is a sham. For how can we be free to choose if the choosing has already been done for us?

"Fate is the endless chain of causation, whereby things are," said Zeno, "the reason or formula by which the world goes on." Ernst Haeckel, German evolutionist, was more forthright. "The freedom of the will," he wrote (*The Riddle of the Universe*, published 1899), "is not an object for critical scientific enquiry at all, for it is pure dogma, based on an illusion, and has no real existence."

It has to be said that there does seem to be a strange inevitability about the way some things happen, as if they were meant to be. In the 1930s, for instance, as events leading up to the Second World War unfolded, it was as if they had a will of their own; as if fate had decreed that war was inevitable. I suspect that the same could have been said about other momentous events in history: the First World War, the French Revolution, the American Civil War, etc., etc. "I go the way Providence dictates with the assurance of a sleepwalker," said Hitler, in a speech in Munich, on September 26, 1938. This remark just about sums up the feeling of inevitability that everyone felt at the time, as one event after the other led inexorably to a seemingly unavoidable catastrophe.

It is, of course, much easier to put the blame on fate than on the wickedness and stupidity of man. " 'Tis weak and vicious people who cast the blame on Fate," wrote Emerson. "No one is made guilty by fate," said Seneca. Given the circumstances at the time—the aggressive expansionist policies of Nazi Germany, the psychopathic personality of its leader, Adolf Hitler, the unstableness of European politics, and the economic problems accentuated by the vindictive Versailles Treaty imposed on a defeated Germany after the First World War—given all this, it would have been surprising, human nature being what it is, had there not been a Second World War. War was inevitable only to the extent that human nature is inevitable.

Writing about Indian thought at the time of the Buddha, Trevor Ling, author of *The Buddha,* says that the Ajivakas sect denied that man had any control over events. "In their view," he states, " . . . all that happened within the universe took place within a totally closed causal system in which all events were completely and unalterably determined by cosmic principles over which there was no control."

"Predestination," says Antony Flew (*A Dictionary of Philosophy*), "is the doctrine that everything that happens, including particularly the making of all choices, has been fixed in advance by God: 'The first dawn of creation wrote what the last day of reckoning shall read.' " Now if everything has indeed been fixed in advance by God (or fate or anything else) then free will surely is an illusion?

It is often asserted, by physicists and philosophers alike, that in a universe subject to the law of cause and effect, it should be possible, given total knowledge of all facts involved, to predict accurately everything that will happen in the future. Which again, would suggest that there is no such thing as free choice.

Precognition, the ability to foresee the future, though not the subject of this chapter, cannot be ignored, impinging as it does on the question of predetermination. For if future events already exist and can be foreseen, then they must be predetermined.

Numerous books have been written on the subject of precognition, and hundreds of apparently genuine precognitive dreams have been recorded. I say "apparently" because no one can ever be absolutely certain of their authenticity. There is no way that such dreams can be positively verified. However, I pass on to the reader two famous examples of precognitive dreams, the first being taken from the late J.B. Priestley's *Over the Long High Wall*: "It was three months before Napoleon invaded Russia that the wife of General Toutschkoff had a strange dream—and not once but three times in one night. She dreamt she was in a small inn she had never seen before, and that her father came into the room, leading her little son by the hand, and telling her brokenly that her husband had fallen at Borodino. In great distress she woke her husband, asked him where Borodino was, and together they tried to find it on the map, without any success. (The battle took its name, like many another, from a tiny obscure village.) Months later, everything happened as it had in the three dreams; she found herself staying in the same room in the same inn; her father came in with her son and announced her husband's death at Borodino, where he had been commanding the army of the reserve. Apparently every detail was identical with what she had dreamt."

If this is a faithful record of an actual dream, it would certainly give credence to the notion that future events can be witnessed precognitively, thus indicating that events are predetermined. Otherwise how could the future's contents be revealed to one of the participants months before they happened?

The second example comes from the celebrated John William Dunne, a former army officer and aeronautical engineer, who wrote about his extraordinary dreams in his *An Experiment with Time*. It was this book that led Brian Inglis, author of *Natural and Supernatural,* to write: "[At school] we were conditioned . . . to be intellectual skeptics: to assume that the supernatural was only superstition. And a skeptic I would probably have remained but for coming across a copy of J. W. Dunne's *Experiment with Time*, with its descriptions of dreams in which he had seen future events. [Dunne's] analogy . . . that we travel through life like passengers on a train sitting with their backs to the engine, able to see only what is past; the future being already there ahead of us, to be glimpsed sometimes in dreams—seemed natural, and quite plausible, even if its implication, that events might be predetermined, was disturbing."

The content of Dunne's dream was as follows: (Source: John Taylor's *Black Holes*): "J.W. Dunne . . . dreamed one night in the autumn of 1913 that he was looking from a high railway embankment at a scene which he recognized as being situated a little to the north of the Firth of Forth Bridge. Below him was open grassland on which groups of people were walking about. The scene came and went several times, but on the last time he noticed that a train going north had fallen over the embankment. He saw several carriages lying near the bottom of the slope, down which large blocks of stone were rolling. He then warned his friends not to travel north by train to Scotland. On April 14, 1914, the 'Flying Scotsman' jumped the parapet near Burntisland Station, about fifteen miles north of the Firth of Forth Bridge and fell onto the golf links twenty feet below."

The morning after the dream, Dunne described it to his sister, who later confirmed it almost in exact detail (the only discrepancies being of a minor order). So here again, we have a future event being "seen" months before it actually happened. In Dunne's book, and in books by other authors, equally striking precognitive dreams are recorded. Now unless one is prepared to believe that all these dreams are either the concoctions of liars and charlatans, the imaginations of unstable minds, or an extraordinary string of coincidences then one is obliged to accept that some people do have a facility for seeing into the future. And remember, it only needs *one* precognitive dream to be genuinely and unambiguously true, for the case for precognition to be proven. I have to say that having read the evidence, I personally am convinced that some dreams are authentically precognitive.

However, my purpose here it not to discuss the phenomenon of precognition, but to ask: If the future can be foreseen, is it predetermined? And if it is predetermined, how meaningful is free will? If, for instance, several months before the "Flying Scotsman" plunged over the embankment near the Firth of Forth

Bridge, someone was able to foresee this event in a dream, then how much free choice did the driver and passengers exercise when they "freely" chose to travel on this particular train? If the dream were genuinely precognitive then out the window goes free choice. And so, it would appear that free will and predetermination cannot be reconciled. Or can they?

I believe that the future *is* predetermined. I also believe in free will. We shall be looking at this apparent contradiction a little later. But first, let us consider the following.

When Abraham Lincoln was assassinated on April 14, 1865, it was a fact that almost a century later, on June 23, 1963, another American president would be assassinated. These two events, like every event in history, were facts not only as they happened and after they happened, but before they happened. Whether viewed from the present, the past or the future, facts are immutable. The only difference between a past fact and a future fact is that the former has been revealed and the latter has not.

The fact that people living in 1865 did not know that a century later President Kennedy would be assassinated, is irrelevent. Know it or not, it was a fact that he would be. How do we know? Because he was! No matter where we position ourselves in time, June 23, 1963 is the date on which President Kennedy was, is, and would be assassinated.

If we could travel forward in time to some specific point in the future, events would unfold precisely as they would do if we were to travel back to the same point from its own future. Suppose a person living in the last century had been able to project himself forward to the present day. Looking back from his new privileged vantage point in time to, say, September 1, 1939, he would see German troops marching into Poland. Suppose now that he then returned to the last century (remembering what he had seen), he would be able to predict with absolute certainty that on September 1, 1939, German troops would march into Poland. Let us take this a step further. If a person living in the year 1900 had projected himself forward to September 1, 1939, whilst a person living at the present moment projected himself back to the same day—both time travellers arriving at the same place together—they would witness the same events. Now it may be objected that it is facile talking about travelling backwards and forwards in time, because it is physically impossible. True. But that doesn't invalidate the point I am making. No one would say that the events of 1939 didn't happen, just because we cannot physically go back in time to see them happening. So why should a person living in 1900 assert that the events that would subsequently happen in 1939, wouldn't happen, just because he couldn't physically go forward in time to see them happening? Obviously he couldn't foretell the actual events themselves, but that doesn't affect the principle of the argument. The events of 1939 did happen. And that is true, whatever position we occupy in time.

Some extraordinary people, like Dunne, apparently do have the ability (occasionally) to draw back the curtain and peek into the future. Why this is so we can only speculate. Perhaps the information concerning all events, past, present and future, is stored in a secret dimension, to which most of us do not have access, and only a few have occasional access.

If this sounds ludicrously farfetched, just consider what happens when an event is filmed and then broadcast later on TV. It is recorded, mechanically stored and subsequently released into the air waves for transmission to our TV sets. Admittedly, I am talking about the storage of present events and not future events, but the principle of storage remains the same.

I am suggesting that the information concerning events exists waiting to be "picked up" by anyone psychically attuned to do so. Maybe in some strange way this is related to that peculiar sense of déjà vu which many, if not all, of us experience at some time or another; that odd feeling of knowing what we are about to do as we do it, as if we are reliving a few moments of "prior existence."

Some think that this sense of "I have done this before" is caused by a forgotten dream suddenly being released into the consciousness. My own personal experiences suggest something quite different. It seemed to me that I was doing something for the "second time." The sensation was far more real than a remembered dream. Could it be that the knowledge of future events is stored in a "universal supernatural psyche," which occasionally, when the mind slips out of gear, we are able to contact? So that future knowledge is effectively dragged out of the future into the present, where we "reexperience" it, having already had a preview of its content? It is not that we have in fact done it before, but that we have the impression we have; as if a pair of "precognitive bellows" were sucking in air from the future and blowing it out into the present. Maybe the explanation is that we have previously (perhaps only a split second earlier) had a precognitive glimpse of the future without knowing it? The event already existed, and in some inexplicable way the mind was already aware of its existence.

I used to experience this sense of déjà vè fairly frequently, but curiously enough I haven't had an occurrence for forty years or more. Perhaps when I was young my mind was more elastic, more receptive to whatever it is that triggers off this kind of experience?

I believe that future events already exist and are lurking in the wings, waiting to come on stage to be enacted. What now happens, what we now do, is what has "already" happened, what we have "already" done—in the "future." The revealed facts of the present are simply the unrevealed facts of the future.

But how, you may ask, can a fact be a fact *before* it happens? Surely at present a future fact is just one contingent out of an infinity of contingents.

This, I feel, is to confuse the fact of the event with the happening of the event. They are not the same thing, as we can clearly see when looking at past events. A football match, for instance, played a week ago, is just as much a fact today as it was on the day it was being played. It didn't cease to be a fact when the final whistle blew. Likewise, a match that is yet to be played is also a fact before it is played. At present it is a future fact. At some time in the future it will be a present fact. And after the match has been played it will be a past fact. We are talking about the same game of football. When it was, is, or will be played is immaterial.

I believe that events, whenever they take place, are ever-present facts. And time, as was argued in Chapter 4, is an ever-present now, in which all events, past, present, and future, take place. The poet T. S. Eliot neatly sums it up with these words from "Burnt Norton":

Time present and time past
Are both perhaps present in time future,
And time future contained in time past.

No event has ever happened in the past; and no event will ever happen in the future. This is self-evident. Because all events happen in the now. A future event will not happen until its "time" is come. And when its "time" is come, its presence, which was previously hidden from us, will be revealed. (In the case of a precognitive dream, the fact of the event is revealed before the event itself is enacted.)

To make the point a little clearer, the reader is invited to carry out the following thought experiment.

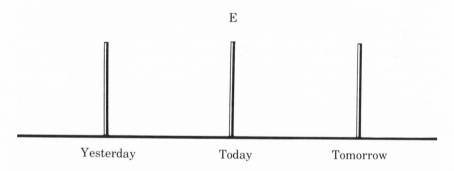

Imagine three time poles: yesterday, today, and tomorrow. Perched on top of the today pole is the letter E, representing an event happening today. Now let your gaze travel forward to the top of the tomorrow pole. From that point in the future, glance back to the top of the today pole. What do you see? You see the letter E. You obviously accept the evidence of your eyes, because you know that when tomorrow really does come you will look back at the events of the day before, knowing full well that they really did happen. Now go to the yesterday pole (i.e., into the past). From there glance forward to the top of the today pole. What do you see? That's right, you see the same letter E (i.e., the same event) that you saw when you looked back at it from the tomorrow pole. So the event is there, whether you look back to it from the future or forward to it from the past.

The reader is probably now thinking: "Ah yes; but when I was really at the yesterday pole, and not just there in my imagination, the letter *E* wasn't there." To which I would reply: Yes, it was; but you couldn't see it, for the simple reason that you can't see into the future. To see the letter *E* from the yesterday pole you would need special "precognitive spectacles," which only a few possess and only occasionally are permitted to use.

I believe that all events are predetermined. "Whatever befalls thee," wrote Marcus Aurelius, Roman Emperor and religious philosopher (121–180), "was preordained for thee from eternity." The following stanzas from *The Rubaiyat of Omar Khayyam*, a poem written in 1237 and beautifully translated by Edward Fitzgerald, sum up the "militantly predestinarian theism of Islam." (Source: Antony Flew's *An Introduction to Western Philosophy*):

With Earth's first Clay they did the last Man knead,
And there of the Last Harvest sow'd the Seed:
    Yes, the first Morning of Creation wrote
What the last Dawn of Reckoning shall read.

Every single event in time, past, present and future, is known to God. He knows whether the sun will rise tomorrow just as surely as he knows that it rose this morning (if he doesn't then he isn't omniscient). And if he does know then that event is preordained.

Now it may be objected to that this is fallacious because the sun, unlike man, does not enjoy free will, it has to rise tomorrow whether it likes it or not; therefore its actions are predictable. Not so. Its actions are only predictable provided nothing unpredictable happens to interfere with natural law as we presently understand it. We believe that the sun will rise tomorrow; we do not know that it will. We believe; God knows. It is not a question of predictability or unpredictability: it is a question of knowledge. If God knows that the sun will rise tomorrow then he knows irrespective of whether that event is predictable or unpredictable (in any case how can anything be unpredictable to an omniscient God?)

If God is omniscient then we have to accept that the future is predetermined—although one doesn't have to believe in God to believe in predetermination. The existence of an all-knowing God is not a prerequisite to all that an all-knowing God would know if such a being existed. If future events already exist then they already exist whether or not there is a God.

It is sometimes asked: Could God alter the future? The question is, of course, a nonsense. God cannot alter the unalterable; truth is inviolate. But isn't God supposed to be all-powerful? Yes but the future is what actually happens; it is what is happening right now; it cannot be changed.

Another point: omnipotence doesn't mean that God can do anything and everything. He can only do what is in his "nature" to do. For instance, a God of truth cannot lie. Not because he hasn't the power to, but because his "nature" forbids it. If a God of truth were to lie, he would cease to be the God of truth. To cite a simple human analogy: a loving mother could not maltreat her children. Not because she hasn't the power to, but because if she did she would cease to be a loving mother.

We shall now consider the question of free will.

Here we find ourselves confronted with an apparently insuperable difficulty. If the future is already determined (as I believe it is); if our future actions are already decided (as I believe they are); how can we be free?

"Spinoza," writes Milton K. Munitz, distinguished professor of philosophy City University of New York's Baruch College, Graduate School, in his *The Ways of Philosophy*, "argues that the belief in free will is a superstition. It derives from a failure to acknowledge the strictly determined pattern that holds for all the parts of Nature.

" 'Thus the infant believes that it is by free will that it seeks the breast; the angry boy believes that by free will he wishes vengeance; the timid man thinks it is with free will he seeks flight; the drunkard believes that by a free command of his mind he speaks the things which when sober he wishes he had left unsaid. Thus the madman, the chatterer, the boy, and others of the same kind, all believe that they speak by a free command of the mind, whilst, in truth, they have no power to restrain the impulse which they have, to speak, so that experience itself, no less than reason, clearly teaches that men believe themselves to be free simply because they are conscious of their own actions, knowing, nothing of the causes by which they are determined . . .' " (III, Prop. II, Scholium.)

Few would argue that free will is paramount. Of course the infant that seeks the breast is actuated by deterministic impulses. Of course the timid man who seeks flight flees because he cannot help himself. Of course the drunkard who says things that afterwards he regrets does so because he cannot control his actions. But it does not follow that in all circumstances we have no control whatsoever over what we do, what we say, and what we think. We are not robots. We do have a will (even if it is not wholly free). And we do have a mind over which we have some (even if not total) control. There is no natural law that says that the drunkard *must* "speak the things that when sober he wishes he had left unsaid." There is no natural law that says the timid man *must* flee, that he *cannot* stand and fight. The reason why in both these examples Spinoza is invariably proved right, is because natural forces conspire to make him right, not because the drunkard and the timid man do not have freedom of choice. If, after several days in the Sahara desert, I come across an oasis, it is certain that I will drink the water and eat the dates, for the simple reason that natural forces will demand it of me. However, that does not mean that I am not free not to eat the dates and drink the water. What if I espy the notice: "Poisoned water, do not drink; poisoned dates, do not eat"? Would not the instinct of self-preservation remind me that I did have a choice?

Does not our everyday experience tell us that free will is not entirely a fiction, that we do have freedom of choice? Even as I write these words, I am undecided as to whether to break off and make myself a cup of tea or to carry on writing. I am perfectly free to choose; I am under no compulsion. Unlike the infant who seeks the breast, I am fully aware of what I am doing and what it is that prompts me to make a cup of tea—I am thirsty. (Yes, Mr. Philosopher, I know that I cannot prevent myself from becoming thirsty and tired and hungry, etc., etc. But the decision to make or not to make myself a cup of tea is entirely mine. Just to "prove" Mr. Spinoza wrong, I could, if I wished, stop eating and drinking altogether. But I don't think I shall go so far as that!)

One part of my nature (the tired and thirsty part) is urging me to stop writing and make myself a cup of tea. The other part (the part that wants me to continue writing) is telling me not to. Which impulse shall I obey? I feel compelled to obey neither. So, with absolute freedom of choice, I will . . . no, I won't . . . yes, I will . . . make myself a cup of tea!

Intermission.

I have now made myself a cup of tea, thus conclusively proving (haven't I?) that I am a free-will agent. Well, perhaps not. The moment of action is irrevocably frozen in time. The only way I can prove that I acted freely is to go back in time and act differently. As this is impossible, I can never know whether my action was genuinely free or whether it was preordained from eternity.

John Searle (*Minds, Brains and Science*) puts the case for the freedom of the will like this: "As many philosophers have pointed out, if there is any fact of experience that we are all familiar with, it's the simple fact that our own choices, decisions, reasonings, and cogitations seem to make a difference to our actual behaviour. There are all sorts of experiences that we have in life where it seems just a fact of our experience that though we did one thing, we feel we know perfectly well that we could have done something else. . . . Human freedom is just a fact of experience. If we want some empirical proof of this fact, we can simply point to the further fact that it is always up to us to falsify any predictions anybody might care to make about our behaviour. If somebody predicts that I am going to do something, I might just damn well do something else. Now, that sort of option is simply not open to glaciers moving down mountainsides or balls rolling down inclined planes or the planets moving in their elliptical orbits."

We are presented here, says John Searle, with a philosophical conundrum, the standard solution to which is that "free will and determinism are perfectly compatible with each other. Of course everything in the world is determined, but some human actions are nonetheless free. To say that they are free is not to deny that they are determined; it is just to say that they are not constrained. We are not forced to do them. So, for example, if a man is forced to do something at gunpoint . . . then his behavior is genuinely unfree. But if on the other hand he freely acts, if he acts, as we say, of his own free will, then his behaviour is free. Of course it is also completely determined by the physical forces operating on the particles that compose his body, as they operate on all of the bodies in the universe. So, free behaviour exists, but it is just a small corner of the determined world."

In *War and Peace,* Tolstoy, in discussing the infinite number of diverse and complex causes that combine to make an effect (e.g., the countless acts of millions of men engaged in the business of waging war), and the concurrence of innumerable circumstances without any one of which no event could take place, says this: "We are forced to fall back on fatalism as an explanation of irrational events (that is to say, events that reasonableness of which we do not understand). . . .

"Each man lives for himself, using his freedom to attain his personal aims, and feels with his whole being that he can now do or abstain from doing this or that action; but as soon as he has done it, that action performed at a certain moment in time becomes irrevocable and belongs to history, in which it *has not a free but a predestined significance*" (my emphasis, Source: Louise and Aylmer Maude's translation of *War and Peace*).

In other words, every act, however earth-shattering and important, or insignificant and trivial, *once enacted*, has a *predestined* effect on all future events.

When it comes down to rock bottom, it would appear that we aren't so very different from the atoms of which we are made. We have controlled freedom. That is to say, we are partially free, free to do and think what we like within certain well-defined parameters. Like the atom, we cannot wander beyond the prison walls. But there is an important difference. *We* know that we are not completely free; the atom doesn't. We can do something about it: the atom cannot.

But we are still left with this niggling doubt. If everything is predetermined; if our every thought, word and deed was, as I believe, written down in the Book of Creation at the very instant the Universe was created, how can we in any sense of the word be free? If it is predetermined that tomorrow I shall dig the garden, then tomorrow, like it or not, I shall dig the garden. I cannot choose not to dig the garden.

Well, it's like this: the key to the problem is knowledge. If I know what I am going to do before I do it then I am not free; I am a slave to that knowledge. If on the other hand I do not know what I am going to do before I do it then I do it freely. It is as simple as that. I cannot see into the future; so I have no way of knowing what my future actions will be. Therefore I am (within certain constraints) free to choose. The fact that God (or fate or destiny) knows what my choice will be, makes me no less free. There is no conflict between free will and predeterminism. My actions, though predetermined, are enacted freely.

God has eternal knowledge. He knows what is happening, what has happened, and what will happen in the length and breadth and depth of eternity—because he is outside the constraints of time. God exists nontemporally (and nonspatially). We exist in a temporal, "time-blinkered" (and "space-warped") environment.

If we could go back in time and see ourselves living our past, we would be watching ourselves acting freely. The fact that we now know what we then did is irrelevant. However many times we rerun an old movie, it always comes out the same, and the actors always exercise free will. The fact that the viewer knows what the actors will do, doesn't alter the fact that what they do (did) they do (did) freely. It is just that the viewer, being in a time-privileged position, is, unlike the actors at the time, aware of what is going to happen.

Our freedom to choose is obviously limited. For instance, I am not free to contest the heavyweight boxing championship of the world—although I would be if I were young enough and strong enough. But I am free to write or not to write these words, free to make or not to make myself a cup of tea!

We are free to do and think whatever is within our competence to do and think—although even then there are influences at work (at the atomic level) over which we have no freedom of choice whatsoever: we are not free to break the freedom chains that bind us. In other words, we are not free to give up free will (even when we act out of fear or under compulsion, we still act freely).

We can only ever be partially free. To be wholly free we would have to have absolute wisdom and absolute power. Only God, who has both, is truly free.

To sum up: everyday experience and intuitive perception tell us that we are free to make choices but only within strictly confined parameters. Our behaviour is very largely determined by the physical forces that act upon the particles that compose our bodies. As these forces are obliged to behave in the way that universal laws decreed that they should since the dawn of creation, then to that extent our behaviour is predetermined and unfree.

Predetermination means that our actions are predetermined by reason of the fact that God knows what they will be. In the words of Aquinas: "If God foresees that this will happen it will happen . . . But it will occur in the way in which God foresaw that it would occur. He, however, foresaw that it would occur contingently and not necessarily." (*Summa contra Gentiles.*) Ergo: we are free!

As for precognition: if future events already exist waiting to be enacted; if our future actions are already inscribed in the Book of Creation, then I believe that it is possible, sometimes, for the human mind to "tune in" and "pick up" that information. But I do not believe that it can be done at will. The conditions must be right. "Signal" and "receiver" must be in complete harmony, on the same "wavelength," "wandering abroad" in the same dimension.

J. B. Priestley, who was keenly interested in the phenomenon of time, and wrote several books and plays incorporating his ideas on the subject, also believed in precognition. He claimed to have had a few memorable precognitive dreams himself, and thought that the future was "partly fixed" and "partly fluid," that "an event on the scale of the Battle of Borodino is already determined, and so inevitable, like the Countess's experience on the edge of it." The part that is fluid, he believed, consists of "possible events," of which only one "can be actualized."

I cannot myself go along with Priestley that the future is "partly fixed" and "partly fluid." Either it is wholly fixed or it is wholly fluid. If God is omniscient then he knows it all, not a part of it. And if he knows it all then it is all predetermined.

It is strange that those who subscribe to fate do not live their lives as if they really believed it. I suppose this is because, although they feel a profound sense of impotence in the face of irresistible natural forces, and sense that there is a universal cosmic plan that governs everything within the Universe —whether stars, moons, mountains, or human beings—they also know that in the ordinary detail of their everyday lives they are free to make choices. They are free to do what they will, but not free to change their destiny. Their future is as fixed as the orbit of the planets.

To use an everyday analogy: it is like participating in a soccer match that has been fixed in advance. The result has already been decided, and the description of the match already written up in tomorrow's sports reports. All we have to do is go out and play the game—to go through the motions, as it were; to score goals, take free kicks, corner kicks, goal kicks and penalties, incur yellow cards and red cards—all in accordance with reports already written.

But here's the paradox! In doing so we act freely, because *we* don't know what's written in those reports. Therefore, we have to accept responsibility for our actions. We cannot blame the referee or the match organizer, or the reporter who has already written up the report (one and the same "person" of course). This all-seeing, all-knowing, all-powerful "reporter" knows the result before the match begins. He knows how many goals we will score, how well or badly we will perform, how many fouls we will commit. We are not privy to this knowledge; so how we play the game is up to us.

Is it not a mercy and a blessing that we do not know the content of the future, all the problems and disappointments, the pain and suffering and sad bereavements we are destined to endure, the exact day, hour, minute of our earthly demise—not to mention the excruciating boredom of knowing in advance precisely what we are going to do, say and think every second of our waking lives? Not knowing the future enables us to live our lives in blissful ignorance of what lies ahead. "Ignorance," said Anatole France (*The Garden of Epicurus*, 1894), "is the necessary condition of life itself. If we knew everything, we could not endure existence for a single hour." Or as the poet Eugene Lee-Hamilton (1845–1907) puts it (*Mimma Bella*):

> Oh, bless the law that veils the Future's face;
> For who could smile into a baby's eyes,
> Or bear the beauty of the evening skies,
> If he could see what cometh on apace?

And the poet Dryden (1631–1700) in *The Indian Queen*:

> Seek not to know what must not be reveal'd;
> Joys only flow where Fate is most conceal'd.
> Too-busy man would find his sorrow more
> If future fortunes he should know before;
> For by that knowledge of his Destiny
> He would not live at all, but always die.

But then, of course, the thought is absurd! If we could foresee the future, we would not be the creatures we are. We would be automatoms, subject only to the whims of fate. "No means of predicting the future really exists," wrote Epicurus (342–270 BC), "and if it did, we must regard what happens according to it as nothing to us." In other words, we must get on with living our lives as free creatures.

If free will is an illusion, it is an illusion we cannot do without. It is because human beings believe that they have (albeit, restricted) free will, and act in accordance with this belief, that they require the status of free-will agents. Belief and action turn the *illusion* of free will into the *reality* of free will. Believe freely and act freely, and we become free. Not wholly free, of course. We are free to rebel against God's will, but not against God's laws. (Whether I choose to jump off the top of the Empire State Building is up to me; but if I do then I can expect to travel in one direction only, downwards, because God's law of gravity will not permit me to fall upwards.)

Is the future predetermined? Are our actions preordained? As I have said, I believe that they are. If they aren't then God

196

isn't omniscient. And if he isn't omniscient then he isn't omnipotent. And if he is neither then how come he managed to create the Universe?

Chapter 7

How Do We Know That Wrong Is Wrong?

Nobody yet knows what is good and evil—unless it be the Creator.
Friedrich Nietzsche

For right is right, since God is God.

Frederick William Faber

"Mankind has always been inclined to believe in the existence of objective forces of evil," says Colin Wilson in his book *Mysteries* . . . "Rationalists are inclined to argue that it is the crime itself that is evil, or socially undesirable, not the person who commits it. If a tree falls down in a storm and kills a passing pedestrian, nobody 'blames' the tree. In the same way, many murderers seem only partially responsible for their crimes. In a recent case [1976] in Germany, the killer not only murdered and raped more than a dozen children, but also carried away parts of their body, presumably to eat. In the public imagination, he became a figure of pure evil. When arrested, Joachim Kroll, a public toilet attendant, proved to be something of an anticlimax; he was a mild absent-minded little man who was unable to recall most of his victims. He was convinced that, after medical treatment, he would be allowed to return home. When the police burst into his room, a hand of his latest victim, a five-year-old girl, was being boiled in a stew with carrots; Kroll regarded his taste for eating small girls as unusual but not reprehensible. The Middle Ages also recognized this frequent disparity between the crime and the criminal, but they regarded it as a proof of the objective existence of evil. If the crime is more evil than the individual who committed it, then it seems to follow that evil has an independent existence."

198

Independent existence or no, it is a self-evident truth that what Kroll did was wrong. But how are we able to come to this conclusion without even thinking about it? We would not say that a man was *self-evidently* 5'10½" tall. We would have to prove that he was, by using a measuring stick. So what measuring stick do we use to prove that what Kroll did was wrong?

It is easy to demonstrate that his actions were socially undesirable; for they were unquestionably opposed to the interests of society. No civilized society could tolerate this kind of behaviour. To do so would invite the destruction of society itself.

But this is to miss the point entirely. The question posed is not "How does one define wrong?" or "How does one recognize wrong?" but "How do we know that wrong is wrong?" In other words: How do we know that such a thing as wrong actually exists?

The reader is probably now thinking: "Why this pedantic splitting of hairs? Does it matter how we know; isn't it sufficient that we do know?" No, it is not. The "How we know" is even more important than the "We do know," as the following imaginary conversation between an atheist (A) and a believer (B) will, I hope, show:

B. Can you tell me how you know that wrong is wrong?
A. Yes. Wrong is wrong because by definition it is wrong. If it weren't wrong we'd call it something else! I presume that what you are really asking me is: How would I define wrong?
B. No, that is not what I was asking you; but please carry on.
A. Human beings are thinking, rational, and social animals, who live in communities and know that the community must defend itself against undesirable antisocial acts that would damage society, and, if unresisted, lead to chaos. In order to protect itself, society makes laws prohibiting such antisocial behaviour as murder, theft, rape, torture, etc., which offends the dignity of man and is diametrically opposed to the interests of society as a whole. These acts are not intrinsically wrong, but inasmuch as they render society unstable and unsafe, and, *in extremis,* unworkable, they are regarded by man as unreasonable, illogical, and unsocial and therefore wrong.

B. I was interested to hear you say that you do not regard wrong acts as *intrinsically* wrong. However, I will let that pass for the moment, as I wish to stick with my original question, which you haven't yet answered . . .

A. I thought I had?

B. . . . which was, "How do you know that wrong is wrong?" With respect, you have told me that in your opinion certain acts—murder, rape, torture, etc.,—are wrong not because they are intrinsically wrong but because they work against the interests of society. But you haven't explained by what process you come to the conclusion that such a thing as wrong actually exists; that what you and society think is wrong, is not in fact right, or at least, not wrong.

A. I'm sorry, but I don't understand what you are getting at. You are surely not suggesting that wrong isn't wrong?

B. No. But then I have good reason for believing that wrong is wrong. What I am curious to know is: by what process, on whose authority, using what measuring stick, are you able to definitively state that wrong is wrong; that is to say, that wrong is not just a word to denote a fashionable, transient view of social misconduct. Let me ask you this: do you think it wrong to kill little children?

A. Of course I do.

B. Why?

A. It is wrong because it is self-evidently wrong: it goes without saying.

B. Kroll didn't think so. Nor did Herod.

A. Oh, come now! I am not talking about inhuman monsters; I am talking about decent civilized human beings.

B. Like you and me?

A. Yes, if you like, like you and me.

B. Why are *you* so sure it is wrong to kill little children?

A. Because my reason tells me it is. Ah ha! Now if you are going to tell me that my reason is the voice of God speaking to me, then I shall have to disagree. God doesn't come into it. Human feelings stem from humanity not from God.

B. What I am suggesting is that your opinion that it is wrong to kill little children is a subjective one, and as such has no more claim to validity than Kroll's or Herod's. What makes you think that you are right and they are wrong? What's so special about you?

A. There's no need to be rude!

B. I beg your pardon; I didn't mean it like that.

A. There's nothing special about me—except that my opinion also happens to be shared by all decent, civilized people—including yourself, I presume.

B. But Kroll and Herod were human beings just like you and me, with as much right to think that they were right, as you have to think that they were wrong. On whose authority are we to make our judgements?

A. On the authority of the consensus of the vast majority of human beings, including the world's great philosophers, humanitarians, and theologians, who set principles of behaviour and ethical standards that have been accepted by everyone except the most wicked in society. Human beings are quite capable of differentiating between right and wrong. The inhuman monsters of this world are in the tiny minority, and are the exception that proves the rule—the rule that the majority of human beings are decent and humane and regard the killing of little children as wrong. So frankly, I still don't understand what you are trying to get at!

B. Please bear with me for a moment while I try to explain. Throughout the ages human beings have perpetrated the most appalling crimes against one another. The history of the human race is one of continuous violence, persecution and war. Millions have been slaughtered in the name of patriotism, freedom, justice, peace, God, and Allah. Millions have been murdered, executed, starved to death, maimed, tortured, boiled in oil, buried alive, roasted over spits, impaled, dismembered, disembowelled, torn to pieces, had their eyes gouged out and their extremities cut off. Towns, villages, and communities have been wiped off the face of the earth, and whole peoples exterminated. (Genocide was not invented by Hitler, it's been going on for thousands of years.) If peace is indivisible, as the Russian diplomat, Maxim Litvinov once declared, then the world has never been at peace. At the present moment the Middle East is in a state of turmoil, and has been for eighteen years. Arabs are killing Jews and Jews are killing Arabs. And in the Lebanon Christian Arabs and Muslim Arabs are killing each other. In Iran opponents of the Islamic revolution, including young girls of sixteen and seventeen, have been shot in their hundreds and homosexuals and adulterers suffer the same fate.

In neighbouring Iraq, now at "peace" with Iran after eight years of bloody conflict, in which the Iraqis not only killed Iranians but also used chemical weapons against their own Kurdish people, and poisoned their drinking wells and food supplies, the human rights record is, if anything, even worse. Men, women, even young children, are arrested by the omnipresent secret police, tortured, and arbitrarily executed as "enemies of the state." And with one million dead and eight years of killing and being killed behind them, their appetite for conquest apparently unabated, the Iraqis invaded the tiny Gulf Kingdom of Kuwait, as if to demonstrate, if demonstration be needed, that whatever else might change, war and aggression will never go out of fashion. As I speak, events in the Gulf are moving towards a bloody confrontation between the U.S. and her U.N. allies, and Iraq. Whether the present conflict will end "peacefully" or explode into a major regional war, with one side using poison gas and the other nuclear weapons, is anybody's guess.*

In El Salvador civil war has raged for ten years; in the Sudan for six; in Ethiopia and Eritrea for twenty-eight; in Mozambique for fourteen. In Chile trade unionists and socialists have been tortured and murdered by the military

---

*Whatever the outcome of the current crisis in the Middle East, there can be no lasting peace in the region until the Palestinian problem is resolved. The will to war—Saddam Hussein or no Saddam Hussein—will not dissipate until the basic needs and aspirations of the Palestinian population have been taken into account. These wretched people cannot, year after year, generation after generation, be made to live and die as displaced persons. Common humanity forbids it. The Jews, no strangers to hatred and persecution, themselves "homeless" for nearly two thousand years, should know this better than anyone else. They fought and suffered and died to create a homeland of their own. What makes them think that the emergent young Palestinians will not do the same? How is the problem to be solved? As the most intellectually and spiritually gifted people in the world, whose religion is based, above all, on justice, it is incumbent on the Jews to give a moral lead. Their faith demands it. From God's chosen people (if they are not chosen to give a moral lead, what are they chosen for?) we should expect nothing less.

regime. And in Argentina, prior to the fall of the military junta after the Falklands war, over 30,000 left-wing sympathizers disappeared, never to be seen again. On the borders of the Iranian Jaya province of Indonesia villages of the primitive "stone-age" tribesmen are bombed with napalm; captured prisoners are tied in sacks and drowned or beheaded or bludgeoned to death; pregnant women are bayonetted and the throats of tribal elders cut. In Guatemala the native Indian population is being systematically wiped out; tens of thousands of these poor, simple folk have been massacred, often hacked to death in front of their children. In the bloody aftermath of the assassination of Mrs. Gandhi, more than a thousand Sikhs were murdered by Hindus, many of them doused in petrol and burned alive. In Sri Lanka racial war rages between the Sinhalese and the Tamil communities. And in Bangladesh 185,000 people have been slaughtered in a local war being waged by the Bengalis and Muslims against a Buddhist tribe of the Chittagong Hill Tracts; Buddhist monks, who have peacefully resisted efforts to destroy the culture of their peoples, have been tortured and murdered by the State's armed forces. Thousands of young delinquents have been executed in China, many in public, for a variety of crimes including theft and molesting women. No one knows how many students were arrested and put to death in the wake of the Tiananmen Square protests in June 1989, but we do know that the Chinese have practiced genocide in the killing fields of Tibet for the past thirty-eight years. Brutal assassinations are the order of the day in Nigeria, and public executions are carried out in the most sadistic manner after peremptory trials by secret military tribunals—the death sentence being mandatory for a whole range of offences which, in the West, would attract prison sentences of a few months. During Dr. Obete's five-year rule in Uganda, it is estimated by Amnesty International that up to 300,00 people vanished or were butchered, a record even worse than that of the bloodthirsty Idi Amin whom Obete succeeded. In South Africa for decades whites have treated blacks like subhumans, and in Zimbabwe blacks kill blacks without mercy. Mass graves uncovered in South Matabeleland a few years ago containing the victims of the notorious Fifth Brigade, show that when it comes to committing atrocities, blacks have little to learn from whites. In pre-Gorbachev Russia dissidents were put into asylums or sent to Siberian labour camps, where the will to survive was destroyed, and death from exposure and starvation was a daily occurrence. In Libya public hangings take place in front of vast jeering crowds. Offenders, many of them young students, are tortured, tried, sentenced, and then taken directly from tribunal to a makeshift scaffold, where they are suspended from a beam and slowly strangulated. And in Northern Ireland men are shot dead in their homes, or blown up on their way to work or whilst having a drink in a pub with their friends.

Not a day goes by without some act of terrorism somewhere in the world.

Only forty-five or so years ago the Nazis shot, hanged, gassed and starved to death six million of their fellow human beings—for no other reason than that they were Jews. Two million gypsies, Slavs, Poles, and Russians were also put to death, because they, too, were considered racially "impure." The atrocities committed by the Nazis in Russia, Poland, Yugoslavia, Greece, Belgium, France, Holland, Denmark—in fact, in every country they occupied—surpassed in bestiality anything previously recorded in the history of mankind. In the decade prior to 1941 the Germans put to death more than 60,000 of their own men, women, and children in the infamous "euthanasia" clinics, because they were considered mentally or physically "inferior."

After the bloody excesses of the Bolshevik revolution in the twenties and thirties millions of the peasant population of the Ukraine were deliberately starved to death on the direct orders of Joseph Stalin—probably, next to Mao Tsetung, the biggest mass murderer of all time, whose crimes exceeded in number even those of the Nazis. In 1940 over 4,000 Polish army officers and NCOs were taken to the Katyn Forest in Poland and murdered in cold blood by machine-gun fire or a single bullet in the back of the neck. When the graves were discovered, the Russians blamed the Germans, and the Germans blamed the Russians. It was almost cer-

204

tainly the work of the Russians, but either way it was perpetrated by members of the human race.*

In Japanese prison camps and on the infamous Burma Railway during the last war, Allied servicemen and civilians were beaten, starved, tortured, beheaded and crucified in their thousands, while Japanese doctors, professors and academics (not psychopathic hoodlums, be it noted) experimented on human guinea pigs with cyanide gas, by deliberately infecting them with bubonic plague and tetanus, by freezing them to death in locked refrigerators, and by dissecting them whilst still alive (all in the interests of medical science, of course). Just over a decade ago, another mass murderer, Pol Pot of Cambodia, took a leaf out of Hitler's book and embarked on a massive programme of genocide, exterminating over two million people, a quarter of the population. And so it goes on, ad nauseum, ad infinitum . . . .

Such is the world in which we live. And it has always been so. Only the names and places change, only the scale and methods vary. The examples I have quoted are just a random selection from the present and recent past. It would be of some consolation to know that only barbarians commit barbarious acts. Unfortunately this isn't so. We have examined the record of the bad guys. Let us now take a look at the good guys—those decent civilized people you spoke about earlier. What is their record?

In the Second World War it is estimated that the Allied Air Forces killed over 800,000 civilians in air raids over German cities. On one night alone, February 13, 1945, three-quarters of a million incendiary bombs were dropped on Dresden, creating a raging inferno in which more than 100,000 men, women and children were incinerated or suffocated. This was one of the many saturation bombing raids instigated by Britain's Commander-in-Chief of Bomber Command, Sir Arthur Harris, whose avowed aim was to reduce Germany to ruins by massive air attacks. Harris received many laudatory congratulations from Churchill and the

*On April 13, 1990, the Soviet Union finally admitted responsibility for the massacre.

American and Soviet leaders, and much praise for his strategy aimed at shortening the war and thus saving Allied lives.

At the time, public opinion was not the slightest bit shocked. Why should it have been? We were at war, and wartime is no time to be squeamish. We were fighting for our lives, for freedom, for civilization, and were only doing to the Germans what they had done to us. Did the murderous Luftwaffe have any qualms when they bombed the citizens of London, Coventry, Warsaw, and Rotterdam? They did not. So, was it not right and proper that our gallant airmen should bring home to the German people the stark reality of the horror and suffering that their megalomaniac leaders had inflicted on others? And when the war was won was it not also right and proper that the victorious Allied nations should take those guilty men—at least, as many as they decently could—and hang them?

On August 6, 1945 an American B29 bomber dropped an atom bomb on Hiroshima, killing 100,000 men, women and children. Three days later, for good measure, a second was dropped on the town of Nagasaki killing another 35,000 innocent civilians. In mitigation, it has been argued (in my view, rightly) that the use of this uniquely horrendous weapon brought about the immediate end to a war which would otherwise have dragged on and claimed the lives of a further million Allied servicemen and two million Japanese. (What has never been satisfactorily explained, however, is why the bomb was not demonstrated on open ground, so as to give the Japanese the chance to surrender, thereby saving much suffering and loss of life. Whether it was because the Americans could not bear the thought of the Japanese going unpunished for their treacherous attack on Pearl Harbour, or because they wanted to see what effect radiation would have on human beings—or whether indeed they regarded the Japanese as human beings—is something we shall probably never know.) Was the Allied action justified? Of course it was. But note how morality becomes a matter of simple arithmetic! Subtract the 135,000 human souls killed by the two atom bombs, from the three million that would have been killed had the bombs not been dropped, and hey presto! we get a credit balance of 2,865,000 lives saved! By this line of reasoning it would have been even more beneficial had Germany's scientists invented the atom bomb for Hitler to drop on Poland in 1939. Think how many lives *that* would have saved!

After the war ended in Europe, the decent civilized British repatriated, literally at the point of a gun, over two-and-a-quarter million Russian citizens, most of whom were immediately shot or subsequently starved to death in the wastes of Siberia. The British authorities knew that they were sending these people to their certain death, but, as it was agreed at Yalta that this should be done, done it was.

In the years that followed VE Day, over 14 million ethnic Germans living in Eastern Europe suffered brutal dispossession and degradation at the hands of the decent civilized Czechs, Slovaks, Poles, Romanians, Hungarians, and Yugoslavs. These ancient German communities were forcibly expelled from their homeland with the tacit approval, at the Potsdam Conference, of the decent, civilized British and Americans. Many were murdered in cold blood, two million simply died by the wayside or were left to starve in the concentration camps abandoned by the Nazis, where their rations were even more meager than those in Belsen.

A little further back in modern history, the decent, civilized British were engaged in unspeakable acts of brutality, torture, and murder against the Indian people. A few years later, the decent, civilized French were doing the same in Indo-China. And in the same country, but now called Vietnam, the decent, civilized Americans were committing the most awful atrocities against the villagers of My Lai. More than 500 helpless children, women, and old men were slaughtered in cold blood. Some had their hands cut off and their tongues cut out. Some were scalped. After four hours of occupation the village ceased to exist.

Another example of the appalling disregard for human life in time of war is a revealed in this report from the *London Daily Mail,* October 8, 1984: "Old soldier Gerald Fitzpatrick, last night feared he may have made a serious error of judgement in telling of a hitherto unrecorded massacre of twenty-seven Burmese villagers in 1942. The Burmese were wiped out, he says, to prevent them revealing the presence of British soldiers retreating before the invading Japanese. Mr. Fitzpatrick, then a twenty-two-year-old second lieutenant with the King's Own Yorkshire Light Infantry, says he knifed the first victim himself. He then ordered three other officers to execute the remaining twenty-six Burmese and dump the bodies in a dry river bed. . . . Dr. Ralph Tanner, then a twenty-one-year-old second lieutenant, now a university lecturer living in Steeple Aston, Oxon, said yesterday: 'It was a question of obliterating anyone who could be a potential menace to us.' "

What these British soldiers did in Burma; what the GIs did in Vietnam; and what others have done in every war that has ever been fought, simply serve to illustrate what human beings are prepared to do when they are convinced that their cause is just. Of course there are differences in degree. To equate the deeds of the Allied airmen who bombed Germany, with the hideous atrocities committed by the Nazis in the concentration camps at Mildenhausen, Belsen, Auschwitz and Dachau would be monstrous. Our airmen didn't put children into gas chambers. But they did blow them to bits and incinerate them. (Ah, yes, but the Germans started the war, didn't they? Who did, the German babies?) When our men set out to bomb German cities they did not willfully intend to kill and mutilate little children. Nonetheless, that is what they did. And the fact that these brave men were decent human beings, risking and losing their lives to rid the world of the evil of Nazism, only serves to highlight the awful nature of what they were doing. One expects evil deeds from evil people. It is the evil committed by good people that is so frightening. Some might protest that to characterize the actions of these courageous young men as evil is quite outrageous. Maybe it is. But how else is one to describe the indiscriminate slaughter of little children? And to suggest that children were only killed by accident is simply not true, as the following letter from a Mr. Bill Williams, in the correspondence columns of the *London Observer*, August 5, 1984 will testify:

208

On 13 February 1945, I was a navigator on one of the Lancaster bombers which devastated Dresden. I well remember the briefing by our Group Captain. We were told that the Red Army was thrusting towards Dresden and that the town would be crowded with refugees, and that the centre of the town would be full of women and children. Our aiming point would be the market place. I recall that we were somewhat uneasy, but we did as we were told. We accordingly bombed the target and on our way back our wireless operater picked up a German broadcast accusing the RAF of terror tactics, and that 65,000 civilians had died. We dismissed this as German propaganda. The penny didn't drop until a few weeks later when my squadron received a visit from the Crown Film Unit who were making the wartime propaganda films. There was a mock briefing. Same crews. Same maps. Same briefing—with one notable difference. The same Group Captain now said "as the marketplace would be full of women and children on no account would we bomb the centre of the town. Instead our aiming point would be a vital railway junction to the east."

And so, the civilian population of Dresden was deliberately bombed, and the lives of thousands of children wantonly destroyed, in order that in the ensuing chaos the Red Army could advance more swiftly into Germany. It is, of course, a tragic fact that people are killed in wartime. And why should the lives of German children be more precious than the lives of the brave Russian soldiers, who themselves had their own babies slaughtered by the Nazi invaders? Compassion, it would seem, is a luxury one simply afford in time of war, when one's country is locked in a life and death struggle with an evil foe.

Since the end of the last war, which itself was fought twenty years after the "war to end wars," the world has been engaged in a continuous carnage of "mini-wars," the total casualties of which amount to over thirty million dead, including as many women and children as combatants, more than the dead of both world wars put together.

And it is not only in time of war that men behave in such unseemly fashion, with little regard for the sanctity of human life. Even today in modern civilized Britain, children are often beaten and killed—sometimes by their own parents—and blind old ladies of eighty and ninety are raped, battered and brutally murdered. There is, it would seem, no depths of depravity to which the human condition cannot sink.

Less than two centuries ago children were executed in England for petty crimes. In 1629 a boy of eight was found guilty and hanged for setting fire to two outhouses. According to Harold Nicholson (*Age of Reason*), "[In England in the first half of the eighteenth century] there still existed on the statute book some 253 offences, the punishment for which was death. A prisoner could be hanged on Tyburn tree if he shot a rabbit, damaged a bridge, cut down a young tree, or stole property valued at five shillings. As late as 1816 there were fifty-eight prisoners in Newgate jail under sentence of death, among them a child of ten."

In the eighteenth century women were burned at the stake or drowned for alleged witchcraft. And it wasn't until the nineteenth century that the sentence of hanging, drawing and quartering was withdrawn from the British statute book. All this, in a country which at the time was regarded, by herself and the rest of the world, as a civilized nation! (Ah, but that was a long time ago, wasn't it?)

Not so long ago, January 28, 1953 to be precise, a feeble-minded, epileptic nineteen-year-old youth, Derek Bentley, with no previous record of violence, was hanged in Wandsworth Prison, London, not for murdering anyone, but for being engaged in a criminal escapade with a sixteen-year-old boy, Christopher Craig, when the latter shot dead a policeman. At the moment Craig fired the shot, Bentley was actually under arrest, in the physical custody of another police officer. Craig, who shot the policeman, was too young to be executed. Bentley, who shot no one, wasn't. Were we right to hang him? The law said we were.

In the summer of 1955, twenty-eight-year-old Ruth Ellis was hanged in Holloway Jail, London, for shooting dead her lover David Blakely. Ten days before the crime she miscarried Blakely's child after being punched in the stomach by her lover in a drunken fury. When she fired the shot, she was suffering from extreme post-miscarriage depression, and had just discovered that Blakely was having an affair with another woman. Here, one might have thought, was a case for the Home Secretary to exercise his prerogative of mercy. Not a bit of it. Ruth Ellis had sinned and must pay the price. Were we right to hang her? The law said we were.

In both these cases there was an intense public outcry against the sentences. No one believed that this unfortunate boy and this pitiful young woman would be hanged. They were wrong. They were. The law decreed that the supreme penalty be paid. And there were not enough who cared, or who cared enough, to prevent the executions taking place.

This chronic catalogue of "man's inhumanity to man," clearly shows that decent, civilized human beings are decent and civilized SO LONG AS THEY HAVE NO REASON TO BE OTHERWISE. Whatever we wish to do, even if it entails the wholesale slaughter of innocent little children, we will find good reason for doing it. The Home Secretaries who refused to recommend the commutation of the death sentences on Derek Bentley and Ruth Ellis; the Allied airmen who killed and maimed children in their thousands; the politicians who sanctioned the use of the atom bombs; the scientists who built it and the men who dropped it; all had one thing in common—they were all *decent civilized human beings*. The slaughter of the innocent is not a unique activity of barbarians. We are all prone to it or prone to condone it. The human race carries the stigma of Cain. To put it bluntly—we are not to be trusted.

What I have endeavoured to show is that human beings, IRRESPECTIVE OF RACE, CREED OR COLOUR, are quite capable of committing, or sanctioning, or encouraging, or tolerating, or turning a blind eye to, the most appalling crimes against humanity. No nation is exempt. Every aggressor in the annals of history has sincerely believed that he was in the right, that God was on his side. No war has ever been fought where both sides were not convinced of the rectitude of their cause. We all like to think that we are civilized and peaceloving. And so we are. Until, that is, we find ourselves in a situation where we are threatened, or fearful, or called upon to fight for our country (or someone else's country), our freedom, our religious beliefs, or simply our own selfish commercial and economic interests. And then the wafer-thin, waxlike mask of civilization, melts in the intense heat of self-interest, hatred and fear, and the inner barbarian, which lies just below the surface like a second skin, is suddenly revealed. It would be foolish to suggest that human beings are all brutes like Hitler, Stalin and Pol Pot. In fact, the vast majority of people are, in ordinary circumstances, perfectly decent and civilized. But we would do well to remember that the evil that lurks in the murderous perverts of this world, is the same evil which motivates us all to a greater or lesser degree. By focusing our attention on the supercrimes of the superbarbarians, we neatly avoid having to think about the lesser crimes that we ourselves commit. Because there are others more demonstrably evil than I, I am able to anaesthetize my conscience and say: "Thank God I am not as other men." But the truth is, I *am* as other men! That is the problem of the human race. Left to our own devices, we act according to our nature—just as the bird does when it eats the worm, and the cat when it kills the bird. If it is not wrong for them to act according to their nature, why is it wrong for us to act according to ours? Fortunately we are blessed (or cursed?) with a conscience. Animals do not have this problem. Not for them the dilemma of choosing between right and wrong. We have freedom of choice. We are, for example, free to help an old lady across the road. We are also free to mug her. The right choice may seem obvious to us, but apparently it isn't to the mugger. And who is to say that the mugger is wrong?

A. I presume that isn't meant to be a serious question . . .

B. Actually, it is.

A. . . . as I am sure you are not suggesting that mugging old ladies can be anything but wrong. Also, I have to say that the picture you have painted gives a totally distorted impression of the human race. The world is not perpetually at war. The majority of people do not spend all their time committing atrocities, battering babies and murdering old ladies. Society is not continually executing nineteen-year-old youths and sick young women—the two examples you cited were isolated cases, which all humanitarians would agree were regrettable mistakes. Most people, most of the time, live in perfect peace and harmony with their neighbours. Just because a tiny minority are capable, on occasions, of committing the most heinous crimes against their fellow men, does not mean that the overwhelming majority of human beings are not fully aware that these acts are wrong. You have completely over-looked the good and noble qualities inherent in human na-ture. As Harold Nicholson pointed out in his book you yourself quoted: "Bacon and Locke had taught that man ... was naturally good and that he had been corrupted by false theory and evil institutions."

B. Really? Who was it that created the "false theory and evil institutions" that "corrupted" man, if not man himself? How then can man be naturally good? Has not man, throughout the ages, demonstrated that, left to his own devices, he is naturally evil, or at least not naturally good? Where do we get this extraordinary idea from that man is naturally any-thing but natural? But I digress. Let me return to my original question, How do we know that wrong is wrong? As a theist, my position is quite clear. God exists; therefore so do right and wrong. If God did not exist then neither would right and wrong. Unless we acknowledge the existence of the Creator of morality (whom theists call God), we cannot know that morality *per se* exists. "If God did not exist," said Dostoevsky, "everything would be permitted." Meaning that without God nothing would be wrong—for the simple reason that there would be no one with the authority to say that it was wrong. Do right and wrong exist? I say that if God exists, then yes, they do. If God does not exist, then no, they do not.

A. Let me get this clear. Are you saying that if God does not exist then no crime, however criminal, no deed, however hei-nous, are wrong? That murder, pillage, rape and torture, are not wrong? That, to quote your own example, to put innocent little children into gas chambers is not wrong?

B. Yes, that is precisely what I am saying.

A. I find that an extraordinary statement coming from someone who professes to believe in God!

B. It is because I believe in God that I believe that these things are wrong. If there were no God, I would have no way of knowing that it would mean anything to say that these acts were wrong. Antisocial, yes. Against the interests of society, indubitably. But wrong—how? When Hitler and the Nazis committed genocide, they were unquestionably indulging in an antisocial act—for the very good reason that to murder a whole race is against the interests of that society. But where do we get the idea from that they were wrong? "Wrong" is not a synonym for "antisocial." Genocide is antisocial, irrespective of whether there is a God or not. But genocide cannot be *wrong* unless there is a God. Society is a man-made organism, therefore man is entitled of his own accord to say that an act is antisocial. But man did not create right and wrong, only his *interpretation of* right and wrong. For instance, not very long ago, homosexuality was generally regarded as a sin. Nowadays, homosexual practices are deemed to be, by many people, including a large number of clergymen, perfectly acceptable, even praiseworthy. Who knows when the pendulum will swing the other way and homosexuality again become morally unacceptable? Now, whether homosexual practices are right or wrong, is a matter of personal moral judgement. But no one, whatever his or her convictions, would say that these practices were not either wrong or not wrong. In other words, whatever our personal interpretation, we would all agree that wrong (as opposed to homosexuality) is wrong, that such a thing as wrong actually exists.

A. Be that as it may, I cannot agree that the existence of morality depends on the existence of God. They are completely unconnected. If morality exists—and however one defines it, it obviously does—then it exists independently.

B. That is like saying that the acorn exists independent of the oak tree; that sunshine exists independent of the sun. Morality exists because God exists. If God doesn't exist then neither does morality. And if morality doesn't exist then nothing is wrong. In which case, it cannot be wrong to kill little children. We kill cockroaches, so why not children?

A. Because children aren't cockroaches!

B. I know they aren't. But why should it be wrong to kill the one and not the other? It is obviously antisocial to kill children (though there could be circumstances in which it might be argued that it wasn't); but why *wrong*? Only God knows whether right and wrong exist, because if there are such values then he created them.

A. That is nonsense. We know that right and wrong exist.

B. Do we? How? We are able to judge the difference in quality between certain acts. But to define some as morally right and others as morally wrong is to use a vocabulary to which we are not entitled, unless we accept that there is a definitive standard by which all acts are judged. Either this definitive standard is God, or it is man (there is no other alternative). Now, it cannot be man, for man is incapable of creating definitive standards—when "man on his own" uses the words "right" and "wrong," he means whatever he wishes them to mean. Let me ask you a question: if every person on earth, including yourself, thought that mugging and murdering were right, would mugging and murdering be wrong?

A. Of course they would.

B. Why?

A. Because there is a standard of morality which says they are; and mugging and murdering would still be wrong, even if everyone ignored that standard.

B. What standard? What morality? If everybody judged mugging and murdering to be right, by whose definition of morality would they be wrong? Not yours. Not mine. Because, like everyone else, we would think that they were right. Quite simply, mugging and murdering could not be wrong by any human definition. By recognizing that such things can be wrong, we are, *ipso facto*, recognizing that God exists.

A. According to that line of reasoning, anyone who doesn't believe in God can do no wrong—because for them right and wrong do not exist!

B. Not so. God's existence does not depend on what you or I or anyone else may think. God exists objectively and independently. And it is for this reason, and for this reason alone, that right and wrong exist.

A. Let me ask *you* a question. If it could be proven beyond a shadow of doubt that God did not exist, would you still believe in the concepts of right and wrong?

B. That is a bit like asking if I would still believe that a mile was a mile if it could be proved that it wasn't.

A. I thought you might try to dodge the question!

B. I wasn't dodging the question; I couldn't answer it, because it is not a valid question. I have already said that I believe that the existence of right and wrong depends on the existence of God. No God, no right, no wrong. And that, I am afraid, is my final position.

A. In that case, we shall have to agree to disagree.

B. One last question: Do you think it right to help others, and wrong to harm them; that love and compassion are infinitely better than hatred and revenge?

A. Of course I do.

B. Then, believe it or not, you believe in God.

This fictional conversation of course proves nothing. As with any discussion about God, it all breaks down at the boundaries of faith. To the atheist, right and wrong are a matter of expediency; nothing is intrinsically wrong; an act is wrong only when it is antisocial, illogical or irrational. To the theist, however, wrong is wrong because it is *intrinsically* wrong: it is wrong *in itself*; and is therefore an offence against God Almighty. The theist believes that evil is a force that needs no intellectual definition—indeed, it cannot be intellectually defined. The murder of millions of Jews, gypsies and Slavs by the Nazis wasn't wrong because it was antisocial, illogical or irrational. It was wrong because it was intrinsically wrong. If one despised these peoples as much as the Nazis did, it would have been irrational *not* to have killed them. It is logical and rational to love one's friends, but totally illogical and irrational to love one's enemies. As for the Nazis being antisocial, according to their idea of what constituted a good society, there was no place for Jews, gypsies and Slavs, so the logical and sensible thing was to get rid of them. Can anyone argue with this on the basis of reason?

Now, it may be a matter of opinion as to whether German society would have been better off without Jews, gypsies and Slavs. But what isn't a matter of opinion is that WHAT THE NAZIS DID TO THESE PEOPLE WAS EVIL. To describe the obscene murder of eight million defenceless human beings as "antisocial"—or any other weasel word the atheists and humanists care to come up with—is a PATRONIZING INSULT TO THE HUMANITY OF THE VICTIMS. Shoplifting is antisocial. Parking on double-yellow lines is antisocial. Driving without a license is antisocial. Herding men, women and children into gas chambers is not. IT IS EVIL.

Let me put it another way: it is a matter of opinion as to whether income tax should be set at X per cent or Y per cent. It is a matter of opinion as to whether the speed limit should be thirty mph or whatever. It is a matter of opinion as to whether smoking should or should not be prohibited in public places. These are matters rightly decided by social agencies, because they are matters that affect society, and no one would suggest that good and evil as such were involved. But whether it is right or wrong to put millions of human beings into gas chambers is not something that can be decided on the basis of "what is good for society as a whole." The "good of society as a whole" is nothing to do with it (Hitler may have thought it was, but he was wrong). One can envisage a situation where it might be considered logical, rational and in the interests of "society as a whole," to liquidate hundreds, thousands, even millions of human beings—BUT IT WOULD STILL BE EVIL. Evil is evil, not because it is antisocial, but because it offends against the nature of the Creator, which is intrinsically good. For "right is right, since God is God," wrote the great English priest and poet Frederick William Faber (1814–1863). In other words, wrong is wrong because God exists AND IS WHAT HE IS.

The fact that we do not know what God is, or that we do not even believe in God, is irrelevant. If that sounds like the voice of faith and not of reason, then I would not argue. Reason may be able to tell us that this particular course of action is more reasonable or more desirable than that, even that it is more ethically acceptable, but never that wrong itself exists. If God does not exist then neither does wrong. And it is because so many people living in this secular age of ours knowingly or unknowingly accept the logic of this statement, AND DO NOT BELIEVE IN GOD, that we have so much "mindless" violence at the present time.

217

If it is felt that by writing these words I am helping to fan the flames of violence by offering those individuals who do not believe in God an excuse, even encouragement, for their violent behaviour, then I am sorry; but I do not feel that I have a duty to put the "fear of God" into unbelievers in order that they might turn away from violence. I am afraid that each individual must take responsibility for his or her own actions; I have enough problems coping with my own sinful nature without having to carry the burden of others!

In conclusion: If God does not exist then the atheist is right in asserting that no act is intrinsically wrong; that wrong is a human concept to describe something of which society disapproves. However, he gives the lie to this belief when, in the deepest recesses of his heart, he knows that it is wrong to put little children into gas chambers. Not just socially undesirable, or unreasonable, or irrational, or illogical, or inhuman—but WRONG, that is to say, *intrinsically* wrong. And he knows this in the same way that we all (theists and atheists alike) know it: the only difference is that the believer knows why he knows it; the atheist doesn't.

How then do we know? In a word: conscience.

Chapter 8

What Is Conscience?

Yet still there whispers the small voice within,
Heard through Gain's silence, and o'er Glory's din;
Whatever creed be taught or land be trod,
Man's conscience is the oracle of God.

Byron

Conscience is the voice of the soul.

Rousseau

"We may open the pages of history almost haphazard," says
Viscount Samuel (*Belief and Action*), "and we shall find num-
berless instances of deeds done by excellent men for the most
conscientious motives which later times have unanimously condemned as acts of cruel persecution and ruthless barbarism.
Every persecution springs from conscience. Further, one man's
conscience will give direction in one way, his neighbour's in the
opposite . . . If it were true that there is a natural instinct, implanted in every human being, which is an independent and
infallible guide to right and wrong, then mankind would always
have been, and would be now, of one mind on every question of
right conduct. Obviously, no such unanimity exists, or has ever
existed. So it is clear that the fact that a man holds, however
sincerely and tenaciously, that 'this is the right thing for me to
do', does not of itself make it so."

It goes without saying that Lord Samuel is right when he
says that sincerity is not necessarily indicative of righteousness.
Some of the most evil deeds in history have been committed by
some of the most sincere men of history. Where, for instance,
were the consciences of those so-called good men of history, the

men of the Christian Church, who, in medieval times, persecuted and slaughtered their fellow theists because they subscribed to a different religion? Who tortured and murdered their fellow Christians because they practiced a different mode of worship? Who spoke in the name of God but acted in the name of the devil? What kind of evil is it that has conscience as its standard-bearer? Far from being a surefire guide to right, conscience, it would seem, is the universal excuse for any kind of behaviour, however frightful, that happens to take man's fancy at any given moment in history.

But Lord Samuel is wrong when he says that "every persecution springs from conscience." It doesn't. It springs from a rejection of God. However pure and noble our motives may appear to be, it isn't conscience that urges one human being to persecute another. It is a confluence of intolerance, hatred, jealousy, and fear; a denial of God's wishes and purposes for man; perverted conscience dressed up to look like conscience.

"Man's conscience is the oracle of God," wrote Lord Byron. Nietzsche disagreed. "The content of our conscience," he said, "is everything that was, during our years of childhood, regularly *demanded* of us without reason by people we honoured or feared . . . The belief in authorities is the source of the conscience: it is therefore not the voice of God in the heart of man but the voice of some men in man." (Source: *The Wanderer and his Shadow*, from *A Nietzsche Reader*, translated by R. J. Hollingdale.)

What manifest nonsense! Nietzsche, like Lord Samuel, was confusing conscience with belief. The uncritical acceptance of what we were taught as children has nothing to do with conscience. Is it seriously suggested that the reason why we believe it wrong to lie, steal, cheat, and murder—even though we may cheerfully indulge in all these activities—is because we were conditioned to believe that they were by our upbringing and education? (Next time, dear reader, you refrain from strangling someone with whom you have a disagreement, or poisoning your grand-aunt for her money, or knocking down an old lady and stealing her purse, remember, your reluctance to do these things is due to what you were taught as a child, and not to the fact that in your inmost heart you know them to be wrong.)

Whilst it is perfectly true that our beliefs are partially, even predominantly, formed by what we were taught as children (and nobody knows this better than the Communists and the Catholic Church) it is equally true that as we grow older we often discard those beliefs and embrace new ones, and rebel against those "authorities" that helped formulate our early beliefs. It may be difficult for a person reared, say, in the traditions of the Catholic Church or under a Communist regime, to renounce the ideologies under which he was brought up, but it is not impossible. In fact, it happens all the time!*

Underlying all our beliefs, whether religious, philosophical or political, whether "forced" on us in childhood or arrived at "freely" in adulthood without indoctrination, below the level of reason and instinct, is that "little spark of celestial fire" (George Washington: *Moral Maxims*) called conscience.

What is conscience?

It is not, I agree, an infallible guide to right and wrong (nothing in life is as simple as that). If it were, then everything would be laid out for us in black and white. All we'd have to do is feed the right software into our morality computer and out would come the right answer. But it is an independent guide to right and wrong. If it weren't independent, it would never oppose our reason, as it so often does.

"A man's conscience and his judgement is the same thing," said the English philosopher, Thomas Hobbes (1588–1679) (*Leviathan*). It isn't. A man's conscience and his judgement can be, and often are, completely at variance with each other—his judgement sending him in one direction, his conscience in another. Judgement is conscious and subjective; conscience, unconscious and independent. Conscience isn't judgement, more a judge of our judgement.

Conscience speaks with an independent voice, almost as if it were another person speaking to us. As Sir Thomas Browne (*Religio Medico*) puts it: "There is another man within me that's angry with me." But why different messages for different people? Why, to paraphrase Lord Samuel, don't we all get the same

*Written before the collapse of Communism in Rusia and Eastern Europe!

221

message? Why does conscience tell one person to do one thing, and another the opposite?

First, the messages we receive have to fight their way through layer upon layer of inherited prejudices and millions of years of morally-infected genes. Sometimes the armour of evil we so readily don is too thick for the messages to pierce, they simply cannot get through.

Second, when the messages do get through, they often strike a discordant note. None of us likes to be told we are wrong; that we are doing something we ought not to be doing; or not doing something we ought to be doing. So the messages receive a hostile reception. Or, more insidiously, we deny their authenticity. Our deeply held convictions persuade us that the conscience is sending us false signals; that we shouldn't listen to them; that conscience is another word for cowardice. If all else fails, we pretend we are deaf.

There are powerful influences at work within us that combine to resist the voice of conscience. But the fact that we ignore the conscience, or stifle it, or misinterpret it, or that sometimes it cannot compete with the more strident, more seductive, more persuasive voices that clamour for our attention—like anger, hate, revenge, malice, greed, selfishness and pride—or that sometimes it malfunctions, even atrophies through constant rejection, or is driven out by an imposter masquerading as conscience, is beside the point. It is the fact that it is there that is important.

Who put it there? And why?

The conscience is a real and vital living force implanted in the human breast. It is there not because of us but in spite of us. We did not create it. It is not something we acquire, like wisdom and knowledge. It is not an intellectual achievement, like a degree in science or mathematics. It is not an accomplishment, like riding a bike or driving a car. We are born with it. It is part of our unconscious psyche. Even as children it is there, waiting to develop as we grow older. (Yes, I know that babies are naturally amoral, and that unless children are taught the difference between right and wrong, they will probably go astray; but nevertheless, the awareness that there is a difference between right and wrong is something that instinctually grows within us, it is not something that is foisted upon us from without.)

More often than not, the conscience is an unwelcome intruder, niggling away when we would wish it to be silent. It has an unpleasant habit of butting in at the most inopportune moment. We may, for example, after much reasoning and internal debate, come to the conclusion that a certain course of action is right, only to find, having embarked on that course of action, a little voice within telling us that what we thought was right is in fact wrong. Whence comes this voice which speaks with such irritating independence? Can it really be Nietzsche's "voice of some men in man"? I do not think so. The voice of God in man? I think that far more likely.

But how are we to recognize the voice of conscience, and distinguish it from those siren voices that so effectively fight for our attention? Perhaps the following may help. We like to hear what we want to hear, and have a remarkable facility for not hearing what we do not want to hear. If the message is irritating and difficult to comply with then the chances are that it is the conscience. If the message is secretly attractive to our prejudicial proclivities then it almost certainly is not. When you hear someone boast that he does something as a matter of conscience, then you can be pretty certain that it is not conscience which motivates his actions. Conscience doesn't boast. It doesn't beat the big drum. Or head the parade. It doesn't drive in at the front gate. It enters quietly through the back door.

To break down the barricades our subconscious erects in order to prevent the conscience getting through, we should stop thinking and start listening. "No man knows what conscience is," said the American lecturer Joseph Cook (1838–1901), "until he understands what solitude can teach him concerning it." If we really want to hear what our conscience is saying, we should empty our minds and open our hearts—AND LISTEN.

Of course, what we do about what we hear is up to us. We can if we wish "muddy" the message, pretend it means one thing when really it means another. We can say, "Get thee behind me, conscience." Being free-will agents, that is our prerogative. But what we are not entitled to say is that we do something as a matter of conscience, when in fact we do it as a matter of conviction. The two often coincide, but then, as often as not, they do not.

If we are honest with ourselves and listen with an unprejudiced ear, most of us know in our heart of hearts when we hear the voice of conscience. "Why," asks Bernard Levin (*Enthusiasms*), "unless we are psychopathically deranged, do we *always* know when we are doing wrong, whether we thereupon stay our hands or not?" We know because the inner voice will not be stilled. It will persist until we either heed its warning or shout it down.

The atheist, however, is unimpressed. He believes that conscience is simply primitive instinct; that our responses are formulated and conditioned by millions of years of environmental evolution, by social mores and codes of conduct handed down from generation to generation. There are others who say that it's all down to genes.

Without doubt these factors all play a big part in the fashioning of human thought and behaviour, and it would be foolish to deny that we are in many ways (if not in all) preconditioned. But there is more to it than that. There is more to us than evolution, environment, and genes. We are not just preprogrammed lumps of matter, creatures without a creative and spiritual will, responding solely to materialistic environmental conditions. If we were, then certainly (after Voltaire) there would exist no difference "between the ideas of Newton and the droppings of a mule."

As for instinct, if that is all conscience is, why does it so often trigger off a dual response? C.S. Lewis (*Mere Christianity*): "Supposing you hear a cry for help from a man in danger. You will probably feel two desires—one a desire to give help . . . the other a desire to keep out of danger. . . But you will find inside you, in addition to these two impulses, a third thing which tells you that you ought to follow the impulse to help, and suppress the impulse to run away. Now this thing that judges between two instincts, that decides which should be encouraged, cannot itself be either of them. You might as well say that the sheet of music which tells you, at a given moment, to play one note on the piano and not another, is itself one of the notes on the keyboard. The Moral Law tells us the tune we have to play: our instincts are merely the keys."

There are here two conflicting instincts at work, one urging us to help the man in danger, the other (that of self-preservation, the strongest instinct known to mankind) urging us to run away. Now there is nothing inherently wrong in seeking to avoid danger, just as there is something inherently right in wanting to help someone in distress. If we are just a product of environmental and genetic pressures, why should we even consider defying the instinct that has ensured the survival of the human race?

Our response cannot be decided by reason, for reason is amoral, it can only tell us whether an act is reasonable or unreasonable, it cannot tell us whether it is right or wrong. Science cannot help, for it doesn't even recognize the existence of right and wrong. So, if it isn't reason or instinct, and it cannot be science, what is it that tells us that the right course of action is to help the man in danger? What "authority" can we rely on to urge us to make the right choice, to decide which of the two conflicting instincts (both of which are "right" but couldn't be more opposite) we should obey? The answer is: the conscience. It is the conscience that transmits to us the content of the moral law; that tells us "the tune we have to play."

We are not simply creatures of our environment, slaves to our instincts and genes. When Saul of Tarsus went down on his knees on the road to Damascus, he had the same hereditary traits, the same upbringing, the same preconditioning, the same education and the same genes after he "saw the light" as he did before. He was exactly the same person. But, as we all know, he wasn't! He was a totally different person. His life was utterly and inexorably changed. Whether he really did hear the voice of Christ, or whether he had an epileptic fit or a hallucinatory experience, is neither here nor there. The fact is that millions of years of evolutionary change and the ubiquitous genes all went by the board, in just the space of a few seconds. What explanation can there be other than that there must be some other explanation?

All religions and philosophies recognize that there is a difference between right and wrong, even though they may differ in interpretation (and they don't differ all that much, which, in itself, ought to tell us something). They all accept that morality exists, even if only as a concept. "There are no moral phenomena at all," wrote Nietzsche, "only a moral interpretation of phenomena . . . There are moralities but no morality." (Source: *Beyond Good and Evil*, from *A Nietzsche Reader*, translated by R. J. Hollingdale.) Nietzsche was wrong, as I shall endeavour to show in a moment. So was Einstein, when he said: "There is nothing divine about morality; it is a purely human affair." With respect to the great man, human beings *set* standards of morality, and *practise* (or do not practise) morality; they do not *create* morality. And if they do not *create* morality then morality cannot be a purely human affair; something other than man must be involved. If morality were a purely human affair then it would be pertinent to ask: Which human being or group of human beings is supremely qualified to set supreme moral standards? The Church (which one?) The Pope? The Archbishop of Canterbury? Plato? Buddha? Karl Marx? Adolf Hitler? (Will candidates please step forward?) If no such human being or human agency exists, then we are obliged to look elsewhere for the someone or something that created the quality we call morality.

There exists an ultimate, absolute, and immutable permanent standard of morality to which all things relate and by which all things are judged. Without this fixed moral standard there would be nothing to aim for, nothing to regress from.

The point is made by C.S. Lewis in his *The Poison of Subjectivism: Christian Reflections*. "Does a permanent moral standard preclude progress?" he asks. "On the contrary, except on the supposition of a changeless standard, progress is impossible. If good is a fixed point, it is at least possible that we should get nearer and nearer to it. But if the terminus is as mobile as the train, how can the train progress towards it? Our ideas of the good may change, but they cannot change either for the better or the worse if there is no absolute and immutable good to which they can approximate or from which they can recede. We can go on getting a sum more and more nearly right only if the one perfectly right answer is stagnant. . . If 'good' means only the local ideology, how can those who invent the local ideology be guided by any idea of good themselves?"

Morality is not a geographical or historical concept; it does not change from one place to another, from one age to another, from one society to another. Our idea or interpretation or understanding of morality may change in the course of time and in accordance with fluctuating fashions, but morality itself does not; it exists as a definitive value.

It is the conscience that enables us to recognize morality as morality. Faulty though our moral judgements may be, it is by reason of the conscience and the conscience alone that we can make them. Reason cannot do the work of conscience. Reason, for instance, sometimes tells us that it is irrational and unreasonable to kill. Other times, that it is both rational and reasonable. Never that it is moral or immoral. Because it cannot. Reason is incapable of making that kind of judgement. The existence of good and evil cannot be established by rational enquiry—in fact, it is only by an act of faith that we can even know that good and evil exist!

"If we are to continue to make moral judgements," says C. S. Lewis (*Miracles*), " . . . then we must believe that the conscience of man is not a product of Nature. It can be valid only if it is an offshoot of some absolute moral wisdom, a moral wisdom which exists absolutely 'on its own,' and is not a product of non-moral, non-rational Nature."

Now if, as Mr. Lewis asserts, conscience is not a product of nonmoral, nonrational nature then this can lead us in one direction only. Which, I need hardly add, is not man!

Conscience, I believe, was built into the human psyche at the beginning of human evolution, like a "sleeper" waiting to be activated; not unilaterally by the Creator; but by the inherent "response mechanism" of the created.

The conscience is a direct link with the Almighty—a kind of spiritual umbilical cord. And, like all means of communication, liable to distortion, misunderstanding and misinterpretation. Human beings, being what they are—selfish, proud, cruel, conceited, and arrogant—it could be no other. However clear the messages may be when they first set out, the quality of reception will depend on the efficiency of the receiver. We cannot expect perfect reception if the receiver is faulty; just as we cannot hope to hear the nightingale singing in the garden if the radio is going

227

full blast in the living room. Most of the time we are too busy listening to what we want to listen to, to hear the things we do not want to hear. Is it any wonder then that the line is engaged when the call comes through?

The Oxford Illustrated Dictionary defines conscience as: "Moral sense of right and wrong as regards things for which one is responsible." Note the last five words: *"for which one is responsible."* Conscience is a personal thing. My conscience tells me what I ought and ought not to do; it does not tell me what my neighbour ought and ought not to do. That is between him and his conscience. As I am not able to see into his heart or to read his mind; as I can never know exactly what he thinks or feels, it is not my right, nor is it in my power, to exercise his conscience for him.

It seems that we are now back where we began: Why should my conscience send me in one direction, and my neighbour's in the opposite? If conscience is the voice of God—why the contradiction?

I shall be dealing with this point directly, but first let me say that we should be very careful how we use the word conscience. Just because someone declares with absolute sincerity that he does something as a matter of conscience, does not necessarily mean that he does. Being convinced that one is right, is not at all the same as saying, "It is my conscience that tells me that this is the right thing for me to do." There have been times in my own life when I was certain that what I was doing was right but failed to heed the warning voice within telling me that what I thought was right was in fact wrong. I can clearly remember the messages coming through, but as they did not fit in with my preconceived beliefs, I refused to acknowledge their authenticity. (How easy it is to delude oneself if one really wants to!)

If my neighbour and I are both travelling to the same destination, but are required to set off from different starting points, then plainly the signposts must point in different directions. And even if we start from the same point, it might be necessary, for a variety of reasons, for us to take different routes. We are not all in the same stage of spiritual development, just as we are not all alike physically and mentally (one would not expect the conscience of a cannibal to be as "refined" as the conscience of

228

a missionary, though I would not want to press the point too far).

It would be a mistake to imagine that conscience can adjudicate between causes, like some kind of industrial arbitrator. As far as conscience is concerned, causes, as such, do not exist. Conscience doesn't recognize "sides." It is concerned only with individual conduct. How could conscience (whose?) decide which "side" is right and which "side" is wrong in an industrial dispute? How could conscience (whose?) decide whether a body of workers engaged in a dispute should accept a pay offer or go on strike? How could conscience (whose?) determine whether the Falkland Islands rightly belong to Britain or to Argentina? Or Gibraltar to Britain or to Spain? Like all disputes, whether international, national, social, or personal, these problems should be subject to rational and ethical debate. Conscience cannot adjudicate between the claims of the parties concerned—although it will have much to say to the individuals involved in such disputes as to how they should conduct themselves in pursuance of their claims. Whether the participants listen to and act upon the advice given them by their consciences (and the chances are that they won't, for vested interests have a way of distorting such delicate messages) is another matter. When a soldier is in imminent danger of having his head blown off, the last thing he will be listening to is his conscience. But that doesn't mean that his conscience is inoperative, simply that he has more pressing things on his mind at that moment!

An individual's conscience tells him, in his personal state of spiritual development, whether *his* actions are right or wrong. Conscience is individual not corporate, singular not plural. That is why it is a fiction to talk of the "national" or "collective" conscience. There is no such thing.

Let us consider a specific example of where the conscience of one individual appears to be in direct conflict with the conscience of another and ask ourselves why this should be so.

Now I personally am against capital punishment. My conscience tells me that it is wrong to take the life of a fellow human being, for any reason, for any crime; that capital punishment is squalid and barbaric, and spiritually degrading to those who administer it (at least, it would be to me, and it is my conscience

229

I am talking about). I hold this view even though it could be proved that capital punishment was an effective deterrent. (This at least indicates that my conscience is not the arm of reason.)

My neighbour, on the other hand, supports capital punishment. He believes that it is an effective deterrent, which, if reintroduced into Britain would save the lives of many innocent victims. And even if he didn't believe this, he would still support the death penalty because, he would say, some crimes are so vile that the perpetrators forfeit all right to live. His conscience also tells him that a just God would approve of just retribution. (Does not the Bible say, "Vengeance is mine, sayeth the Lord"?)

It is not for me to say that I am right and he is wrong; it is for me to say what my conscience tells me. (I am, of course, assuming that our responses genuinely reflect what our consciences are telling us, and that I am not being motivated by a sense of squeamishness, and he by a primitive desire for revenge. [What's wrong with that? he might ask.])

We have now to face the fact, however, that God appears to be telling me through my conscience, that capital punishment is wrong, and my neighbour through his conscience, that capital punishment is right. The messages couldn't be more contradictory. So how can they originate from the same source?

Impasse!

Not being able to implant myself inside my neighbour's psyche, I cannot possibly know how, and in precisely what form, he receives his "messages." But I must assume that he receives them in the same way as I receive mine. Why, then, do our consciences conflict? Does God speak with forked tongue?

I believe the answer is this: I hear God telling me that it is wrong to take the life of another human being; whereas my neighbour hears God telling him that some crimes are so heinous that the perpetrators deserve to die. We both receive similar messages emphasizing the sanctity of human life, but we "translate" them (or rather, our unconscious psyches "translate" them for us) with a different emphasis. I would not disagree with his translation, and I think that he would not disagree with mine. In fact, I am sure he would not, because he feels so passionately about the sanctity of human life that he is prepared to take the lives of those who wantonly destroy it. (The difficulty that conscience encounters in the matter of "interpretation" is high-lighted by a remark by Dietrich Bonhoeffer, the German Christian pastor, who was engaged in a war-time conspiracy to remove [i.e. kill] the infamous Adolf Hitler. "No actions," he wrote in his *No Rusty Swords*, "are bad in themselves—even murder can be justified." Often in this life we are faced with a choice of evils. Whatever choice we make, we know that what we do is wrong, that is to say, *intrinsically* wrong, although in the circumstances in which we find ourselves, our conscience tells us that we have made the "right" choice.)

So you see, my neighbour and I come to opposite conclusions, though we are both motivated by the same message, that which tells us that human life is sacred. This would indicate, or so it seems to me, that we are both "tuned in" to the same "station," but as we are not in identical states of spiritual evolution, it is inevitable that our responses will not always be identical. And, of course, we must not forget those many perverting influences I spoke about earlier that the messages have to contend with. When it comes to a battle between the rampant ego and the passive conscience, the former invariably wins.

I also believe in the relativity of the conscience (and, by extension, the relativity of morality). By this I mean that conscience is not an objective, definitive arbiter of right and wrong (how could it be?); it is relative to, and cannot be separated from, the "individual with the conscience." So that, what might be the "right" action for one person in a given situation, could be the "wrong" action for another in the same situation. As we are all different, it might be necessary for God to speak to each one of us in a different "tone of voice." Otherwise we could have difficulty in understanding what he was saying. As an analogy, a Scotsman speaking broad Scots might have a problem trying to communicate with a Cockney unfamiliar with the Scottish dialect (and vice versa). Right conduct is the individual's subjective interpretation of the moral law, which alone is objective and immutable.

With individuals whose conscience are comatose or extinct, there is no problem of interpretation. It is hard to believe, for instance, that Ian Brady, the infamous Moors Murderer, was ever troubled by conscience. Why such people should be born

231

with a malfunctioning conscience (as presumably they are) we cannot know. Perhaps, just as some are born bodily deformed or mentally defective, others are born with a spiritual abnormality. If that is so then such human monsters are to be pitied rather than condemned.

But human monsters are not all the same. Some, like Brady, are insane; they do not know the difference between right and wrong. Others, like Hitler and Stalin, for instance, do not have the excuse of madness; they are sane and ought to know better. (I must add this rider, however: it is difficult to know precisely where the line between evil and insanity is to be drawn. I am not a psychiatrist, but I do know that there is a difference, however subtle, between congenital insanity and pure evil.)

As I have said, if the conscience is continually ignored or suppressed, it will atrophy to the point of extinction. And if it persistently meets with strong resistance from the ego, it doesn't stand much of a chance anyway. "We must suppose," says Mary Kenny (*Why Christianity Works*), "that those who worked the concentration camps for the Nazis had successfully suppressed or wiped away their feelings of conscience. How could one usher a child into a gas chamber without feelings of guilt? Since it has been done, and since many other brutalities have been done and continue to be done without such feelings of constraint or inhibitions to stop them, this indicates that normal criteria of good and evil and the consequences thereof can be suppressed in human consciousness."

Not to know that one has a conscience is probably the worst misfortune that can befall a human being. And for a sane man to experience the inner voice telling him that what he is doing is wrong, and that by persisting in his actions he runs the risk of alienating himself from God, is a folly of the highest magnitude—more than a folly, it is spiritual suicide.

I can vouch for this from my own personal experience, which is almost too shameful for me to relate. When I was in my teens, I was anti-Semitic. (Oh, yes, I had good reason to be—don't we always have good reason for disliking someone we dislike?) I subscribed to a pernicious form of racial prejudice, for which I have never forgiven myself. I can clearly remember my conscience telling me at the time that I was wrong. But I did not listen.

(Not true; I did listen, but did not heed—not until, that is, the full horror of the Nazi extermination camps was revealed.) Even now, over fifty years on, I still feel intense guilt. But why should I feel guilty? I did not harm any Jews. My anti-Semitisim did not manifest itself violently. Nevertheless, I am haunted by the thought of what I might have become had I been born in Germany and brought up under the Nazi regime. In disliking Jews, I had taken the first step. How many more would I have taken? Where would I have stopped? When I think of the odious degenerates who operated the gas chambers, I do not see inhuman Nazi thugs, I see myself. For that is where racial prejudice, if unrestricted, leads. To the gas chambers and extermination camps. The first step is the one that should be resisted. If we do that then we are safe. The Nazis did not start off by gassing children. They worked up to it. Had they resisted the first step, there would have been no Holocaust. At first the Nazis disliked Jews. Dislike turned to hate (someone had to be blamed for the post-war state of the German economy; and who better than the "alien" Jews?). But even worse than hating Jews, the Nazis despised them. "Vermin," they called them (subtle noun that, for we all know, don't we, that it is not wrong to kill vermin). Nazi thugs smashed Jews' windows, destroyed their synagogues and burnt their books (it was Heine, in 1823, who said, "Wherever they burn books they will also, in the end, burn human beings"), put yellow stars on their clothing, and consigned them to the concentration camps.

I cannot believe that the Nazis were born without consciences. Their evil deeds emanated partly from (as so many do) ideals that were not wholly unworthy—to build a strong and prosperous Germany, a Germany that, according to their Führer, Adolf Hitler, would last a thousand years. But what shortsighted, bigoted claptrap this turned out to be! As if a brave new Germany—a brave new anything could be built on the gas chambers and crematoriums of Auschwitz and Treblinka. Oh, if only they had not taken that first fateful step!

The first step on the road to Auschwitz and Treblinka was taken when one man and his small group of followers refused to listen to their consciences, and, partly through the "loftiness" of their ideals and partly through the evil genius of their leader, managed to persuade millions of their countrymen to do likewise.

I cannot speak for others, but I have to say that I know when my conscience speaks to me. I always have known, "whether or not I thereupon stayed my hand." And I know full well that this inner voice is not mine. Nor is it, as Nietzsche so foolishly said, "the voice of some men in man." I was not brought up to dislike Jews. My anti-Semitism sprang from a deep-lying personal prejudice, which at the time I was not able to rationalize. The small voice within (or moral instinct, if you wish) that warned me I was wrong, did not originate from "authorities" I "honoured" or "feared" during the course of my formative years. It emanated from elsewhere.

Conscience is not man-made. Nor is it an arm of reason or a product of man's will. It is a sovereignly independent voice. It is Emerson's "private door" by which God "enters into every individual."

Now the skeptics may scoff at such belief, but they themselves offer no convincing explanation of what conscience is, if not some kind of "mechanism" for the reception, deciphering and transmission of God's messages to man. I do not profess to understand how this "mechanism" works (but then, I have no idea how a computer works, or the pacemaker that a surgeon implants in the heart of the patient). But this I know: work it does!

The intellectually condescending atheist tries to make believers look naive and foolish by implying that they see God as some kind of telephone-operator-in-the-sky frantically trying to get in touch with his billions of subscribers all at the same time. In fact, of course, we do not see God like that at all—though even if we did, we could be forgiven for finding this childish analogy helpful in trying to comprehend the incomprehensible. I myself believe that the "messages" we receive are already there, built into the human psyche, waiting to be released into the spiritual consciousness. Our responses inhere in the situation in which we are involved, and are triggered off automatically by the conscience, in the same way that an alarm clock goes off at a pre-set moment. It is by way of this spiritual alarm clock that God speaks (or rather, has *already spoken*) to us. When the alarm fails to go off, it means that something has gone wrong with the mechanism; when the sound is muffled, it is we who do the muffling.

It is a curious fact that not even the most militant atheist denies that such a thing as conscience exists (though denying its origins, of course). But why does it exist? What function does it perform? It is not a requisite for survival. Reason and instinct take care of that. It serves no utilitarian purpose whatsoever. We could manage perfectly well without it. It is not necessary for the survival of civilization—art, music, literature, and poetry would still flourish, albeit on different "levels."

"Without the conscience that underpins reasonable guilt," says Mary Kenny (*Why Christianity Works*), "we would be nothing but psychopaths." True. But what's *wrong* with being psychopaths, to have no moral sense? If there is no God then nothing is wrong. So whenever we assert that conscience tells us that this is the right thing for us to do (whether or not that which we are about to do is in fact right or wrong, is irrelevant), we are testifying to the existence of God.

Finally: what purpose does the conscience serve if not to tell us the difference between right and wrong? And even more important, WHY DO WE NEED TO KNOW THE DIFFERENCE?

Chapter 9

What Is Faith?

Faith is the subtle chain
Which binds us to the infinite; the voice
Of a deep life within, that will remain
Until we crowd it thence.

Elizabeth Oakes Smith

Faith is a quality which the scientist cannot dispense with.

Max Planck

Everyone has faith. The theist has faith in God. The philosopher in the power of reason. The mathematician in the equation that tells him that two and two make four (in spite of the fact that the rabbit constantly proves him wrong!). The atheist in unfaith. The skeptic in skepticism. The agnostic is agnosticism. And the nihilist in the belief that the mind that tells him there is nothing, would be able to tell him there is nothing, if in fact there were nothing.

It is, however, in the religious sense of the word that I am here discussing faith—the faith that leads one to say: "I believe in God."

But first, who is this 'I' that says "I believe"? "A mind and a body very intimately conjoined," says Descartes. A spiritual or mental or thinking substance, say other philosophers. "The unitary consciousness . . . the abiding 'I,'" says Kant. "When I enter most intimately into what I call *myself*," writes Scottish philosopher David Hume (1711–1776), in *A Treatise of Human Nature*, "I always stumble on some particular perception or other, of heat or cold, light or shade, love or hatred, pain or pleasure. I never can . . . observe any thing but the perception."

Hume believes that the self (or mind) is "a bundle or collection of different perceptions": love, hatred, pain, pleasure, etc., and not a "thing" that we can observe. He doesn't say that the self is meaningless, simply that it doesn't exist in the way that we think it does. In point of fact, he asserts that our perceptions are not just in the mind, they *are* the mind.

Whatever else the self is or is not—a real "thing" or a fiction—it is the sum total of our personality, personal awareness, ego, and being. The "whatever-it-is" that makes you you, and me me.

We are all unique; no two persons are alike; yet we all experience the same sense of personal identity. You feel that you are you in the same way that I feel that I am me. But I would go further. I would say that your you is exactly the same as my me, not similar to, but the same as. That is to say, if I were able to take over your total self and not only experience what it is like to be you but to actually be you, I would find that being you was the same as being me. I would, of course, be aware that I had a different personality, different likes and dislikes, different thoughts and ideas, etc. But the new *I* would be the same as the old *I*. I would be the same person, but different.

Who or what then is this *I* that we all are? Am I the same *I* that I was on the day I was born? At six years, sixteen years, sixty years? Am I the same *I* now at 5'8½" tall, weighing ten and a half stone, as I was when I was eighteen inches long, weighing ten and a half pounds? My body is bigger. So is my brain. But am *I* bigger; is there more of *me?*

A continuous process of change takes place in the human body. Old tissues die, new tissues are born, old cells decay, new cells take their place. I am a different person now from what I was when I was a child. During my life my body has been replaced many times over—in fact, every seven years or so—except, that is, for my brain, which unlike other organs in the body, does not produce new cells. (Perhaps that is what gives the self its sense of continuity?)

We are all individuals, with our own individual personality, ego, psyche, and spirituality but all sharing a common, "collective" identity. In that sense we are one, or perhaps "extensions" of one another, separated only by an individual sense of selfhood, like blood corpuscles flowing through the same corporate body.

This is very much in line with Buddhist thinking, where the concept of the individual is discouraged, and the boundaries between one so-called "individual" and others are regarded as artificial (vide Trevor Ling's *Buddhism*).

The human body is made up of countless billions of atoms. And as the atom consists almost entirely of empty space then that, I suppose, is what I mainly am, empty space!

According to the chemist, I am about ninety percent water and ten percent calcium and salt. Anything else? No, that's the lot. Funny, I didn't know that water, carbon, and salt (and empty space) could think, feel and love. If our chemist friend were to measure out my exact ingredients, put them in a vat and stir, would they turn out to be me? No, they would not. Why not? Well, I suspect that there is more to me than water, carbon, salt, and empty space. In other words, I am more than the sum of my atoms.

According to the atheist-biologist, I am simply the product of evolution and chance variations. The nihilist goes one better. He believes that I am a nothing from nowhere, with no primal source, no primal purpose and no primal meaning. Such a degree of negativity is so completely at odds with our experience of nature, which is so creatively positive, that it is difficult to understand how anyone can believe that the positivity of nature can have been produced by the negativity of nihilism.

What does Christianity have to say about this *I*? It is very specific. It says that I was created by God in his image. By "image" is meant the living, thinking, personal and loving God as revealed in the life and person of Jesus Christ. I am thus invited to believe that there is in me something, however tiny and insignificant, that is in some infinitely remote degree similar to the nature of God. And that, worthless though I am, I am of infinite value in the eyes of the Creator. In a family every child is (or should be) of equal value, and enjoys (or should enjoy) the same degree of love from its parents. In the imperfect human family this is not always so, but in the universal family whose Father is God, we may be sure that it is.

When the Christian talks about the "image" of God, I think

he means something like this: the human heart, wicked though it often is, is also capable of immense love and compassion, and it would be wholly unlikely to have this capacity if it were nothing at all like the Creator of love and compassion. Similarly, the human mind which has the ability to examine, investigate and understand the laws which govern the Universe, is equally unlikely to have this capability if it had nothing whatsoever in common with the Mind that created those laws.

I must say that I find this more compelling than the notion that I am nothing more than a handful of chemicals, a bucketful of water, and empty space. If that is all I am, if I am of no significance—a useless appendage, a "nothing" from "nowhere"—how come I spend so much time wondering who I am, why I am, and who it was that made me? (Does a motor car spend its whole life trying to figure out what it is and why its maker made it?) And if the Universe is a meaningless nonentity, how come it produced me? As C.S. Lewis (*Encounter with Light*) puts it: "How could an idiotic universe have produced creatures whose mere dreams are so much stronger, better, subtler than itself?"

But, alas, we are no nearer to discovering who this mysterious *I* is that inhabits my body. I can be sure only of what I am not. I am not nothing. I am not merely a piece of matter like a rock. Even though the Universe is my physical home, I feel as if a part of me originated elsewhere.

Even so, even though we do have a "destiny" outside ourselves, even though we do have a relevance in the scheme of things, that doesn't prove that "God" is anything more than a simple-minded superstition, inherited from our simple-minded ancestors. There are to be sure no scientifically verifiable proofs that point irresistibly to the existence of God. So where do we go from here?

Enter faith!

"You can do very little with faith," wrote Samuel Butler the Younger, English philosopher (1835–1902), "but you can do nothing without it."

"Faith," said Swiss philosopher Amiel (1828–1881), "is a certitude without proofs." (Which is what it has to be; for if something can be proved, it doesn't need faith to believe it.)

239

"Faith has no merit," wrote St. Gregory (590–604), "where human reason supplies the proof." H. L. Mencken (*Prejudices*), however, thought differently: "Faith," he said, "may be defined briefly as an illogical belief in the occurrence of the improbable." Neatly put. But what does he mean by "illogical"? Is it illogical to believe that, just as an earthly child must have an earthly father, so must the human race have a heavenly Father? Must we have to choose between reason and faith? Cannot we have both?

If belief in God can be proved then it is not faith: if it cannot be proved then (says the skeptic) it is unreasonable.

It seems that we are between the devil and the deep blue sea. If there is no such thing as reasonable faith then what credence can a reasonable person give to beliefs, however sincerely held, that cannot be verified by scientific proofs or precise logical reasoning? Certitude is no substitute for proof. I cannot be expected to believe everything I am told just because the person who does the telling is convinced that what he is telling me is true. For all I know, the Loch Ness monster, flying saucers, and fairies at the bottom of the garden, may all be true (I cannot prove they are not), but I shall continue to disbelieve them until somebody offers me conclusive proof that they really do exist. Faith alone is not enough. And what happens when faiths conflict? Which are we to believe? The one that shouts the loudest? The one that has the biggest battalions? The one that sounds the most attractive?

Isn't faith just another word for superstition? Sometimes—when it is based on illusion. For instance, if Jesus Christ was indeed an actual historical person (and therefore not an illusion), then belief in Jesus *as the Son of God* is a matter of faith. But if Jesus Christ was not a real person but a mythical character (i.e. an illusion), then belief in Jesus, either as the Son of God or anyone else, is a matter of superstition. Faith, even if misplaced, is real if grounded in reality and authenticity, but it is superstition if based on fantasy or illusion.

To many in this modern scientific age, faith is a bit of a dead duck, unfaith seeming so much more reasonable than faith. Benjamin Franklin, himself a believer, said (*Poor Richard*): "The way to see by Faith is to shut the Eye of Reason." So what is the

240

believer, whose beliefs have no scientific validity, and which sound like pie-in-the-sky wishing thinking to the atheist, to say to the hard-headed, feet-on-the-ground skeptic, who is not susceptible to naive assumptions, who has no time for childish superstitions, and is only prepared to believe that which can be proved by scientific experimentation? Nothing. Faith is a personal thing. "Certitude without proofs" derives from knowing not from proving. For example: I do not need the evidence of blood tests or gene scans to prove that my mother and father were my natural parents. I know that they were. Not just because I trust my instincts, but because I have faith in my mother and father. I do not require proofs. To ask for them would be to confess that my faith was fraudulent. Yes, I know the old saying, that it is a wise man who knows his own father, but in the present case I am able to say with absolute certainty that I *know* that my mother and father were my mother and father. The reader will have to take my word for it, or reject it as he wishes, which he would not do IF HE HAD KNOWN MY MOTHER. If the reader has the same faith in his mother as I had in mine, he will understand what I mean, and he will know that such faith is born of truth not superstition. Such an instinctively held truth is as true as any scientifically verifiable truth. Truth is true whether it can be proven or not.

The reader will now know (if he did not know before) what it means to have an unshakeable faith, and he need never again feel diffident about acknowledging faith. Even the most skeptical scientist will not demand scientific proofs if he has a similar degree of faith in his mother.

What it comes down to is belief in the authority of the source. If we have absolute confidence in the source of our information, even though the information cannot be scientifically verified, then we are entitled to believe. "Ninety-nine percent of the things you believe," says C. S. Lewis (*Mere Christianity*), "are believed on authority. I believe there is such a place as New York. I have not seen it myself. I could not prove by abstract reasoning that there must be such a place. I believe it because reliable people have told me so. The ordinary man believes in the solar system, atoms, evolution and the circulation of the blood on authority—because the scientists say so. Every historical statement in the world is believed on authority. None of us has seen the Norman Conquest or the defeat of the Armada. None of us could prove them by pure logic as you prove a thing in mathematics. We believe them simply because people who did see them have left writings that tell us about them: in fact, on authority."

It is much the same way with faith in God. If we have faith in the authority of our source we will believe. Faith is not faith if it needs the support of proofs.

But again I have to say, faith is a personal thing; it comes from within, it cannot be imposed from without.

Many people regard religious faith as "old hat," a relic from the past. As we saw in Chapter 1, new exciting discoveries in the field of science have prompted some physicists to assert that we are now on the threshold of discovering a wholly scientific explanation of the Universe. I even heard one physicist on TV declare: "Science has now made God redundant." Well, well! Hurrah for science! Bully for the physicists!

Does this clown really believe that, if the scientists do ever get to the end of the road, that will be the end of the road? That even if they do discover how the whole thing works, that will tell them who or what decided that that is the way the whole thing should work? Before these arrogant buffoons start talking about "redundant Gods," let them first make a human brain, a human mind, a human soul. And when they have finished telling us about the energy in the atom, let them explain how it got there in the first place. Far from making God redundant, I would have thought that these new scientific discoveries made God more necessary than ever. I mean, the old, pre-Copernican, comparatively uncomplicated Universe, might possibly have been made by a "second-rate" God; but this new, post-Einsteinian, multidimensional Universe, with its timewarps and spacewarps, black holes and exploding stars, and God knows what other mind-boggling phenomena yet to be discovered—never!

And not only is God more necessary, but more relevant! As the greatest achievement of modern science (which some are now calling "the new superstition"), is the invention of the means of destroying the whole human race in one fell swoop, perhaps it might be better if we looked elsewhere for the inspiration we need if we are to avoid turning this beautiful planet into a nuclear desert, and mankind into a biological freak. It seems to me that the greater our scientific achievements, the more desperate our need for spiritual guidance.

To whom then should we turn? If not to the scientists who gave us the bomb, then most certainly not to the politicians who, although having no intention of dropping it again, nonetheless reserve the right to drop it should they ever decide that it would be morally right to do so.

Perhaps we should turn to the man who said "Love one another." But here we must be careful; for if we are to heed the words of Jesus, then not only will we be required not to drop nuclear bombs, but also not to fire rifles! The fundamental problem facing the human race is that it has always found it much more difficult to love than to hate, and so much easier to pull the trigger than to turn the other cheek. (This is not an argument for pacifism; nor even for nuclear disarmament; it is a simple statement of fact. The reader must draw his own conclusions as to what Christ meant by "loving one another.")

Science cannot help us in our moral dilemma. For science is amoral. We need something more than an arid search for a mathematical explanation of the Universe. We need the *idea of God* more than we have ever needed it before. Because God alone can save the world. (If the reader is inclined to snigger at this last remark, I would like to ask, who are *you* going to put in the place of God? Man? If so, which man?)

Now if God is necessary, then so is faith. Because God cannot exist for us except in faith. Without faith, the idea of God degenerates into a sterile intellectual and philosophical debate. "To believe only possibilities and probabilities," wrote Sir Thomas Brown (1605–1682), "is not Faith but mere Philosophy."

Faith transcends reason. "Reason saw not," said Dryden (*Religio Laici*), "till Faith sprung the light." In any case who wants to believe in a God that can be proved? Where's the excitement, the wonder, the awe? St. Augustine didn't ask for proof. "For what is faith," he wrote, "unless it is to believe what you do not see?" Nor did the French theologian Jean Daniélou. "Faith," he said, "is the only means of knowing what is beyond knowledge."

A God that needs to be proved is not God. I personally would cease to believe in God the moment his existence were proven.

Some things have to be taken on trust: even if we believe in nothing, we are obliged to trust the very reasoning power that tells us that there is nothing. But this doesn't mean that faith is naive and unreasonable. Am I being naive and unreasonable when I say that without God nothing makes sense? That without God there is no purpose? That everything is for nothing? That birds sing for nothing? Flowers bloom for nothing? All our experiences, good and bad, happy and sad are for nothing? All our kindness, caring, love, and compassion are for nothing? All our striving, suffering, sacrificing are for nothing? That a man lays down his life for another for nothing? That Jesus Christ was born, lived, suffered, and was crucified for nothing? And yes, that all the wickedness, cruelty, and hatred in the world are for nothing?

Does all this nothingness make sense? If it does then that is the end of the matter. If it doesn't, if it places too great a strain on our credulity, then we have no alternative but to believe in something.

What?

It is, of course, possible to believe in something without necessarily believing in God. Buddhists do. So do humanists. They see the humanities and the advancement of the welfare of the human race as an end in itself. Now in my view this comes pretty close to saying that man is God. For how can anything less than the ultimate be an end in itself? Humanism asserts that man's purpose in life is the development of the human intellect, the promotion of human interests, the betterment of the human condition. It is not to decry these worthy aims to say that there must be more to our existence than this. If the only reason we are here is to make our stay on Earth happier, longer, and more intellectually satisfying then man does indeed become an end in himself, a definitive being, an object of worship—God!

Humanism takes no account of man's persistent need for something other than material advancement and intellectual achievement. Man's constant search for some kind of meaning to his existence, other than satisfying his sensibilities and indulging his sensuality, points to an inner need for something else besides. If there is nothing else, why the need? Why the insatiable curiosity to find out who he is, what he is, and why he is? Why the consuming restlessness to reach for the stars, to delve deeper and deeper into the atom to discover why it behaves in the way it does? And why this deep yearning for a spiritual dimension to his existence? If there is nothing for him to yearn for, why the yearning?

Humanism does everything to make more of man, but nothing to make man more than man. Only an inspirational source higher than man can do this. And the only means we have of reaching this source is through the medium of faith. Not naive, superstitious faith, but, in the words of Hans Küng (*On Being a Christian*; trans. by Edward Quinn), faith "rooted in reality, justified in the light of reason."

Faith bridges the gap between belief and reason. At the end of the gallery I see a picture, not very clearly, but clearly enough to see that it is a picture. As I get nearer, the detail becomes more distinct, and the colours more vivid. I get closer still and I see that this is no ordinary picture but the work of a master artist. Reason tells me that I am looking at a masterpiece, an incredible work of art. But it is faith that tells me WHOSE SIGNATURE IT IS ON THE CANVAS.

The function of science is to determine facts by observation and experiment, and to make reasonable deductions from those facts. Observation, experimentation, deduction and reasoning are all activities of the intellect. Now, if there is a Supreme Intelligence directing, controlling and organizing the Universe then it is, I suppose, remotely possible that one day intelligent man will be able to identify this Intelligence. But if that Intelligence is more than Intelligence; if intelligence is not the whole but part of the whole, then we shall need more than intelligence to reach it. So where does that leave science?

Religious faith runs like a vein of gold through human nature. All religions have this in common—faith in something other than man. Now if they are all wrong, if indeed there is nothing, if man is the highest there is, then man's deep intuitive instinct, which tells him there is something and not nothing, has been sending him false signals from the beginning. I cannot believe that nature would play such a trick. Our observations of the unerring and uncanny instinct of animals, who, after all, have only instinct to go on, suggest otherwise. If animals are "guided" by some unseen influence that is relevant to their needs, is it not equally likely that man is "guided" by some influence relevant to his needs? Superstitious nonsense? I do not think so, although I freely admit that in the end it all comes down to faith, the positive faith of the believer versus the negative faith of the unbeliever.

Faith or unfaith? Which is it to be? It is for the reader to reach his own decision. For my part, I would rather have faith in someone or something which cannot be proved, than have faith in nothing at all. Trust is an essential part of the human psyche. A person completely devoid of trust is, by definition, insane. As the Protestant theologian, Wolfhart Pannenberg, so eloquently puts it: "Only trust allows the soul room to breathe . . . Even the most distrustful man cannot avoid trusting. Not of course all the time. He can refuse to trust here and there, but not everywhere at all times."

The person who trusts completely and indiscriminately, "everywhere at all times," will often be wrong. But sometimes he will be right. On the other hand, the person who trusts no one and nothing will often be right, but one day, *when it matters most*, he will be wrong. Better, I say, faith misplaced than no faith at all! By this I mean that by habitually withholding faith we run the risk of missing what faith is all about. Take Father Christmas, for instance. To millions of children all over the world, Father Christmas is real. In point of fact, he *is* real, but not in the way children think he is. The red coat and white beard may be false, the coming-down-the-chimney bit a fable, but the love of the children's parents (the bit that really matters) is real, there is nothing false about that.

After writing the above, I came across a story in *The London Daily Mail*, December 13, 1986, which I thought apposite. The paper reported that a certain clergyman had held a quiz about "The truth of Christmas," which had apparently caused considerable distress among some of his younger listeners when he said: "We all know that Santa doesn't exist." The newspaper admonished the reverend with these words: "We all know the vicar is wrong and here's why . . . Eighty-nine years ago in

America, a little girl called Virginia O'Hanion was also told there was no Santa Claus. Desperately upset, she wrote to *The New York Sun* asking whether this was true. The paper replied to Virginia with an editorial. It is one of the most famous in newspaper history and has been reprinted all over the world. This is what *The New York Sun* said in 1897: "Virginia, your friends are wrong. They have been affected by the skepticism of a skeptical age. They do not believe, except what they can see. They think that nothing can be which is not comprehensible by their little minds.

"All minds, Virginia, whether they be men's or children's, are little. In this great universe of ours, man is a mere insect, an ant in his intellect, as compared with the boundless world about him, as measured by the intelligence capable of grasping the whole truth and knowledge.

"Yes, Virginia, there is a Santa Claus. He exists as certainly as love and generosity and devotion exist, and *you* know that they abound and give to your life its highest beauty and joy.

"And how dreary the world would be if there was no Santa Claus. It would be as dreary as if there were no little girls.

"There would be no childlike faith then, no poetry, no romance, to make tolerable this existence. We should have no enjoyment, except in sense and sight. The eternal light with which childhood fills the world would be extinguished.

"Not believe in Santa Claus? You might as well not believe in fairies. You might get your papa to hire men to watch in all the chimneys on Christmas Eve to catch Santa Claus, but even if they did not see him coming down, what would that prove?

"Nobody sees Santa Claus but that is no sign that there is no Santa Claus. The most real things in the world are those that neither children nor men can see.

"Did you ever see fairies dancing on the lawn? Of course not, but that's no proof that they are not there. Nobody can conceive or imagine all the wonders there are unseen and unseeable in the world.

"You tear apart the baby's rattle to see what makes the noise inside, but there is a veil covering the unseen world which not the strongest man, nor even the united strength of all the strongest men that ever lived, could tear apart.

247

"Only faith, fancy, poetry, love, romance, can push aside that curtain and view and picture the supernatural beauty and glory beyond. Is it all real?

"Ah, Virginia, there is nothing else real and abiding.

"No Santa Claus? Thank God he lives, and he lives for ever. A thousand years from now, Virginia, nay ten times ten thousand years from now, he will continue to make glad the heart of childhood."

I have reproduced this beautiful piece of prose in full, as it reveals a deeper religious understanding of the meaning of faith than all the books on theology ever written.

Like the child's faith in Santa Claus, man's faith in God is real, although his perception and understanding of God and his purposes will change as he, too, "grows up." The content of faith evolves, but the attribute of faith—absolute trust—remains constant and unchanging. There is no halfway house with faith. One either believes (in which case proof is superfluous), or one doesn't (in which case proof is unnecessary).

(Interpolation: I was taken to task by a very good friend of mine who read these words in draft form before publication. "That is far too cut and dried," she said, "and does nothing to help those whose faith has taken a battering, and who are struggling with their doubts." Objection sustained. In defence, however, I would explain that the words were not written to help those whose faith was under pressure. They were meant as a simple, subjective statement of what faith means to the writer. You see, faith is more than belief. A person will say: "I believe in God." But what does that mean? I believe in Mount Everest and the Taj Mahal. Because I have read about them, and have seen them. [Not in the flesh but on TV, and you can't get better proof than that!] I also believe in William the Conqueror, Henry VIII and Napoleon. Not because I have direct evidence of their existence, but because I have confidence in the historians who have written about these famous historical figures. But that kind of belief is not faith, at least not the kind of faith that Jesus had in the Father, or the Saints in Jesus. Having faith in God is more than believing that God exists. It is a total commitment of the whole person—mind, body, psyche and soul—to the proposition that God exists and is what he is: that is to say, whatever

248

he is to the individual concerned. It is a faith that takes possession of the believer totally. It is not just an intellectual affirmation that such a being as God exists. I hasten to add, in case I am misunderstood, that I am not talking about goodness or godliness, but faith. End of interpolation.)

I would like to tell you a story.

First, it is necessary to explain that, as a Christian, I have never quite been able to come to terms with that dreadful cry from the cross: "My God, my God, why hast thou forsaken me?" What did Jesus mean? Did he really believe that he had been forsaken by the Father? Did his absolute faith in God waver at the very moment he needed it most? If so, what does this say for his claim to a unique relationship with God? (If you can't trust your father, whom can you trust?)

My own faith in God was not affected by this dilemma, simply my faith in Christ's relationship with God. (After all, nearly two thousand years of commitment to the Christian religion has depended solely on its founder's claim to a unique relationship with the Father.)

Some believe that Jesus, in his final moments of agony, was seeking comfort in reciting the old Hebrew psalm, which would have been familiar to him from his childhood days, and which began with those pregnant words, "My God, my God, why hast thou forsaken me?"

Personally, I have never been able to accept this explanation. Mainly, I suppose, because I have always resisted the temptation to believe something simply because I wanted to believe it.

It is fruitless to speculate as to what went on in the mind of Jesus as he hung dying on the cross. However, forsaken or not—and it is indeed possible that Jesus was ordained to suffer a unique depth of despair, which only the Son of God would be able to experience—what we do know is that Jesus did not lose faith in the existence of the Father. He would not have asked a nonexistent Father why he had forsaken him. Nor would he have cried out, "Father, into thy hands I commend my spirit," to a Father whom he did not believe existed.

Nevertheless, for years the "cry from the cross," niggled away at my faith. I don't know why it should have; but it did.

So I recently resolved to try to settle the doubt in my mind, one way or the other, once and for all.

First I contacted an eminent biblical Greek scholar, to see whether there could have been any discrepancy in the translation from Aramaic through Greek into English. There wasn't. So I decided to study the psalm from which Christ had quoted. That, I thought, was where the answer would be. Not having an Old Testament in the house, I went along to my local library, took a copy of the Bible off the shelf, sat down, and then realized that I didn't know where to look. (Truth to tell, and embarrassed as I am to admit it, I didn't even know it was a psalm!)

I searched the pages for quite some time, without success. Eventually I gave up, replaced the Bible on the shelf, and then, without conscious thought, absentmindedly took down the book next to it, snapped it open, and there staring me in the face were the words, "My God, My God, why has thou forsaken me?"

I was absolutely taken aback. My head swam and I literally staggered to a chair. It wasn't that what had happened was so unexpected; it was the way that it had happened. I realize of course that it could have been a coincidence. But at the time, I had a distinctly eerie feeling that it wasn't I who had found the psalm, but the psalm that had found me. (I have to say that, during the course of writing this book, many similar extraordinary "coincidences" have happened to make me suspect that I have been "led" towards something which I have been seeking. I am not saying that God intervenes directly in our affairs, but I am suggesting that in some inexplicable way guidance inheres in the *seeking* of guidance, it does not come in the form of "unearned income;" that "intervention" is *built into* the situation and our *reaction to* the situation.)

And so, having been, as I thought, "guided" to the psalm, all I had to do now was to read it and all would be revealed! I did. And it wasn't. I read it very carefully half-a-dozen times. Nothing. If there was a hidden message then it was hidden from me, too.

Feeling somewhat disappointed, I got up and left, and started to make my way home. Why, I wondered, had I been "guided" to what I had been looking for, only to find that what I was looking for wasn't there? The whole thing seemed pointless.

250

What appeared to have meaning turned out to have no meaning at all. *Oh well,* I thought, *you can't win 'em all.* So I dismissed the matter from my mind, crossed the road, was about to enter a shop when, out of the blue, the following words floated into my mind: "THERE IS NO ANSWER, SO STOP LOOKING."

End of story.

Now, the reader may make of this what he will. I have described what happened, exactly as it happened, without embellishment. (I recorded the events the moment I got home, so as not to have to rely on my memory at a later date.)

"THERE IS NO ANSWER, SO STOP LOOKING," seemed a strange sort of message. "There is no answer" is rational enough. But, "so stop looking," what is that supposed to mean? Aren't we expected to look for answers? That is what I found so puzzling.

It certainly wasn't the kind of "revelation" I had expected. (Which at least shows that I wasn't trying to delude myself!) I tried to rationalize what had occurred; but without success. It just didn't make sense. I should have felt cheated; but curiously enough I didn't. I had a peculiar feeling that I had been taught a very important lesson, that I had received the right answer. It had that kind of quality.

Now the reader may conclude that my little story means nothing, that I had built up a simple (and not all that unusual) coincidence into something portentous, and that my imagination did the rest. And he may be right. But that is not the way I see it. The episode was far too important to me for it not to have meaning. Rightly or wrongly, it seems to me that what I was being told was this: FAITH THAT RELIES ON PROOF IS NO FAITH AT ALL. For decades I had, in effect, been saying: Give me a rational explanation of the "cry from the cross," and I will believe. Now what sort of faith is that? Faith cannot be rationalized. Either we have faith, or we have not. That, I think, is the message I was given. Reason is but one of man's faculties; faith is another. And we have as much right to rely on the latter as on the former. If I am to believe only that which can be scientifically proven or rationally affirmed then that puts me in the same boat as the atheist.

Another point: even accepting that it was a coincidence and

nothing more, who is to say that what was originally a coincidence, and therefore meaningless, was not *retroactively* turned into something meaningful by *my reaction to that coincidence?* In the circumstances at the time—i.e. my searching for an answer to something that was affecting my faith—perhaps it was certain that this coincidence would trigger off the reaction it did. Now, I am fully aware that natural law demands that cause must precede effect; but how do we know that something that is originally meaningless cannot be made meaningful *retroactively?* As meaning and reason have no atomic structure, maybe they are not subject to the universal law of causation?

I accept that subjective experiences only mean something to the subject. To an outsider, my story may sound trivial. But it wasn't to me. And after all, I am the one who had the experience. What this story does prove, if nothing else, is the importance of faith to the individual. I had found the answer to something that had bothered me for over forty years. That, to me, was important, So important, in fact, that it was this little episode that prompted me to write this chapter on faith.

Believers are often regarded as naive simpletons. This is understandable. If you haven't experienced something yourself, you cannot be expected to understand what such an experience can mean to somebody who has. (Incidentally, I have yet to hear Christ described as a naive simpleton!) But it would be a mistake to think that faith is all plain sailing. It isn't. It encounters many stormy seas, and many sturdy ships have foundered on the rocks of uncertainty and despair. But then again, some ships are unsinkable; they simply refuse to go down. "A man can maintain his faith even in utter darkness. As a young Jew wrote on the wall of a Warsaw ghetto. [vide Hans Küng's *On Being a Christian*]:

> I believe in the sun, even if it does not shine.
> I believe in love, even if I do not feel it.
> I believe in God, even if I do not see him.

Faith gives us hope when we have lost all hope, when there is nothing left to hope for. When the human lot becomes unbearable and there is no one left to turn to, we are forced to turn to God. For there is nowhere else to go. In the dark moments of suffering and doubt, when we are all alone, defenceless and helpless, faith takes us by the hand and shows us the way.

Nothing taxes our faith more than the problem of suffering. Being the creation we are, suffering is inescapable. Why God created man thus is the sixty-four thousand dollar question. Unfortunately there is no sixty-four thousand dollar answer.

The plain fact is that we do not know why God so arranged the world that human suffering is inevitable. We do not know why man was made to mourn. And it's no good pretending we do. Of course, if God is the malign despot that Nietzsche accused him of being then the answer is clear: God couldn't care less! Whenever there's an earthquake, a famine, a plague, a Holocaust, a war, a plane crash, an old lady mugged or a baby battered to death, God is in his element—literally! For these things are the inevitable result of the way God made the world and the way he made us. And God knew when he made the world and us that this is how it would be. No wonder the American satirist, Henry Louis Mencken (1880–1956), was moved to write: "I see little evidence in this world of the so-called goodness of God. On the contrary, it seems to me that, on the strength of His daily acts, He must be set down a most stupid, cruel and villainous fellow." (Source: *DURANT, On the Meaning of Life.*)

This does, however, present us with a philosophical difficulty: If that is what God is then man is better, more moral, more loving than his Creator. Is this credible?

But suppose that God is not malign, simply disinterested, indifferent, and impotent. Here again, we have a problem. To go to all the trouble of inventing and making the Universe, and then being disinterested in, and indifferent to, what goes on within it—like some absentee landlord—is hard to accept. As for being impotent, that is the most ludicrous charge of all! A God that can do what he's done—impotent?

Suppose on the other hand that God is what theists believe him to be, all-good and all-powerful, then that means that there is an answer, albeit one that is beyond our ability to comprehend. This should come as no surprise to those of us who know that so many of the great truths of this world do not lend themselves to rational explanation, though this may be of little comfort to those who suffer.

Without wishing to minimize "the overwhelming reality of suffering in the history of mankind" (the words are Küng's), I do not think that suffering can be quantified in this way. The suffering of a million people is of the same order as the suffering of one person, it is not a million times greater. We each do our own suffering—and no one else's. When we suffer at the sight of our loved ones suffering, the pain we feel is ours not theirs. C.S. Lewis makes this point cogently in his book *The Problem of Pain*: "We must never make the problem of pain worse than it is by vague talk about the 'unimaginable sum of human misery.' Suppose that I have a toothache of intensity x: and suppose that you, who are seated beside me, also begin to have a toothache of intensity x. You may, if you choose, say that the total amount of pain in the room is now 2x. But you must remember that no one is suffering 2x: search all time and all space and you will not find that composite pain in anyone's consciousness. There is no such thing as a sum of suffering, for no one suffers it. When we have reached the maximum that a single person can suffer, we have, no doubt, reached something very horrible, but we have reached all the suffering there ever can be in the universe. The addition of a million fellow sufferers adds no more pain."

The sum total of suffering in the Universe is of the same order as the suffering of one person experiencing the extremity of mental, physical and spiritual pain, every moment of human existence. Horrendous as that may be, no individual suffers it. That is to say, no human being is called upon to suffer continuous pain for all time. This doesn't make human suffering any easier to bear (when a person is suffering he is, to all intents and purposes, suffering "for all time"); it doesn't explain suffering; but it does put it into a more realistic perspective.

We all know from personal experience that when we are suffering we do not identify with the suffering of those whose degree of pain is less than our own. Their suffering is not added to ours, our suffering is not increased. (Even if it were, the cumulative suffering would still be ours). Anyone who has lost a loved one will testify that the pain is not increased one jot by the knowledge that around the world there are millions who are suffering likewise. It is not that we don't care, just that our personal suffering is paramount and cannot be added to. Where universal suffering is concerned, the multiplication factor doesn't work. Add boiling water to boiling water and it is still boiling water, it doesn't get any hotter.

It is a curious fact that when we look back on a period of personal suffering we see it differently from the way we saw it when we experienced it. A painful episode when we were young is now regarded as character building. A time of anguish we bore with courage and fortitude is now something we are proud of. A period of deprivation and hardship stoically endured now gives us a sense of satisfaction. All these things are now perceived as "good things." But that is not the way we perceived them at the time. When suffering is relegated to the past, it is perceived differently.

Nothing remarkable about that, you may think. Once pain is ended, it is ended. We can't suffer when we are not suffering. True. Except that I am not talking about suffering. I am talking about our *perception* of suffering. What we at the time perceived as "bad," we now perceive as "good." Yet we are talking about the same item of suffering. Nothing has changed—except time.

Penelope Tremayne, author of *Nor Iron Bars a Cage,* who was kidnapped by Tamil terrorists in Sri Lanka, interrogated and threatened with execution and then unexpectedly released, says of her terrifying ordeal: "As for what happened to me, I am glad of it, on balance, because . . . " Now I am sure that Ms. Tremayne did not think at the time that what she was experiencing was a "good thing," not even "on balance"! I have heard many other similar remarks made by Jewish dissidents released after being tortured and threatened with death in Soviet psychiatric prisons.

Looking back on my own life, there is not a moment's suffering I (now) regret, though I very much regretted it at the time. In fact, I (now) wish that on some occasions I had suffered more. Let me explain: I loved my mother dearly, and when she died I felt her loss acutely. But when my father died I felt nothing. I now wish that I had suffered as much when my father died as I did when my mother died. I WISH THAT I HAD LOVED

MY FATHER ENOUGH TO SUFFER. So instead of regarding suffering as an evil, I now perceive it, *in that particular circumstance,* as a blessing.

If then I am able to regard suffering in certain circumstances as a blessing (i.e. a "good thing"), how can I believe that suffering *per se* is an evil? I daresay we would all like to spend our lives in pain-free bliss, and if we knew that ahead of us lay a period of intense suffering, we would want to avoid it, if at all possible. But suppose as a corollary of this we would no longer suffer at the loss of a loved one, no longer feel pain on witnessing the pain of others, no longer experience horror when contemplating the horrors of Auschwitz. Would we not perhaps consider this too high a price to pay for our immunity to suffering, too high a price to pay for our pain-free bliss? It would seem that if we are to dispense with suffering, we must also dispense with love and compassion. What ought we regard as the greater evil—a suffering-less world, or a loveless and compassionless world?

The ambivalence of suffering is highlighted by Malcolm Muggeridge in his *A Twentieth Century Testimony.* "Contrary to what might be expected," he says, "I look back on experiences that at the time seemed especially desolating and painful with particular satisfaction. Indeed, I can say with complete truthfulness that everything I have learned in my seventy-five years in this world, everything that has truly enhanced and enlightened my existence, has been through affliction and not through happiness, whether pursued or attained. In other words, if it ever were to be possible to eliminate affliction from our earthly existence by means of some drug or other medical mumbo jumbo, as Aldous Huxley envisaged in *Brave New World,* the result would not be to make life delectable, but to make it too banal and trivial to be endurable."

To Mr. Muggeridge, life without affliction would be "too banal and trivial to be endurable." That is the way he sees it. But it will be noticed that it is in retrospect that his afflictions did their ennobling, he did not feel ennobled at the time. At the time, his afflictions seemed "especially desolating and painful"; but now that the suffering is over, he looks back on them with "particular satisfaction."

I am not questioning Mr. Muggeridge's sincerity, simply

emphasizing the point I made earlier about our perception of suffering: it is the "time-value" of suffering that I find intriguing.

If we never suffered we would never be free from suffering; because we would not know what it was like to suffer (or not to suffer). In other words, we would not be human. Suffering is an integral part of the human condition; we cannot avoid it. Without wishing to sound frivolous, consider these words from P. G. Wodehouse's novel *The Man with Two Left Feet*: "Henry belonged to the large circle of human beings who consider that there is acute pleasure in being suddenly cured of toothache than in never having toothache at all." Now that's philosophy for you!

Beyond the realms of lay philosophy, and deep into the heart of true theology, come these words from that modern saint, Mother Teresa of Calcutta (*A Gift for God*): "Suffering, if it is accepted together, borne together, is joy . . . suffering shared with Christ's passion is a wonderful gift."

Suffering a joy? A wonderful gift? Good Lord! does the reverend Mother know what she is saying? Well, you may disagree with her, consider her words religious hyperbole, but please, please, do not accuse her of not knowing what she is talking about. This lady is surrounded by suffering, involved and immersed in it every minute of every day. She has spent the past thirty-five years ministering to the needs of the diseased and the dying, bathing their sores, comforting them in the final moments of their agony. So you have better believe that she knows what she is talking about!

Again, from the same source: "Without suffering our work would just be social work, very good and helpful, but not the work of Jesus Christ, not part of the Redemption. Jesus wanted to help by sharing our life, our loneliness, our agony, our death. Only by being one with us has he redeemed us.

"We are asked to do the same: all the desolation of the poor people, not only their material poverty, but their spiritual destitution, must be redeemed. And we must share it, for only by being one with them can we redeem them by bringing God into their lives and bringing them to God."

I don't know what the reader will make of these words. He may, following contempory secular opinion, regard them as high-flown religious rhetoric. If he does then he will be making a big

257

mistake. For what he will fail to understand is that Mother Teresa has conquered suffering. Not come to terms with it, but *conquered* it. She hasn't beaten poverty and disease (she never set out to; that's a job for the doctors and nurses, the scientists, the economists and politicians). She has done something far, far greater. She has shared in the loneliness, the affliction, the agony, the death, of her fellow human beings, brought them spiritual comfort and united them with God through her Lord Jesus Christ. None of which she could have done without faith. So now, perhaps, you are beginning to perceive the importance of faith?

The curious thing about faith is that it is more likely to falter when we witness the suffering of others than when we are suffering ourselves. Watching others suffer—especially little children, victims of a so-called "act of God"—our faith is often stretched to the breaking point. Yet strangely, even perversely, those who actually do the suffering often find that it is their faith alone that enables them to endure. It would seem that suffering undertaken vicariously is the greater test of faith!

No event in modern history has tested the faith of believers more crucially than the recent famine in Ethiopia. As the full horror unfolded night after night on our TV screens, few witnessing these agonizing events could have failed to experience some pang of doubt as to the existence of a loving God. If God really did love his children he certainly had a funny way of showing it. (Did the haunting images haunt God, I wonder?) "Suffer little children to come unto me," seemed to many just a sick joke.

When interviewed by *The London Daily Mail*, Michael Buerk, whose filmed reports first alerted a shocked world to the human catastrophe that was taking place in Ethiopia, said that he was asked by his ten-year-old son, "Why does God allow this to happen, Daddy? Why does God allow babies to starve to death?" Michael Buerk said, "I gave him the only answer I had, the honest one. I said I didn't know. I don't have an answer." Buerk went on to say: "An all-powerful God of good who has allowed children to die from hunger in their tens of thousands? Even the Catholic missionaires to whom I spoke in Ethiopia oscillated between faith and their rejection of it."

No, Mr. Buerk, faith isn't easy.

We watched Mr. Buerk's reports and our hearts nearly broke. So what did we do? We held back our tears, blamed God, sent off our donation to Oxfam, and then got on with our lives. What else could we do? We couldn't give up our jobs, pack up our bags, leave our wives and children and descend on Ethiopia in our millions. Of course not! Apart from the impossible logistics of the situation, we would only have been in the way. What good could we have done? (Probably none, but did we ask? I didn't, did you?) Yet in the last war, millions of Allied servicemen gave up their jobs, packed up their bags, left their wives and children and descended on Germany to fight the Nazis. ("Ah, but that was different; we were at war." Precisely. That is the point I am making; when it comes to fighting and killing, we can make the effort, but when it come to saving and healing, the difficulties are too great to be overcome).

This is not meant as criticism of any nation or individual persons, simply an indictment of human nature as a whole.

And when we sent off our donation, how much did we send? I will tell you. Less than we could afford. Did we give up one single meal, one morsel of bread, because our donation was too large? If we didn't then we gave not enough.

By now, the reader is probably thinking: "Why all this cynicism? Okay, so we're not as good as we ought to be. We could have done more. But we did do something. In fact we did quite a lot, a damn sight more than the Ethiopian's own government did. Had it not been for the generosity of the West, the disaster would have been far greater. We gave money, food, and medical supplies. The charity relief organizations were overwhelmed by the generosity of millions of ordinary people, including pensioners and children, who contributed their meager savings. The Irishman Bob Geldof inspired and organized the Live Aid TV spectacular, the biggest and most successful charity performance ever held anywhere in the world; and the supportive efforts of those much-maligned pop stars, so often accused of setting a bad example to the young, put to shame the efforts of every government agency in the world, including my own. When all is said and done, we did as much as our flawed human nature would allow us to do. If it wasn't enough, it's because we're only human. What about God? What's his excuse?"

We are now at the heart of the dilemma. "Kill a man," wrote Jean Rostand (*Pensées d'un biologiste*, 1955), "and you are a murderer. Kill millions of men, and you are a conqueror. Kill everyone, and you are a god." This is the unanswerable logic of the biologist. If God is good, why does he allow such appalling catastrophes to happen? Why did he so create the world that human suffering would be inevitable? My answer is the same as Michael Burek's: I don't know. If I knew the answer, I wouldn't need faith to believe that there was an answer. But I do know this: if the sight of starving children is going to destroy our faith in God then at no time in human history has anyone ever had any reason to have faith. For children have always starved. And been murdered, tortured, bombed, gassed, and napalmed. If we are to believe in God only when we are cosy and warm and free from pain; when our children are happy and well fed; when the poor little mites in Ethiopia, who are dying in their thousands, with flies crawling all over their beautiful little faces and emaciated bodies, are doing their dying discretely away from the TV cameras, then our faith is not the kind that will stand up to the realities of life and death and suffering. Children have always suffered. In their millions! Starvation is nothing new. The only thing that's new is that pictures of starving children are now inconveniently beamed into our living rooms, often while we are engaged in feeding our faces.

If we are to have faith, then we had better understand what it is up against. If our response to the heart-rending scenes of suffering children is, "I can no longer believe," then fair enough. But in that case we had no right to believe in the first place. We have to be able to look suffering straight in the eye, see the worst that life can offer, and then say, if we can, "I believe."

No glib words about suffering (and whatever these words are, they are certainly not that, for they are being written whilst the tragic TV pictures are currently appearing on our screens), can satisfactorily answer the poignant question, "Why does God allow babies to starve to death?" But of this I am sure: these precious little children would not be precious *if there were no loving God.* It is only the existence of a loving God that makes them precious. If the reader understands what I am saying, he will know what I mean. If he doesn't, then I am sorry but that is the best I can do.

When I saw on TV the gentle, uncomplaining, suffering souls, with only a few hours or days to live, reaching out to touch the hand of the Christian bishop who had flown out "to see for myself what conditions were like" (yes, they were the exact words that fell haltingly from the lips of the embarrassed and bewildered prelate as he watched the starving people dying around him); when I read of the dying woman who, in the words of Michael Buerk, "pushed her emaciated baby into my arms and then knelt down and kissed my feet"—this I know with an unshakeable faith: such nobility of spirit could have been conceived only in the womb of nobility, it could not exist OF ITSELF AND BY ITSELF.

And the famine relief workers, those Catholic missionaries who "oscillate between faith and their rejection of it," who don't get time to break their hearts only their backs, whose only thought is to help, save and succour—whence comes their love and compassion, if not from the God of Love?

And the rest of us, who, deficient though our spirituality is, nonetheless do care and were deeply moved by what we saw—whence comes our compassion? Whatever our shortcomings as a species, there could not have been one single person, of whatever nationality, political persuasion, religion or no religion, who did not feel some degree of compassion, who did not shed one little tear at the plight of those suffering children. WHY COMPASSION AND NOT PLEASURE? There is no *rational* explanation as to why we were disturbed and not elated; sad and not happy. There is no *rational* explanation as to why the relief workers, missionaries, doctors and nurses give up their time, their creature comforts and personal well-being to dedicate their lives to the suffering of others. There is no *rational* explanation as to why we should feel guilty at not helping more than we do. NOR IS THERE ANY *RATIONAL* EXPLANATION AS TO WHY GOD ALLOWS SUFFERING.

The explanation, if there is one, lies deeply embedded in our spirituality, inaccessible to reason. It cannot be rationalized or intellectualized; we can only reach it by faith.

When everything is going well and there isn't a cloud in the

261

sky, we can manage quite comfortably without faith, thank you very much. But when the storm clouds gather, when our loved ones suffer and we suffer ourselves, then faith ceases to be a luxury and suddenly becomes a necessity. (A crutch, you say? Maybe, though I am sure a cripple doesn't regard a crutch as a "crutch." Nor is he ashamed to use it to help him overcome his disability.)

When faced with overwhelming suffering, the believer finds himself wrestling with the age-old question: How can there be a loving God, for no such being would allow such suffering?

There is no satisfactory answer to this question. We have to face the fact that if there is a loving God then suffering is inexplicable. However, there is another question which, in my view, is equally unanswerable: How can there *not* be a loving God, for without such a being suffering is meaningless.

You see the paradox? If there is a loving God then suffering is inexplicable. But it is only in the context of an existent loving God that suffering can have meaning. Now if I am to choose between the inexplicable and the meaningless, then I am compelled to choose the former. I have no difficulty in accepting the inexplicable (we do it all the time; so many of the things that are true are also inexplicable), but impossible to believe in the meaningless. The concept of meaninglessness is as unacceptable to me as the concept of nothingness. So for me, faith in God is faith in reason!

Does suffering disprove the existence of a loving God? On the contrary, says Malcolm Muggeridge (*Jesus Rediscovered*), "Simone Weil would say, as I consider justly, that not only does affliction not disprove God's existence, it uniquely manifests his presence. If every affliction were to be eliminated from our mortal existence then and then only, God really would be dead." In another context (ibid), Muggeridge says: "I think [suffering] is part of the pattern of life. What's more I think it's an essential part. Imagine human life being drained of suffering! If you could find some means of doing that, you would not ennoble it; you would demean it." And later: "If God had created man perfect, man without pain, man without sin, there would have been . . . no creation. . . The life we know, with all its pains and ecstasies, wouldn't have existed. If you imagine your life made by a different God, made perfect, it wouldn't be life . . . the pursuit of perfection is via imperfection. . . . This is how it is, and this is the majesty of it, and why it is interesting. This is why there is literature, why there is art, why there is thought, and how we may know there is a God—a loving God—whose children we all are."

This is not an easy proposition to accept—especially for the disabled, the bereaved, those in constant pain or agonizing over the suffering of a loved one. I doubt whether many of them find life "interesting" or "majestic."

Nonetheless, I believe that Muggeridge (and Simone Weil) see right through to the heart of the dilemma. Without a LOVING God, suffering is senseless. Without suffering, there would be neither good nor evil. Without good and evil, God would not exist.

The existence of God is necessary to explain suffering (even though it cannot be explained). The existence of God is necessary to justify suffering (even though it cannot be justified). The existence of God is necessary to overcome suffering (even though it cannot be overcome). Suffering only becomes meaningful in the context of a living and loving God in whom suffering can be conquered. The little children who are starving in Africa, the little children who were napalmed in Vietnam, the little children who were incinerated in Dresden, the little children who were gassed in Auschwitz—do these things make sense? If there is a loving God then very little. If there is no loving God then none whatsoever. The difference between "very little" and "none whatsoever" is faith.

I do not believe that suffering in itself is senseless. It may be inflicted thus, but it is not endured thus. Faith is our only hope, our only means, of coming to terms with suffering, of accepting it and conquering it. If suffering is senseless and meaningless, then faith can help us transform it into something sensible and meaningful. We cannot do this by ourselves; only with God's help is this possible.

The wonderful thing about faith is its universality. It is available to us all, irrespective of who we are or what we are: the lowliest as well as the highest, the weak as well as the strong, the uneducated as well as the educated, the foolish as well as the wise, the rich as well as the poor, the young as well as the old, the wicked as well as the good. If faith were available only to the holiest, the wisest and the cleverest, it would be elitist, out of reach of all but a tiny fraction of mankind. Truly could it be said that faith is equality of opportunity *par excellence*, and—dare I say it?—the creation of a benevolent being.

Unless we use our capacity for faith, it will fossilize. Faith is a living thing and, like all living things, will atrophy if unused. Those who are blest with this precious gift should consider themselves fortunate indeed. Those who aren't and are quite happy to live without it, then jolly good luck to them! But to those who do not possess faith and would wish to acquire it, or to those whose faith is like a sickly child, without vitality and strength, unable to weather the storms of a hostile world, I would simply say this: If you really want to acquire faith, or to strengthen your ailing faith, you can do so. Not by going to church. Not by reading the Bible. Not by doing good works. But by praying for it—AND MEANING IT. And keep on praying for it—AND KEEP ON MEANING IT.

It will come, I promise you.

Postscript: After completing this chapter, believing I had written all I could on the subject of faith, I was privileged to see a video recording of a BBC2 TV film called "Mother Teresa," which I had unfortunately missed when it was broadcast earlier in the year.

I have often heard Mother Teresa speak of her faith. But I have never seen her at work and frankly was not prepared for what I was about to see.

I will not attempt to describe the film, words would only diminish the content—even the sensitive narration by Richard Attenborough was in some way an intrusion. There was, however, one simple incident that will forever remain engraved on my heart and mind. It was this: Mother Teresa was comforting a young boy convulsed with shock in war-torn Beirut. At first there was no response, but then, gradually, almost imperceptibly, the stricken boy responded to her touch, and the love that flowed from the good Mother to the boy and back again, in a kind of holy cycle, seemed to unite them in one spiritual conflation.

At that moment—for me, a rare moment of enlightenment—I realized that love and faith are, in reality, one and the same thing. That just as time and space are united in one space-time continuum, so love and faith are fused in one spiritual continuum. That love is a confession of faith, and faith a confession of love. Mother Teresa's love and faith are infinite. Her finite heart is so full of the infinite love of Jesus, and faith in the God of Love, THAT THERE IS NO ROOM FOR ANYTHING ELSE, neither worldliness nor doubt nor reason. When Jean-Paul Sartre wrote: "Faith, even when profound, is never complete," (*Words 1964*), he was wrong. In Mother Teresa it *is* complete. The cup of infinity is full to overflowing; it cannot be added to. To the good Mother, faith is nothing less than knowing. And nothing less than knowing is worthy of her Jesus and her God. Unreasonable? Perhaps. But then, faith has little to do with reason.

Love, for Mother Teresa, is not a self-centered, self-indulgent, self-worshipping emotion. Nor is it an abstract theological concept. It is the acting out of faith, a harsh reality, the reality of the cross. When Mother Teresa stroked and comforted that poor demented boy in Beirut, she was in some mysterious way transported back in time to the Hill of Golgotha, and in reality was stroking and comforting the body of the stricken Jesus.

> Inasmuch as ye have done it unto one of the least of these my brethren, ye have done it unto me.
>
> Matthew 25:40

I now realize that true faith is loving God to the utmost of one's being, and had I not seen this film, I would have missed having my question "What is faith?" answered in such a dramatic fashion.

Thank you, Mother Teresa, and thank you, Marion, for showing me the film.

Chapter 10

Was Christ the Son of God?

He saith unto them, But whom say ye that I am? And Simon Peter answered and said, Thou art the Christ, the Son of the living God.
                                                        Matthew 16:15–16

If Christ wasn't the Son of God, he ought to have been.
                                                        Peter Hare

I begin this chapter with trepidation, with no certain belief in the divinity of Jesus. This may seem a strange thing for a Christian to say, but the fact is that I do not even know what it *means* to say that Jesus was the Son of God. I know what it means to say that I am the son of my father. It means that I was conceived as a direct result of an act of cohabitation between my father and my mother. But Jesus? In what way was he the Son of his Father? (In any case, aren't we all supposed to be the children of God? Whether we spell son with a small *s* or a capital *S*, a son is a son, and a daughter a daughter.)

However, had the relationship between Jesus and the Father not been perceived as unique, the life and death of Christ would have been just another minor historical event; it would never have had the earth-shattering effect it has had on the history of the world and on the lives of millions of Christian men and women over the past two thousand years. Whether or not Christ was the Son of God, there is little doubt that Christians have always believed that he was. And believed it so sincerely and so passionately that they have persistently suffered persecution, torture, and death, rather than deny their Christian faith—and erected thousands upon thousands of churches, monuments, statues and crucifixes, produced countless works of art,

266

and composed a multitude of hymns, poems and pieces of music—all to the glory of the man whom they call the Son of God.

Who, then, was this so-called "Son" of God?

Surprisingly little is known of the historical Jesus. He was born in Bethlehem, a small town near Jerusalem, to Mary, a young woman in Nazareth, and her husband Joseph, a local carpenter and builder. His family were conventional working people, neither rich nor poor. He had a normal Jewish religious upbringing and was educated at the local synagogue school. Apart from Luke telling us (2:42–7) that, at the age of twelve, Jesus was to be found in the temple, "sitting in the midst of the doctors, both hearing them, and asking them questions," virtually nothing is known of his activities until he reached the age of about thirty, when he appears seriously to have begun his ministry—though it is difficult to believe that Jesus was religiously inactive during the previous decade when he was in his twenties, the most vigorous period of a young man's life.

Within a few short years, probably three or four at most, Jesus was dead, executed for blasphemy.

It is important to understand that Jesus was a devout Jew, steeped in the traditions of Judaism. He was not, if I may put it this way, a Christian. He radicalized the historical Jewish faith and, in doing so, created a new, universal perspective on an old nationalistic religion. This new version of Judaism, we call Christianity. Strictly speaking, it is not correct to say that Jesus founded Christianity. It was St. Paul who created Christian theology.

The Jews were expecting a Messiah: a man specially chosen by God to deliver Israel from its enemies. Such a Messiah, Jesus was not!

Jesus preached about the kingdom of God. But what precisely he meant by this is not clear. We know what the Jews meant by the kingdom of God; for them it had only one meaning: an earthly not a heavenly kingdom, where Judaism, led by the Messiah, would triumph over the gentiles and establish God's reign on Earth.

It is certain that this is not what Jesus had in mind when he preached about the kingdom of God. Christ's kingdom was not of this world. He was not interested in earthly power; he was not in competition with Caesar. I think he came to terms with this early in his career when, in the words of Malcolm Muggeridge (*Jesus Rediscovered*), "Christ withdrew alone to the desert to fast and pray in preparation for a dialogue with the Devil. Such a dialogue was inescapable; every virtue has to be cleared with the Devil, as every vice is torn with anguish out of God's heart. Christ found the Devil waiting for him in the desert, but what took place between them was really a soliloquy. When we talk with the Devil WE ARE TALKING TO OURSELVES." (My caps.)

The disciples came to see Jesus not just as a good man, not just as a holy prophet, but as someone uniquely related to God. "Lord and Master," which is what the disciples latterly came to call Jesus, is almost equivalent to saying "God." Jesus was obviously different, but just how different not everyone would agree!

"Jesus had few real supporters in his lifetime," writes Colin Wilson in his *A Criminal History of Mankind*. "He was a minor and rather unpopular prophet; if he had lived to be seventy and died in his bed, he would probably now be totally forgotten."

It is difficult to believe that these are the words of a serious writer. First, Jesus did *not* live to be seventy and he did *not* die in his bed. He lived to be little more than thirty, and he died on the cross. So why the gratuitous speculation? One might just as well say: If Jesus had not lived the kind of life he did, not uttered the kind of words he did, not died the manner of death he did, and not "appeared" to his disciples after he had been crucified, he would not have been worshipped as the Son of God. Obviously not! Second, as for Jesus being now totally forgotten had he lived to be seventy and died in his bed, how can Mr. Wilson possibly know that? Muhammad lived to be more than seventy and died in his bed. So did Buddha. Are they now forgotten? Furthermore, should it surprise us that Jesus had few real supporters in his lifetime, considering the impossible nature of the gospel he preached? It was only after the resurrection and the post resurrection "appearances"—and with the benefit of historical perspective—that Christians came to see that Christ's way, the impossible way, was not only possible but mandatory if we are to find God. A rather unpopular prophet he may have been (in his lifetime) but *minor?* What a singularly condescending remark to make about the founder of the world's major religion!

The Apostle St. John saw Jesus rather differently. "In the beginning was the Word," he said, "and the Word was with God, and the Word was God . . . And the Word was made flesh, and dwelt among us . . . full of grace and truth." (1:1,14). John was saying that God revealed himself to the world *in the person of* Jesus Christ, that Jesus was God incarnate, the only begotten Son of the Father. Now we are beginning to see what the capital *S* is all about!

The Christian doctrine of the Trinity—God the Father, God the Son, and God the Holy Spirit—the "three-in-one" God, as it were—grew directly out of the New Testament, out of the teachings of Christ and the impact his life and death had on first generation Christians. It is a theological concept conceived by Christians to explain the mystical union of God, Jesus Christ, and the Holy Spirit. As the Nicene Creed puts it: Christ is "of one substance with the Father." Of one substance! That's pretty close to saying that Christ *is* God, isn't it?

This "oneness" is something that Jews, the most spiritually perceptive people on Earth, can neither accept nor understand. Rabbi Hugo Gryn (Gerald Priestland's *Priestland's Progress*) said that " 'no religious Jew could possibly justify the Trinity or see how it could function. No matter how often the creeds said God was one as often as they said God was three, one, surely was one. The Hebrew word we use [said Gryn] is a very strong *one*: it is unity, uniqueness, indivisibility. It brings together matter and spirit, form and content, creator and creation.' "

One Jew, however, who has no such difficulty, is the Rumanian Christian Richard Wurmbrand. "[The] assertion that God is one," he says (*Christ on the Jewish Road*), "is part of the mystique of numbers. . . . If God is identical with the number one, He must have qualities in common with this number. This shows how useful mathematics is to an understanding of divine truths. All the philosophers, from Plato and Pythagoras to Augustine and Boethius, have maintained that no man who is ignorant of mathematics is capable of understanding divine things. . . . There is no such thing as absolute one. 'One' simply represents a synthesis of conflicting forces. . . . If I maintain that

God is one, I maintain that He is divisible, because the number one is divisible. He can be the Father, the Son and the Holy Spirit. . . . The number one is also capable of being multiplied. But it is unlike all other numbers because, however much one multiplies it by itself, it always remains one. . . . Likewise, the number one is the only number whose square root is equal to itself. That is why Jesus, a man, was able to say: 'He that hath seen me hath seen the Father' (John 14:9)."

The concept of the Trinity does not derive its authority directly from the teachings of Christ, although there are definite trinitarian overtones to many of his sayings. Jesus clearly believed that his relationship to the Father was unique. "I and my Father are one," he declared. (John 10:30.) The following utterances, too, are quite unambiguous:

"The Father is in me, and I in him." (John 10:38.)
"I am the way, the truth and the life: no man cometh unto the Father, but by me." (John 14:6.)
And, when Simon Peter said, "Thou art the Christ, the Son of the living God." Jesus replied: "Blessed art thou, Simon Bar-jona: for flesh and blood hath not revealed it unto thee, but my Father which is in heaven." (Matthew 16:16–17.)

But Jesus said nothing to imply that he was God. In fact, he said the opposite!

"If I honour myself, my honour is nothing: it is my Father that honoureth me." (John 8:54.)
"I go unto the Father: for my Father is greater than I." (John 14:28.)
"Why callest thou me good? None is good, save one, that is, God." (Luke 18:19.)

And, finally, his dying words:

"Father, into thy hands I commend my spirit. (Luke 23:46.)

These are not the words of someone who thinks he is God. Jesus may have been (if the reader will pardon the expression) a chip off the old block, but he certainly did not claim to be the

Old Block himself. He left us in no doubt as to who was the Guv'nor!

Christ expressed in the simplest and most direct words, who and what he believed he was. Yet what would have sounded appallingly arrogant and outrageous coming from another, seemed a simple protestation of faith falling from the lips of Jesus.

What was so extraordinary about Jesus—and this shows very clearly in the pages of the New Testament—was his very ordinariness. He was so normal. Yet there was nothing ordinary or normal about him. In fact, he was quite extraordinary and abnormal!

In considering the persona of Jesus, many learned commentators have argued that there are only three alternatives open to us: (1) He was a liar and a charlatan; (2) He was mad; (3) He was who he said he was.

First, I do not think that anyone would give credence to the suggestion that he was a liar and a charlatan. Because clearly he wasn't. What beliefs he held, he held with absolute sincerity. You don't go and get yourself crucified for something you don't believe in!

The second proposition is also a nonstarter. Far from being mad, Jesus was obviously sane, in my view, the sanest person who ever lived. Even if the reader is not prepared to go so far as that, I am sure he would not suggest that the utterances of Jesus, rich in wisdom and deep in meaning, were the ravings of a lunatic. Jesus showed none of the classical signs of insanity. He didn't froth at the mouth. He didn't rant and rave. He didn't think he was Napoleon (actually he went one better, he thought he was the Son of God!) And he wasn't a "Jesus freak." What he said made sense, though it has to be admitted that he did say some pretty awesome things, such as: "I am the way, the truth and the life: no man came unto the Father, but by me." Yet these words, coming from Jesus, sounded neither insane nor even untoward. HE WAS THAT KIND OF MAN.

In his day Jesus was loved and hated, vilified, derided, cursed, and called a blasphemer. But he was never humoured or pitied or patronised or laughed at. Which he surely would have been had he been mentally deranged. There is nothing more pathetic than someone putting on airs and graces, acting above his station, pretending to be better than he is. But there was nothing pathetic about Jesus. On the contrary, the response to Jesus has, in all ages and all circumstances, been serious. Even skeptical scholars and militant atheists treat Jesus with respect.

This leaves us with hypothesis number three: that Jesus was indeed who he said he was.

C. S. Lewis, the great Christian lay thinker, rejects the idea that Jesus was simply a great moral teacher: "Either this man was, and is, the Son of God: or else a madman or something worse. You can shut Him up for a fool, you can spit at Him and kill Him as a demon; or you can fall at His feet and call Him the Lord and God" (*Mere Christianity*).

Jesus claimed to be divinely authorized to forgive sins. This is probably the most incredible (many would say preposterous) claim he ever made. I mean, it is one thing to forgive someone who trespasses against you, but quite another to forgive someone who trespasses against someone else. As C. S. Lewis (ibid) puts it: "You tread on my toe and I forgive you, you steal my money and I forgive you. But what should we make of a man, himself unrobbed and untrodden on, who announced that he forgave you for treading on other men's toes and stealing other men's money? . . . Yet this is what Jesus did . . . [which] makes sense only if He was the God whose laws are broken and whose love is wounded in every sin." God alone can universally forgive sins. So if Jesus was uniquely able to forgive all sins then, Mr. Lewis asserts, he must himself have been God (or a plenipotentiary of God, a point Mr. Lewis appears not to consider).

Now, far be it for me to cross words with such a formidable and learned a scholar as C. S. Lewis. However, I cannot agree that by rejecting the first two hypotheses—that Jesus was a liar and a charlatan, or a madman—we are obliged to accept the third: that he was the Son of God. There is a fourth hypothesis: namely, that Jesus was mistaken. He wasn't a charlatan. He wasn't insane. He was simply mistaken in believing that he was the Son of God. Subjectively real though his sense of Sonship was; subjectivity valid though it appeared to be, it was not objectively true. I am not saying that I necessarily subscribe to this view myself, at the moment of writing, I have yet to make up my mind, but it is one that must be considered. In fact, if we are to judge the evidence on a rational basis alone, this would appear to be the most likely explanation.

However, rationality is not the only consideration. Many of the great and glorious universal truths are not open to rational explanation. Love has no atomic structure, yet it is as real (perhaps more real) than the atom itself. There are dimensions of reality that cannot be understood by normal, rational thought processes.

No other religious leader in history has pointed to himself as the way to salvation. This alone makes Jesus unique. Consider the following utterances and ask yourself whether or not they are the words of one whose relationship with God was, if you object to the word "unique," at least very special:

"I am the bread of life: he that cometh to me shall never hunger; and he that believeth on me shall never thirst." (John 6:35.)

"For I came down from heaven, not to do mine own will, but the will of him that sent me." (John 6:38.)

"I am the resurrection, and the life: he that believeth in me, though he were dead, yet shall he live: And whosoever liveth and believeth in me shall never die." (John 11:25,26.)

"I came not to judge the world, but to save the world. He that rejecteth me, and receiveth not my words, hath one that judgeth him: the word that I have spoken, the same shall judge him in the last day. For I have not spoken of myself; but the Father which sent me, he gave me a commandment, what I should say, and what I should speak. And I know that his commandment is life everlasting: whatsoever I speak therefore, even as the Father said unto me, so I speak." (John 12:47–50.)

These are not, I suggest, the utterances of an ordinary human being. Does not one sense the innate authority and absolute, unquestioning faith, with which the words were spoken; and the certainty Jesus felt that he was in God, and God in him to a degree that makes it impossible to separate one from the other?

Having agreed (as I hope we have) that Jesus was neither a charlatan nor insane, we are left with but two alternatives:

273

(1) He was the Son of God. (2) He was a religious genius who believed he was the Son of God.

There was no ifs or buts with Jesus. He knew, or thought he knew, who he was and who it was that sent him: "I am the way, the truth, and the life: no man cometh unto the Father, but by me." Note: *I* am the Way; not *this* is the Way. "No man cometh unto the Father, but by me." BUT BY ME! Did Jesus really believe that the *only* way to God the Father, was through Christ the Son? Apparently he did. But isn't that just a wee bit arrogant? NOT IF IT'S TRUE. But how can it be true? I mean, what about the billions upon billions of human beings who were on this Earth before Christ was born? Were they denied, purely by historical accident, the opportunity of finding God? Not at all. "Before Abraham was, I am," said Jesus. If Christ was truly the Son of God then he existed before the world began. And will exist after the world has ended. This means that anyone, whatever his time in history, who heeds the words of Christ and carries out his commandments, finds God *through Jesus*. This is what Christians mean by the *living* Christ!

But what about other religions? Have they no validity? Do Christians seriously suggest that Christianity is the only faith that leads to God? I cannot speak for other Christians, but this Christian believes that where love is, God is; and where God is, Christ is. And that they who worship the God of love, worship the God of Christ. When a Jew or a Hindu or a Buddhist or an agnostic or an atheist "loves his neighbour as himself," he is carrying out Christ's commandment. I am not saying he is a Christian. I am simply saying that he is carrying out the will of God—the will of "him who sent me"; and in doing so, finds God THROUGH JESUS. Simone Weil (*Waiting on God*) sums it up perfectly: " . . . one can never wrestle enough with God if one does so out of pure regard for the truth. Christ likes us to prefer truth to him because before being Christ, he is truth. If one turns aside from him to go towards the truth, one will not go far before falling into his arms."

Jesus Christ was the greatest revolutionary this world has ever seen. But he made it quite clear that his kingdom was not of this world. He said the craziest things: "Love your enemies" . . . "Resist not evil: but whosoever shall smite thee on thy right cheek, turn to him the other also" . . . "Love thy neighbour as myself."

These things are crazy because they are unnatural. It is unnatural to love your enemies, unnatural to turn the other cheek, unnatural to love your neighbour as yourself. Christianity is all right in theory, say its critics, but in practice it just doesn't work. (Remember the little problem we had in Chapter 2 regarding selling all we have and giving to the poor?) In this world you have to stand up for yourself and for the rights of others. What would have happened if we had not stood up to Hitler? Probably the whole of Europe would still be under the jackboot, and not a single Jew alive in Europe today. And where did turning the other cheek get Jesus? Nailed to a cross, that's where!

Yes, he was crazy all right! But that is the paradox of Jesus. It is the alternatives that are crazy, that don't work. We have been trying them ever since the day we first discovered the difference between right and wrong. And where have they got us?

Christ came to save sinners: "I am not come to call the righteous, but sinners to repentance" (Matthew 9:13). The full implications of this statement are not generally understood even till this day. Jesus did not die for a religious belief or a noble cause. He did not die to create a better world, a new social order, a new system of ethics. He did not die to help the poor, the oppressed, or to overthrow tyranny. He died for one reason, and one reason alone—*to redeem sinners*. Now in case the enormity of this statement is lost upon the reader, let me spell out in plain, unequivocal English, precisely what it means. It means that Christ allowed himself to be humiliated, whipped, tortured and to suffer an agonising death, willingly, not to save the little children who were gassed at Auschwitz, but THE MEN WHO GASSED THEM.

That, whether we like it or not, is the meaning of the cross, the reality of Calvary. Throughout history, men have laid down their lives for their friends, their loved ones, their country, their faith. But only one has laid down his life for the Hitlers, the Barbies, the Eichmanns, the Stalins, the Pol Pots, and all the

275

other evil perverts, sadists, torturers, rapists, child molesters, baby batterers, and muggers and murderers of this world.

Almost indecent, isn't it? Yes, until you really think about it, and then you realize just how much God loves the human race, each and every one of us, without exception, whoever we are, whatever our sins. For if God loves me, then he loves Hitler. Because Hitler was a human being just like me (and I do mean me).

"That's all very well," you may be thinking. "But you can't just allow mass murderers to go around mass murdering, rapists to go around raping, muggers to go around mugging." Agreed. "And as for loving your enemies, surely you are not suggesting that the Jews who lost their loved ones in the gas chambers of Auschwitz, should not only forgive the Nazis for perpetrating those evil deeds, *but love them as well?*" No, I am not. BUT JESUS DID. Now, perhaps, you are beginning to understand what an impossible person Jesus was? And what it means to say he was unique?

Such love is so unnatural that it borders on the insane. For human beings, this degree of love is impossible. But then only an impossible faith can lead to eternal truth. The impossible, which by definition is unattainable, is alone worth attaining. A possible God is not possible. To be real, God must be impossible. And for Christ to be the Son of God, he must be impossible too.

Calvary was about redemption, saving sinners. Hitler, no doubt, was more in need of redemption than most. But how can I be sure of that? I do not know what made him the kind of man he was; how much he was product of his time, his environment, his genes; to what extent he was responsible for the evil impulses within him. And, not knowing, how can I judge? If Hitler's need for redemption was so much greater than mine, then Christ died especially for Hitler. But, of course, Christ also died for me and you. Because like Hitler, we are sinners too.

The truth is that Christ died for one sinner, ME, the universal "me" that we all are. "Jesus, whose being was as closely united to that of God as any truly human man's could be," writes Colin Morris (*Get Through till Nightfall*), "was held on the cross by the adhesive power of God's love for everyone who has ever lived. And such is the mystical arithmetic of his love that should teeming humanity be miraculously reduced to one unnoticed wretch, say you or me, Jesus would still have stayed on the cross."

That is the "mystical arithmetic" of Christ's love. He died for one person me, you, Hitler, and every sinner who ever lived or ever will live.

I would now like to discuss the most controversial aspects of the dogma surrounding the person of Jesus: namely, the Virgin Birth, the Miracles, and the Resurrection.

I do not intend spending much time on the Virgin Birth. Because I do not think it important. It has no relevance for me, or, as far as I can see, for anyone else, including Jesus himself.

I believe that Jesus was born in the normal way, as a result of sexual congress between Mary and Joseph. To have been conceived without the union of the male seed and female egg would have been a violation of universal law. And, as I have said elsewhere, I do not believe that God would make a law then break it himself.

God decreed that the human race should procreate the way it does. Biologists may be able to influence the natural process, by artificial insemination and the like, but they cannot change the law, the law that says that the female egg must be fertilized by the male seed. Neither the male seed nor the female egg can create a child on its own. And that, as far as I am concerned, is that. I cannot agree with those who, like Richard Wurmbrand (*Christ on the Jewish Road*), assert that in the twentieth century "the word 'impossible' no longer exists." Because it does. Universal laws aren't like piecrusts; they weren't made to be broken.

I do not know why the dogma of the Virgin Birth was introduced by the Christian Church. I suspect that the religious establishment did not take too kindly to the idea of the Son of God being conceived by way of sexual intercourse, especially as Christ's parents were unwed at the time. To be sinless, the Son of God would need not to have been conceived in "sin." Well, if the dogma of the Virgin Birth helps the Church to come to terms with the ambivalence of sexuality then that is a matter for them. For my part, I find the idea unnecessary and unnatural. Unnecessary, because it serves no purpose. (Why introduce a new

277

system when there's nothing wrong with the old?) Unnatural, because if Jesus was not born through the union of the male seed and the female egg, then he was genetically defective, a physical freak: in short, he was less than human. This I cannot accept. Far from being less than human Jesus was, in my view, more than human: superhuman not subhuman.

The significant thing for Christians, surely, is not the manner in which Christ was born, but the fact that he was born at all, that he suffered and died that each and every one of us might find our way to God! As I see it, the way in which he was conceived is no more relevant than the colour of his eyes.

Now, the resurrection is a different matter altogether. It is at the very heart of the Christian religion. Without it the New Testament would not have been written, the Christian faith never have been born. "If Christ be not risen," said Paul, "then is our preaching vain, and your faith is also vain." (1. Corinthians 15:14.)

What really happened at that first Easter? Did Jesus indeed physically rise from the tomb? Or is Christianity based on a fraud or a fable? Because if Christ did not rise from the dead, if the resurrection is a myth, then indeed "is our preaching and our faith vain."

The first thing one has to say is that, as recorded in the gospels, the resurrection stories, with all their discrepancies and contradictions, cannot all be true in every detail. But then, one would not expect them to be. Even had the apostles been disinterested bystanders, which obviously they weren't, and not been directly involved in the drama of the events, human frailty alone would have ensured that the stories could not be accurate in every respect. The gospels were written many years (two to seven decades, perhaps) after the events they were describing. It would have been impossible for the apostles to have remembered everything exactly as it had happened all that time before. We know from everyday experience that even eyewitnesses' statements given immediately after an incident, invariably contradict one another in matters of detail. We have to remember, also, that the Easter stories are not meticulously constructed accounts written by professional historians. They are testimonies of faith written by men consumed by the passion of that faith, men incapable of writing objectively about subjective mystical experiences. If the apostles had been objective reporters, they would not have been the kind of men who would be subject to mystical experiences.

To admit that the stories surrounding the first Easter are not objectively accurate accounts of the Easter events, is a far cry from saying that they are untrue or made up. But what puzzles me is: why should a religion that puts so much emphasis on *spiritual* truths be so obsessed with the *physical* resurrection of the material body? "I do not see how one *can* be a Christian," says A. N. Wilson (*How Can We Know*?), "if one does not believe Christ rose from the dead, and that in an objective and absolute sense . . . To be Christian, a person must believe, or come to believe, that Jesus broke the bonds of death and rose from the tomb . . . Of course, the Christian must accept that there was an empty tomb, and that this was not the result of mere trickery or body-snatching."

Agreed that Christians must accept that Jesus did indeed rise from the dead. But why must they believe that the tomb was empty by reason of a *miraculous ascension* of the *physical body?* Does the reality of Jesus—his unique relationship with the Father—depend on the supernatural disappearance of the body of Jesus by direct intervention by the Father? Why should the truth of reality depend on the fantasy of unreality?

In effect, Mr. Wilson is saying: If Christ's body was physically removed from the tomb by body snatchers (or if it were never put there in the first place) then the resurrection is untrue, and Jesus was no more the Son of God than I am or you are. But this is nonsense. If Christ rose from the dead, then he rose from the dead WHEREVER HIS BODY HAPPENED TO BE AT THE TIME. The geographical location of Christ's dead body had nothing whatsoever to do with the truth of his identity and spirituality. What had trickery or body-snatching to do with Jesus? When he foretold his death and resurrection, he did not add the rider, "Oh, by the way, if anyone should physically remove my body from the tomb, I will not be able to rise from the dead." Put like that, we can see just how absurd the resurrection-by-courtesy-of-the-empty-tomb really is.

Suppose that Christ's body was removed from the tomb and

secretly buried elsewhere and subsequently did physically rise in the way that Mr. Wilson and most Christians believe that it did—no one would ever have known! Are we asked to believe that the Christian faith depends on such a trivial accident of history?

The "empty tombers" are putting the (material) cart before the (spiritual) horse. It is the resurrection not the empty tomb that is at the heart of the Christian religion. The empty tomb is an idol, a false god. Accept the miracle of the resurrection, and the tomb, empty or otherwise, is an irrelevance, as irrelevant as the Turin Shroud.

If we need the disappearance of Christ's mortal remains, literally into thin air, to convince us that Jesus rose from the dead, then all I can say is that there is something wrong with our faith. Nowhere, at no time, has God offered us proof of anything—either of his own existence or of the divine nature of Jesus Christ. Is it conceivable that the Creator of the Universe would revoke the irrevocable laws of the Universe, JUST TO PROVE THAT CHRIST WAS HIS SON? O, ye of little faith!

No, the miracle of the resurrection does not depend on the magic of God. God is not a magician, and Jesus was not a magician's assistant. To have atomized the body of Jesus would have meant breaking natural law by direct intervention. Yes, I agree that it is possible—nay, certain—that there are universal laws as yet undiscovered; but I would point out that the "empty tombers" do not base their belief on the existence of a yet to be discovered universal law, rather on the breaking of an existing one. This is an important point, because, whereas an undiscovered universal law would apply to everyone, direct intervention to change an existing law on behalf of the Son of God, would apply to Jesus Christ alone, thereby inviting the charge of divine nepotism. (I am reminded here of a remark made by Colin Morris in his book *Get Through till Nightfall*. Speaking of supplicatory and arbitrary prayers, which we sometimes address to God for personal gratification and selfish advantage, he says: "Such requests are pleas to God to interfere with the order of nature . . . God wouldn't do it for Jesus. He won't do it for you." Although Dr. Morris wasn't talking about the resurrection and the empty tomb, he might just as well have been.)

We are, however, still left with the mysterious disappearance of Christ's body. For there is little doubt that the tomb was empty. Those are four, and only four, possibilities, which we shall now consider.

1. Christ's body did literally, physically, and miraculously rise from the dead.
2. The body was not placed in the tomb at all, but somewhere else.
3. The disciples stole the body after it was placed in the tomb, and secreted it elsewhere.
4. Somebody other than the disciples removed the body and got rid of it.

Let us examine these hypotheses.

It is impossible to discuss the first rationally. There were no eyewitnesses to the resurrection. No one claimed to see Christ's body actually rise. One either accepts the physical resurrection as an article of faith, or one rejects it as a physical impossibility. So, for the purposes of this discussion, I would ask the reader to set aside this hypothesis and concentrate on those possibilities that are subject to rational consideration. If the reader is not prepared to do this, if the dogma of the physical resurrection is too firmly rooted in his beliefs to permit an unprejudiced explanation of the evidence, then he should skip the rest of this section.

The second possibility is not, in my view, really credible: one burial place is as good as another, and Joseph's specially prepared tomb ("a new sepulchre wherein man was never laid") was as good as any. Furthermore, why should Joseph pretend that Jesus was buried there if he wasn't? What had he to gain by such duplicity? Why deceive his friends by keeping the real burial place a secret? In any case, the subsequent actions of the disciples prove beyond any shadow of doubt that they really believed that Jesus had been buried in that particular tomb.

The third hypothesis is even less credible. Why would the disciples want to steal Christ's body? The only possible reason is that they wished to create the impression that Jesus had physically risen from the dead. But this is nonsense. If they had removed the body, they would have known that it did not disappear miraculously: even if they had deceived others, they

281

would not have deceived themselves. After the resurrection, the disciples regrouped and risked imprisonment, torture and death. (Peter himself was crucified upside down.) Would they have done this for a belief they *knew* to be false? That is not the way faiths are created.

The Christian Church may have been founded on a Big Myth, but it certainly wasn't founded on a Big Lie, a Big Deception, a Big Fraud. The empty tomb, coupled with the post resurrection appearances, was to have such a dramatic effect on the disciples' lives that it is inconceivable that it was they who removed the body. One last point: If it is true, as Matthew says, that a guard had been placed at the sealed tomb, then the disciples could not have stolen the body, even if they had wanted to.

The fourth hypothesis, that Christ's body was removed by someone else, is the only one that makes sense. If we rule out the disciples; if the body really was put there in the first place; if it did not rise miraculously; then, by the process of elimination, we are left with the only possible alternative—someone other than the disciples removed the body.

Who? And why?

"It would be ludicrous," says Michael Green (*Empty Cross of Jesus*), "to suppose that the [authorities] moved the body of Jesus. They had at last got him where they had long wanted him, dead and buried. They would never had given colour to the resurrection preaching . . . by so crass a folly as removing the body. And if, by some egregious blunder, they had done just that, they would easily have been able to produce the moldering corpse as soon as the Christians began to claim that he was alive. And that happened very soon. *The third day* is strongly embedded in the earliest references to the resurrection. That is embarrassingly early."

Sorry, Canon Green, but I think you are mistaken. The authorities may have been stupid to remove the body, but that is not good enough reason for supposing that they didn't! Since when have authorities been immune to acting stupidly? With hindsight, and the benefit of nearly two thousand years of Christian faith in the resurrection behind us, we may regard such an act as "crass folly," giving as it did the resurrection story impetus and validity. But the authorities were not to know just how important the resurrection was to become. They had other things on their mind at the time. They were more concerned with the possible repercussions the execution of Jesus would have on his followers. Jesus had been a dangerous revolutionary. His teachings had threatened the whole fabric of the religious (and civil) establishment. The "King of the Jews" was dead, but what effect would his death have on the disciples? Any signs of an incipient uprising would need to be swiftly nipped in the bud. The authorities had executed the leader but they weren't out of the woods yet!

We are told that the high priests and the Pharisees warned Pilate that the disciples might try to steal the body. ("Sir, we remember that that deceiver said, while he was yet alive, After three days I will rise again. Command therefore that the sepulchre be made sure until the third day, lest his disciples come by night, and steal him away, and say unto the people, He is risen from the dead." And Pilate's reply: "Ye have a watch: go your way and make it as sure as ye can. So they went, and made the sepulchre sure, sealing a stone and setting a watch." (Matthew 27:63–66.)

On the face of it, this may not seem an unreasonable fear on the part of the high priests and the Pharisees. But is it too farfetched to suggest that they were cleverly creating an "alibi" for themselves, by planting the thought in the minds of others that the disciples were conspiring to do what they themselves had already decided to do? Cannot you hear them afterwards protesting: "Didn't we tell you that the disciples would steal the body?"

If the authorities really did believe that the disciples had stolen the body, why did they not have them arrested, interrogated and prosecuted? More to the point, why did they not search for the body? How do we know they didn't? Simple. With all the resources of the church and state at their disposal—the Roman armed forces, the secret police, quislings, paid informers, undercover agents—it would have been a simple matter to discover where the disciples had hidden the body. Is it not significant that the authorities did not even look?

Canon Green's argument that, had the authorities been so

crass as to remove the body, they could have quickly rectified their mistake by producing the corpse, assumes that they would want to. Maybe they considered that the damage to their reputation and authority had they done so, would be far greater than the problems caused by the disciples claiming that Christ had risen from the dead. After all, how many would believe such an unlikely tale? Even if they did, it would only be a nine-day wonder.

Bear in mind also, that the high priests could not possibly have bargained for the post resurrection "appearances." It cannot be overemphasized that it was the "appearances", not the empty tomb as such, that convinced the disciples that Jesus had risen, and which had such a fantastic effect on the embryo Christian Church.

Having surreptitiously removed the body, there was no going back. Church dignitaries could hardly admit to being body-snatchers, liars and cheats! But why move the body in the first place? What purpose did it serve? I believe the answer is this: Having made a martyr of Jesus, the authorities were not prepared to run the risk of his burial place becoming a shrine and a rallying point for Christians and future revolutionaries. So they removed the body at the dead of night (what could have been simpler?), secreted it in an unmarked grave or destroyed it, and then blamed the disciples!

Has it not been the nature of authorities the world over, having vanquished a hated and dangerous ideological enemy, to set about expunging all trace of his existence, in order to thwart any attempt by his followers to create a shrine for their defeated leader? In 1945, for instance, when the Russian army overran Hitler's bunker in Berlin, the charred remains of Hitler's body were removed and the whole area bulldozed. Later, when the Nazi war criminals were hanged in Nuremberg, their bodies were immediately cut down and cremated, and the ashes secretly disposed of. To this day the burial place has never been revealed, although it is widely believed that the ashes were scattered over the North Sea by an American army plane.

(Later: On August 17, 1987, Hitler's deputy, Rudolf Hess, committed suicide in Spandau prison, West Berlin, where he had been incarcerated for the past forty years. It was reported in the press the next day that the British authorities were going to demolish the prison and develop the site "to prevent it becoming a shrine for neo-Nazis.")

The high priests and Pharisees had every reason to fear a shrine being set up for the crucified Christ. But little did they know, how could they, that the cross, the murder weapon itself, was to prove more potent than the tomb?

No amount of speculation can tell us what really happened on that first Easter. Of the four possibilities outlined, this writer finds the last the most believable. Many Christians start from belief in the physical resurrection, and then fit the evidence to suit that preconception. Convinced as they are that God miraculously intervened, they shut their minds to the other possibilities, because for them they were too fearful to contemplate. In short, they believe what they want to believe.

This Christian, however, much as he would like to believe in the physical resurrection, cannot, because the natural law regarding dead bodies can no more be violated than can the natural law of gravity. God would not break his own laws for anyone—least of all for his own Son! It is for the reader to choose which explanation is the most reasonable. (I have deliberately ignored those fatuous theories put forward by some fatuous commentators, that Jesus was taken down from the cross, unconscious but not dead, patched up by a physician and smuggled out of the country to Kashmir or Turkey, where he lived the rest of his life in splendid anonymity. Or that somebody [a disciple? a well-wisher?] took his place on the cross, while Jesus legged it to Jerusalem . . . etc., etc.)

I, myself, am obliged to accept what reason dictates. Christ was a human being. He was born like anyone else, bled like anyone else, felt pain like anyone else, died like anyone else—and his corpse rotted like anyone else's. As a Christian, I feel under no obligation to believe superstitious and unreasonable dogma.

Finally: all four gospels are unanimous on one salient point: the stone was rolled back. Now if the body of Jesus had *supernaturally* risen, why was it necessary to *physically* roll back the stone? Is it not reasonable to assume that the stone was physically moved in order to facilitate the physical removal of the body? If it isn't, why was the stone moved?

We shall now turn to the postresurrection appearances, which, we are told, occurred over a period of forty days after the death of Jesus.

Did the disciples really see and hear and speak to and eat with the risen Jesus? Or did they suffer from delusions or hallucinations? Or were they simply lying?

There were so many reported appearances, to such a wide variety of individuals, including a crowd of five hundred people gathered together at one time, that we would be unwise to dismiss these reports as the meanderings of demented or impressionable people, or the concoction of liars.

I believe that the disciples were telling the truth—the subjective truth, that is, the truth as they saw it. They were as sure that they had encountered the risen Jesus, as Paul was a few years later on the road to Damascus. But why the discrepancies in their stories? Why did Jesus appear "in disguise," as it were, unrecognizable as a "gardener," a "stranger"? Why did the risen Jesus look so different from the earthly Jesus?

The first thing these discrepancies tell us is that the witnesses weren't lying, there was no collusion. Had they been lying they would have made sure that their stories matched. Furthermore, they would have reported seeing Jesus *as he appeared when he was alive*. It would never have occurred to them to talk of "gardeners" and "strangers." (A gardener? A stranger? A likely story!) It is the discrepancies that give the stories verisimilitude, that make them credible, a true recollection of the events as they appeared to the participants at the time.

We have to remember that these were traumatic times for the followers of Jesus. Their beloved leader, the Son of God, no less, had been seized, put on trial and executed—all within the space of less than twenty-four hours. The disciples were shattered—physically, mentally, emotionally, and spiritually. Is it surprising that in these quite extraordinary circumstances they should have witnessed something quite extraordinary?

The manner in which the disciples experienced the presence of Jesus, raises all sorts of metaphysical questions. For example, was Jesus actually present *in person?* What does "in person" mean? Does a person have to have flesh and blood before he can be a person? Did Christ's corpse, whilst mouldering in the grave, "step out" of itself and present itself to witnesses, in what Paul calls a "spiritualized" or "glorified" body? After death, does the body still exist in an "immaterial" form, does it merely cease to have substance, and cease to be visible? In other words, does it still exist *nonsubstantially* and *nonvisibly,* rather like the hole that remains after a figure has been cut out of a piece of cardboard. The cut-out figure and the corresponding hole match perfectly, but the figure is substantial and visible, whereas the hole is nonsubstantial and invisible; if the "positive" substantial figure is destroyed, the "negative" unsubstantial hole remains intact. Do we exist in a similar fashion—"positively" and "negatively," "substantially" and "nonsubstantially"?

After death, do body and soul merge into one rarified glorified continuum? Indeed, are they so merged in life? The body and soul have usually been regarded as two separate entities, with independent realities. But are they? Have not the modern sciences shown that the frontiers between body and soul are fictitious? That a person's moral character can be affected by a physical malfunction? That human behaviour may be changed by an operation on the brain?

If Paul was right, if the "glorified body" is a reality and not just a meaningless spiritual metaphor, then "resurrection" does have a meaning. If Paul was wrong, then the body—the corporeality through which our spirituality manifests itself—is nothing more than a heap of dust. It may well be that the dead body is simply a heap of dust. But it wasn't when it was alive! How do we know, then, that the "embodied self" does not retain its "embodied self-ness" after it has ceased to express itself through the corporeality of the physical body? In other words, "embodied self-ness" may perfectly well exist outside the material flesh-and-blood body we inhabit when we are alive.

That the disciples experienced the presence of Jesus after he had been crucified is, in my view, certain. Exactly what happened is an inexplicable mystery. But it is not unusual for someone who has lost a loved one to sense the presence of that loved one in a way that defies all rational explanation. Love has a way of penetrating death. Perhaps I may give a personal example.

Several months after the death of a friend of mine, his widow wrote to me as follows: "I had a very strange experience when I visited Chichester Cathedral. I was looking at a very fine stone picture dated about AD 1000 of the raising to life of Lazarus. I stood there looking at it and feeling very bitter inside—saying, yes, *he* was helped but nobody helped poor Doug [her husband], and quite suddenly just for a flashing second he was there beside me in his anorak and cap, but absolutely bouncing with joy of life and health. It was over in a couple of seconds and I probably imagined the whole thing but it was the happiness and health that came over so vividly."

A few months later I received another letter from her: "Today, when I was standing outside the Concourse of Bletchley . . . Doug suddenly walked round the corner and came to meet me. Obviously, I don't mean that I saw him, yet I do mean that I saw him, in his old navy anorak and cap and carrying the inevitable carrier bag . . . It was lovely just to have him for a little while."

And this from their daughter: "I was on the ritual evening walk that my youngest son demands before bed and it was very hot and I was tired and out of sorts. I stood in the shadow of a tree whilst David for the hundredth time inspected a car parked at the side of the road and my thoughts were all centered on how quickly I could persuade him to move homewards. Suddenly, a light breeze blew all around me and touched every part of me, and Dad put his hand on my shoulder. I turned round and smiled at him. He was there, not to see, but he *was* there with me and it was so wonderful."

Now, I have no intention of trying to explain or rationalize these "appearances." Because I cannot. What's more, I do not want to. Such revelations defy analysis. What happened to my friend's wife and daughter cannot be explained in rational terms. What, then, did happen? I will tell you. What happened was what they said happened. Nothing more. Nothing less. How you interpret what happened is up to you. What I do know is you cannot analyze or rationalize love. Love is the most potent energizing force there is; at its most powerful, irresistible. It is said that love conquers all. And so it does—even death!

The love that existed between Jesus and his disciples was

of such magnitude that it, too, penetrated the barrier of death. But why Jesus should have appeared to Paul, an archenemy of the Christians at the time and no lover of Jesus, I do not know. Between Paul and Jesus there was no bond of love (at least, not on Paul's side), so it is difficult to see why the persecutor Paul should have experienced the presence of Jesus on the road to Damascus. Could it be that Jesus "made contact" with Paul through the medium of Paul's conscience? That the realization of his wickedness in persecuting the Christians suddenly hit Paul with such force—like a spiritual bolt from the heavenly blue—that it was as if Jesus were talking to him in person: the sledgehammer of Jesus hitting the anvil of Paul, as it were? What we do know is that, from being a persecutor of Christ, Paul became Christ's most devoted and most effective apostle. Whatever explanation we care to come up with, there is no denying the world-shattering effect of what Paul deemed to be a direct intervention in his life by Jesus.

The "great light" which, Paul said, "shone from heaven," physically blinded him and he had to be led by the hand to the city of Damascus where he had been on his way to persecute a new group of Christians.

You may doubt that Jesus intervened directly in Paul's life. You may doubt that Paul had a supernatural experience. But what you are not entitled to doubt is that Paul *believed* that Jesus intervened directly in his life, that Paul *believed* he had a supernatural experience. Something profound must have happened to Paul on the road to Damascus. You don't go and change your whole life and everything you believe in; you don't do a complete religious somersault, risk imprisonment, banishment and death, for no reason at all!

There is no reasonable explanation of Paul's "blinding light." There is no reasonable explanation of the post resurrection appearances. There is no reasonable explanation of the resurrection. One either accepts these events as being in some inexplicable way true or rejects them as being false. Either way, you will need to exercise faith, because there is no proof.

I believe in the resurrection. Not a magical physical resurrection of the here-and-now, flesh-and-blood body, but a miraculous supernatural resurrection of the "glorified" body-soul continuum. A resurrection quite beyond the mind of man to imagine. And what holds for Jesus, holds also for the rest of mankind. Yes, even the Hitlers and Stalins of this world.

We shall now turn our attention to the miracles.

First, I think a clear distinction should be drawn between the healing stories and those miracles that depend on the breaking of natural law. The multiplication of loaves and fishes, walking on water, and turning water into wine, cannot, in my opinion, be accepted literally. They must either be treated allegorically or dismissed as untrue. As reasonable people we should apply the test of reason. Is it reasonable to assert that five loaves and two fishes defied the laws of arithmetic and multiplied themselves a hundred-fold? It is not. Is it reasonable to assert that a person may defy the law of gravity by walking on water? It is not. Is it reasonable to assert that six pots of water can defy the law of nature by changing into six pots of wine? It is not.

What need have we to believe in phoney miracles when we are surrounded by real live miracles every minute of the day—such as, for example, the conception and birth of a baby? Any competent magician can turn a glass of water into a glass of wine (they do it all the time on TV); but only God can create a baby from the gleam in two lovers' eyes.

Christ did not indulge in cheap illusions. To suggest that he did is, if you take the view that he was divine, little short of sacrilegious. When the rain that droppeth gently from heaven upon the place beneath, seeps up through the vine, and, with the help of the burning rays of the summer sun, transforms itself, through the grape, into wine, that, my friends, is a miracle.

"A miracle," said Petru Dumitriu in his novel *Incognito* (translated by Norman Denny), "is an everyday event which brings us into direct contact with the meaning of the world, and of God. If we are conscious of the divine nature of every happening and every fact, then everything is miraculous." Also, this extract from John Austin Baker's *The Foolishness of God:* "When we consider the simplicity of some basic unit of the universe such as the hydrogen atom, and the fact that its potential for change is apparently limited to the rise and fall of its energy level . . . and reflect that with this were made the hummingbird and the whale, the mind of an Aristotle and Einstein, a Kierkegaard, the music of Handel and the utterances of Shakespeare, the Wiltshire Downs and the green mountains of Vermont, Michelangelo's David and the courage of good men, no miracle, no portent, can ever arouse more wonder than the fact of the natural order and the mystery of the human soul."

Then there is the miracle of love. Richard Wurmbrand relates (*If Prison Walls Could Speak*) that, whilst he was languishing in a Communist prison in his native Rumania, a fellow Christian, who was being interrogated, was asked by his inquisitor: "Where is your God? Why doesn't he perform a miracle?" The Christian replied: "You have a great miracle before your eyes, but you are blind. You mock and beat me. I look at you with love. That is the miracle."

Almost the last words of Jesus from the cross were: "Forgive them Father, for they know not what they do." But the crucifiers of Christ knew very well what they were doing. The miracle inherent in Christ's words was not that he asked God to forgive them, but that his love was so strong that he made excuses for their behaviour.

Miracles that call for the reversal of God's laws are out. If just one natural law could be revoked, where would it all end? Reverse the behaviour of the atom and the whole Universe would be destroyed. The Universe was made to run on its own, with no pilot at the controls, no navigator on the bridge, no captain at the helm. Would it not be foolish to mess around with such an exquisite "self-regulating" system?

"The laws of the Universe," wrote the late Leslie D. Weatherhead in 1944 (*The Will of God*), "which are themselves an expression of God's will were not set aside for Jesus, the beloved Son. The laws which govern the hammering in of nails held on the day of Crucifixion in just the same way as they do when you nail up a wooden box. If bombs are dropped from an aeroplane over the closely built dwellings in a city, they pierce the roof of the godly and of the ungodly, and if nails are hit with a hammer wielded by a strong arm, they pierce the flesh even of the Son of God; and because the laws of the Universe are operating and because these laws are an expression of God's will, when Christ's flesh was lacerated on the Cross, the laws of God in regard to pain operated just as they do when we get hurt."

If God would not set aside universal laws to save Jesus, is it likely that he would have permitted Jesus to set aside universal laws just to provide enough wine at a wedding feast, just to see that his followers had a square meal, just to . . . need I go on?

The healing stories are, however, a different matter. It is a medically acknowledged fact that the mind has a powerful effect on the body. Many miraculous cures have been brought about by sheer willpower and faith. Patients with terminal illnesses have recovered in a way that has completely baffled the medical profession. Incurable cancers have shrivelled and disappeared, healthy tissues replacing the diseased. But such cures are not miracles in the sense of direct divine intervention to reverse the laws of nature. They are not supernatural events. Willpower and faith make a dynamic combination, capable of reversing the natural effects of disease *naturally*. If people can will themselves to die (which they can), they can will themselves to live (which they do).

Christ had a dynamic, charismatic persona, and it should come as no surprise to learn that he also had the power of healing, though I do not accept all the healing stories exactly as recorded. Christ's ability to heal the sick would depend on the sick possessing faith in his powers to heal. It was the faith between healer and healed that did the healing, not Christ's power to heal. Christ was a faith healer not a witch doctor. As for those who were raised from the dead—Lazarus, for example—reason tells us that they could not have been well and truly dead. The well and truly dead remain dead. For my part, I am prepared to believe (and do believe) those healing stories that do not offend against reason. Further than that, this skeptical writer is not prepared to go.

We are now ready to begin our summing up. For the writer, this is the moment of truth. The identity of Jesus is something that has intrigued me for more than fifty years. Brought up as a Christian, I accepted the dogma of the divinity of Jesus until I was well into my teens. It wasn't until then that I began to seriously question what I had been taught as a child.

I could not believe that a human being, however good or

holy, could be God. But then, of course, Jesus did not say he was God. In fact, as we have seen, he said that he wasn't. Hurdle number one over!

Jesus did, however, imply that he was the Son of God, the capital S being inferred when he said: "No man cometh unto the Father, but by me." This brings us back to the question: What does it mean to say that Christ was the Son of God?

It simply isn't good enough for me to keep saying that I am a Christian if I don't know what it means to say that I am a Christian. It is time now to come off the fence.

I have never doubted that Jesus was unique. Yes, I know that, as we are all different, we are therefore all unique. But Jesus was uniquely unique. There has never been anyone like him in the recorded annals of history. But that is not the same as saying that he was the Son of God. Son of God? Definition, please.

Now, I guess that if I had any sense, I would end this chapter right now. For I have asked a question that only God can definitively answer. (But then, perhaps he has, through his Son; Jesus Christ?)

But that would be intellectual cowardice, I have to reach some kind of subjective truth, even if it is not objectively true. So, knowing the impossibility of trying to answer an unanswerable question, this is what I shall endeavour to do.

First, let us get this one out of the way straightway: Jesus was not God. He couldn't have been. Being human, he was limited. He was not a master mathematician, a master geometrician, a master physicist, a master biologist—all of which he would have to have been if he were God. God is not only love, he is other things besides. Omnipotence. Omniscience. Omnipresence. Only the last of these attributes could Christians reasonably claim for Jesus.

Christ was a man of and for his times. He was a first-century Jew, with a first-century mind, living in a first-century world. He related to his contemporaries in a way that they could understand. His knowledge of this world was finite, as was his knowledge of the next. How could it be otherwise? He was a human being, with all the limitations that this implies. He knew and understood only what his human nature allowed him to know and understand. He was restricted to the capacity of the human mind, the human heart, and the human soul.

As I have said, it is my belief that Jesus was born the natural son of Joseph and Mary. But as he grew from childhood through youth to adulthood, I think he must have gradually become aware of an acute sense of oneness with the Father (he may even have felt it in the cradle, without of course knowing what it was that he felt). He knew, or thought he knew, that he enjoyed a unique relationship with God, and that his mission in life was to reveal to the world the nature of God—or at least, that part of God's nature which we humans, in our limited way, are capable of understanding.

I do not think that this mission was thrust upon Jesus. He accepted it voluntarily. He could have refused had he wished, although being what he was, it would have been impossible for him to have done so. In other words, the choosing was his but the choice wasn't. That is the paradox: He had no choice but to BECOME the Son of God. He wasn't *born* the Son of God, he *became* the Son of God.

I think the die was cast in the desert, when for forty days Christ wrestled with the devil (the devil in his case being the humanitarian and humanistic impulses within him), finally uttering those fateful words: "Get thee hence, Satan." How easy it would have been for Jesus to have become the kind of Messiah his countrymen had been expecting. To have led a populist uprising against the Roman oppressors. To have devoted himself to good works and social reform instead of spiritual redemption. At that moment, Jesus decided to reject the world of Caesar and all that it had to offer, and to give his life ineluctably to the kingdom of God.

I do not believe that God deliberately interceded in the affairs of man at that particular time, at that particular place. That would be to see God in human, temporal, and spatial terms. I do not think that these things happen that way. What happened, happened when it did and where it did, because that is when and where Jesus was born. Jesus was the spiritual catalyst. His appearance on the cosmic scene flowed naturally and supernaturally from the necessity of spiritual evolution.

Jesus was born to be the Son of God, just as, in an earthly

sense, Prince Charles was born to be king but wasn't a king when he was born, and can, if he wishes, refuse kingship if and when it is thrust upon him. Similarly, Jesus, in a spiritual sense, was born to be the Son of God but could have rejected Sonship had he wished. Christ's inheritance inhered in his being who and what he was, but the inheritance did not become effective until it was consummated by his acceptance.

Jesus wasn't born with a spiritual spoon in his mouth. He earned the right to become (or to be: the past, present and future are all one in the world of the spirit) the only begotten Son of the Father, by virtue of his unique God orientatedness, his absolute loyalty, dedication, and devotion to the Father, and, most important, his unique insight into the God-man relationship—how man was meant to relate to God and to his fellow men. He grew into Sonship (although it could be argued that if his spiritual genes were inherent, so was his Sonship.) Jesus "adopted" God as his Father, and, in doing so, God became his Father, his supernatural Father, and he God's supernatural Son. We are not talking here about sons and fathers in an earthly sense, with mortal flesh and blood and chromosomes. Having sprung from the loins of Joseph and the womb of Mary, Jesus could not have been anyone's earthly son but theirs. We are talking about immortal, supernatural genes, where the laws of inheritance are different. Jesus inherited his Sonship retroactively, a case of effect coming before cause and, in achieving Sonship, acquired Sonship AT BIRTH in a way not possible in this time-structured existence of ours.

The miracle of Jesus is that he was not God but an ordinary human being. If he were God, there would have been no merit in his being what he was, and we would never have known the exquisite heights to which man's spirituality was capable of rising. By becoming the Son of God, he showed us the possibilities open to humankind. If a human being can get that close to God without actually being God, then there is some hope for the future of the human race.

Was Christ, then, the Son of God?

The reader may feel that I am shilly-shallying, that I am avoiding answering the question directly. The problem is that most meaningful questions are not given to straight yes or no answers. So let me try again: If by Son of God is meant that Christ was God or co-equal with God or God in person, then my answer is an unequivocal no. But if is meant that Christ was uniquely at one with (though not one and the same as) God, that he communed with God on a level or in a dimension unfamiliar to other mortals, that he revealed to the world the nature of God, not as it is in its objective entirety but AS IT RELATES TO HUMAN BEINGS, then the answer is an unequivocal yes. In short, my feelings can best be summed up in that mind-tingling aphorism of Gerald Priestland's: "In Jesus, God is saying: 'I am like this. I am *so* like this that, so far as you can understand, I *am* this.'"

To sum up: I think that Christ was born the son of man (and woman) but died the Son of God. He inherited Sonship when he accepted Sonship. And in accepting, his acceptance was "backdated" to the day he was born.

The relationship between God and Jesus cannot be defined; language is inadequate for such a task. Perhaps John V. Taylor (vide *Priestland's Progress*), speaking of the likely thoughts of the disciples after the death of Jesus, came as close as we ever can:

WHATEVER IS TRUE OF GOD, WE HAVE SEEN IT IN THIS MAN. THERE IS A LINK BETWEEN THIS MAN AND GOD THAT IS CLOSER THAN ANYTHING WE HAVE EVER KNOWN.

Postscript:

It is Christmas Day 1987, and I have just come across the following passage in Malcolm Muggeridge's *Conversion: A Spiritual Journey,* which so perfectly encapsulates my immediate mood that I make no apology for introducing it here.

"And you? What do I know of You? A living presence in the world; the One who, of all the billions of the human family came most immediately from God and went most immediately to God, while remaining most humanly and intimately here among us today, as yesterday and tomorrow; for all time. Did you live and die and rise from the dead as they say? Who knows, or, for that matter, cares? History is for the dead, and You are alive. Similarly, all those churches raised and maintained in Your name, from the tiniest, weirdest conventicle to the great cathedrals rising so sublimely into the sky—they are for the dead, and must themselves die; are, indeed, dying fast. They belong to time, You to eternity. At the intersection of time and eternity—nailed there—You confront us; a perpetual reminder that, living, we die and dying, we live. An incarnation wonderful to contemplate; the light of the world, indeed."

These sublime words show just how irrelevant the question "Was Christ the Son of God?" really is. As if it matters whether Jesus was the Son of God or the son of a carpenter. How foolish to spend so much time trying to unravel a mystery that cannot be unravelled. The important thing for Christians, surely, is: to respond to Jesus and live their lives AS IF HE WERE the Son of God.

Son of God? Light of the world? What's in a name? When we feel the beautiful rays of the summer sun shining down on us on a lovely summer's day, does it matter who put the sun in the sky and why it shines so gloriously? It may matter intellectually to the physicist, but does it matter to the sun worshipper lying on the beach soaking up the sun? And when we soak up the spiritual rays of the Son of the Father, does it matter whether we spell "Son" with a capital *S* or a small *s*?

"For me," says Hans Küng (*Does God Exist?*), "Jesus of Nazareth is the *Son of God*. For the whole significance of what happened in and with him lies in the fact that in Jesus . . . . the God who loves men is *himself present and active: through him, God himself has spoken, acted, definitively revealed himself.*"

Son of God? Son of man? What does it matter?

Chapter 11

Is There Any Future for Mankind?

From now on every generation will be aware that it could be the last generation on earth.
Stuart Blanche, Archbishop of York (Feb. 10, 1983).

The Stone Age may return on the gleaming wings of science.
Winston S. Churchill

"Is there any future for mankind?" is not the rhetorical question it used to be. The threat of nuclear annihilation hangs over the world like a sword of Damocles. It has often been said that man is at the crossroads; but this time he really is. One false move and it could all go sky-high. We can no longer take the survival of the human race for granted.

It took Homo sapiens millions of years to evolve, and a few thousand years to come of age. Yet since we first split the atom less than sixty years ago (yes, that's all it is) we have advanced technologically further than we did in the whole of our previous history. Unfortunately we have advanced morally and spiritually not at all. Had our spirituality kept pace with our technological progress we would have now entered a new golden age, instead of which, we stand poised on the brink of oblivion. How ironical it is that man's greatest technological achievement is the invention of the means to commit suicide.

The good old days when we could cheerfully decimate a whole generation without batting a (spiritual) eyelid, are over. It only needs one error of judgement, one miscalculation, one act of insanity, for the road to come to an abrupt halt, a literal dead end. Can it be avoided? The whole of human history would suggest that it cannot. Some day, somewhere, it seems inevitable

298

that some lunatic will press the button. And the human race will go the way of the dinosaur, which, after all, was around for some forty million years before evolution decided to call it a day.

But man is not entirely evil. Nor is he entirely stupid. "Looking at the violence of man," writes Karl Jaspers (*Philosophy is for Everyman*), " . . . it is a miracle that men have ever produced anything but hordes of bandits. Yet they have managed to create orderly political conditions, have founded constitutional states, communities of citizens. Mighty forces of quite a different order must be at work in them to produce these capacities."

But will these "mighty forces" be mighty enough? Frankly, if we have to rely on the *morality* of man to deter us from pushing the self-destruct button then I am afraid there is little hope that I can see of saving the human race. There is absolutely no chance that men will turn to God in such a dramatic fashion. Damascus road conversions do happen, but only with individuals, not with mankind en masse.

The glimmer of hope is self-preservation, the most powerful instinct within the human breast. We all want to live; no one wants to die; and you don't pull the trigger if the gun is pointing at your own head. Better of course that the gun didn't exist, but it does; it cannot be disinvented. The policy is called Mutual Assured Destruction, MAD for short. Whether it is quite so mad in practice is a matter of political judgement, something outside the parameters of this discussion, which is concerned only with the relationship between humankind and God, not with political or national considerations.

The world is living on borrowed time, and knowing that this generation really could be the last generation on Earth, is it beyond the wit of the world's leaders to build on that? After all, they are human beings, just like us, with as much vested interest in survival as we have.

But it is not just to the wit of the world leaders we should be looking. We all have a duty to take a long hard look at ourselves—yes, ourselves, not our perceived enemies—and ask what contribution we in our hearts make to world peace. For it is in the hearts of men not on the battlefields that wars begin.

The perceived belief that wars are caused by one particularly evil and aggressive nation bent on world domination, or by a power-mad dictator, a handful of crazed fanatics, or by forces intent on economic and financial aggrandisement, is a fallacy. That such influences do indeed exist and do variably contribute to the causes of war, is undeniable. But the unpleasant truth is that violence is endemic in human nature, and war is simply an extreme form of violence.

This is not to suggest that human beings actually want war or enjoy war (though it is true to say that some do). But it is a fact that the nearer we are to the battlefield the less we enjoy it; and the further we are from the battlefield the less we oppose it. Now I am not saying that it is wrong to defend oneself, one's family, one's country; or that one who kills in defence of his homeland, his hearth, his loved ones, is as culpable as one who kills in attacking someone else's homeland, hearth, and loved ones. The problem is, however, that we don't always know whether we are attacking or defending. Wars aren't usually so clear-cut as that. How many wars have been fought where both sides did not sincerely believe that their cause was just, that the other side was the aggressor? A question to the reader, whoever you are, whatever your nationality: Has *your* country ever fought an unjust war? (What—never?)

The causes of war are multifarious. And the circumstances and conditions that lead to war, and that includes terrorism and urban violence, can never be analysed with complete dispassion and objectivity. Inevitably one's analysis will depend on one's nationality, one's political views, one's religious beliefs. It will also be influenced by one's status, whether one is privileged or underprivileged, the oppressor or the oppressed, a "have" or a "have not." While there are wrongs (real or imagined) to be righted, there will never be a shortage of men willing to resort to violence to redress the wrongs perceived to have been committed against them. One man's freedom fighter is another man's terrorist. Not all freedom fighters are terrorists. And not all terrorists are freedom fighters.

In any dispute—international, regional, political, or personal—no one country, party or person is ever one hundred percent right, and the other one hundred percent wrong. If the reader thinks that his country or political party or particular point of view is always right and never wrong, or that his opponent is always wrong and never right, then he must be extraordinarily foolish and arrogant and know nothing about human fallibility.

Most people want to live their lives in peace and tranquility. Yet it is equally true that most of us are prepared to go to war or approve violence carried out in the name of the state should the cause be just. (Whether or not the cause is just is always a matter of opinion.) And what cannot be denied is that all wars, defensive or aggressive, rely implicitly on the violence endemic in human nature for their successful prosecution. (How else could we have defeated Nazi Germany? How else could the Falklands have been recaptured?)

One can, of course, argue that it is a good thing there are men and women prepared to fight and die for freedom and justice. But what if the freedom and justice fought and died for are bogus and not real? And even if they are real, is it morally right to take the lives of others in order that freedom and justice might prevail? It is not an easy question to answer. At least, it isn't for this writer.

Someone once said—I think it was C. S. Lewis—that unfortunately the man who is prepared to die for a cause is also the man who is prepared to kill for a cause. The brute fact is that were it not for the stratum of violence that lies just beneath the surface of human nature, it would not be possible to wage war of any description, neither aggressive nor defensive. It is man's sad contradictory nature that makes war not only possible but inevitable. "Drain the blood from men's veins," said Tolstoy, "and put in water instead, then there will be no more war."

Why are men so attracted to violence? Why do we get a vicarious thrill out of violent deeds committed on our behalf? Why are we so willing to commit violence by proxy when we are too fastidious, to cowardly, to do it ourselves? Why for that matter do little boys like playing with guns? (Little boys instinctively play with guns, just as little girls instinctively play with dolls. When I was a child I can clearly remember the pleasurable feeling of power and aggression that welled up within my young breast. Of course, it is possible that if little boys were forbidden to play with guns, within a few generations the desire to play with guns would be directed into other channels. But the basic aggressive instinct would not disappear; it would simply manifest itself in other destructive ways.)

It in only in time of war that man gets the opportunity of expressing his total nature. No other form of human endeavour allows him to gratify all his instincts, base and noble, so completely. Climb Mount Everest and my desire for conquest and achievement is completely satisfied. But what about the darker side of my nature? That will not be satisfied by climbing a mountain.

War is evil, barbaric, and obscene. But it also produces enormous acts of courage and self-sacrifice. In war, man is able to indulge the darker side of his nature without attracting the stigma attached to barbarous acts committed in time of peace. Kill a man in peacetime and you are sent to prison. Kill a man in battle and you are given a medal.

Throughout man's history, war has been regarded (by noncombatants, at least) as heroic and glorious.

Pride, pomp, and circumstance of glorious war!
Shakespeare (*Othello*)

Battle's magnificently stern array!
Byron (*Childe Harold*)

You may think there are greater things than war. I do not; I worship the Lord of Hosts.
Benjamin Disraeli (*Coningsby*)

Terrible as is war, it yet displays the spiritual grandeur of man daring to defy his mightiest hereditary enemy—Death.
Heine (*Wit, Wisdom and Pathos*)

Ye say, a good cause will hallow even war? I say unto you: a good war halloweth every cause. War and courage have done more great things than charity.
Nietzsche (*Thus Spake Zarathustra:
Of War and Warriors*)

War is elevating, because the individual disappears before the

302

great conception of the state . . . What a perversion of morality
to wish to abolish heroism among men!

Treitschke (Politics)

Once more unto the breach, dear friends, once more;
Or close the wall up with our English dead.
In peace there's nothing so becomes a man
As modest stillness and humility:
But when the blast of war blows in our ears,
Then imitate the action of the tiger,
Stiffen the sinews, summon up the blood . . .

Shakespeare (Henry V)

Yes, war is glorious, all right! Unless, that is, it is your
bayonet that is stuck into someone's stomach; or someone else's
bayonet that is stuck into yours. (Funny how it is the poets and
thinkers who glorify war, never the mothers and wives of the
sons and husbands who have to do the dying. Funny also, how
age and proximity to the battlefield affect our attitude to war.
Who was it that said that wars are started by old men and fought
by young men?)

War brings out the worst and the best in human nature.
Hate and intolerance, love and sacrifice, they are all there in
infamous and glorious abundance. The paradox is enough to
make one weep!

Not wanting war is not quite the same as wanting peace,
just as not wanting to die is not the same as wanting others to
live. We ought to be motivated by more than self-interest. If we
were truly and passionately dedicated to peace, other's as well
as our own, we would be more concerned about ending the conditions that lead to war. (Hitler may have started the last war
but who created the conditions that created Hitler? And who
created the conditions that spawn the murderous psychopaths
of the IRA?) Wars will only cease when there is a fundamental
change in human nature. But how can we change our nature if
we don't know that it needs to be changed?

There is no clear dividing line between peace and war. The
line is not just blurred; it doesn't exist. Light greys run into dark
greys; dark greys into blacks; there are no whites. Wars are like
volcanoes. They rumble away beneath the surface until, unable

303

to restrain the pent-up ferocity of inner tensions, they erupt in an orgy of destruction. Violence is always there, like a wild beast waiting to be unleashed.

Violence has a long pedigree. And, like a river, it has many tributaries. It is all of a piece. We cannot extract one tiny particle, put it under the microscope and examine it without reference to the other particles that go to make up the whole. The ingredients are always the same—anger, greed, frustration, jealousy, hatred, fear—only the mix is different.

Violence begets violence. One act of violence leads to another, and another . . . the sequence is endless. "For what can war but endless war still breed?" (Milton: *Sonnets: To Lord Fairfax.*) We are quick to condemn violence and the men of violence, but not so quick to recognize that we all, in one way or another, in one degree or another, help to produce or sustain the conditions in which violence flourishes. Everyone who encourages or condones violence, or whatever scale, in whatever form, physical, mental, social, psychological or verbal; everyone who tolerates injustice or fertilizes the soil in which the seeds of violence take root; everyone who indulges in hatred, malice, intolerance or a desire for revenge; helps stoke up the boiler which, when overheated, explodes into confrontation, violence and war. And when a civilized society resorts to violence or war in the common good or for a noble cause, with the justification that it is the lesser of two evils, let us never forget that that is what it is—an evil.

If war, then, is undeniably evil, are not the pacifists right? Should we not refuse to fight, whatever the circumstance, however just the cause? Did not Jesus say "Love one another," "Turn the other cheek," "Blessed are the peacemakers"?

Yes. But he never specifically condemned war. Why not? Because Jesus refused to legislate, and it would be quite improper for me or anyone else to legislate on his behalf.

The Christian nonpacifist is now getting a little hot under the collar. He is beginning to feel stifled by the absolutism of the commands of Christ. How can anyone, he asks himself, possibly justify the obscenity of war? How can the wholesale killing and mutilation of innocent human beings be anything but evil?

But, of course, it's not quite so easy as that, as the following dialogue (real, not imagined) between me and myself will show.

Me:	You know as well as I do that war is evil; so why don't you condemn it unequivocally? Why all this nauseating nonsense about Christ not legislating?
Myself:	Well, he didn't.
Me:	You are not suggesting, are you, that Jesus was not against war?
Myself:	No.
Me:	Surely the reason why Jesus didn't legislate was because he didn't need to? He didn't specifically say that it was wrong to kill babies, but we may reasonably assume that he thought it was?
Myself:	Of course.
Me:	And when Jesus said "Love one another," may we not also assume that he didn't regard the dropping of bombs on one's fellow human beings as an appropriate way of expressing that love?
Myself:	Agreed. But . . .
Me:	What do you mean, "But"? Here we are living in the shadow of nuclear annihilation, looking to Jesus for a way out of our appalling predicament, and all you can say is "Jesus didn't legislate!" These theological niceties may have been all right in the days of the bow and arrow, but frankly, in these desperately dangerous nuclear times, I find them quite obscene. A direct question and a direct answer, if you please! Do you think it could ever be morally right, in any circumstances, for any reason, for any cause, however righteous, however just, for any person or any nation to press the nuclear button and obliterate millions of men, women, and children, even perhaps the whole human race?
Myself:	No.
Me:	So at least you are against the use of the nuclear bomb?
Myself:	Yes—and bows and arrows.
Me:	So you are an out-and-out pacifist?
Myself:	No.

Me:	What do you mean, No?
Myself:	It's bit complicated.
Me:	Try me.
Myself:	When Christ said "Love one another," he was giving an absolute command which allows of no deviation. You see, Jesus dealt with absolutes. "Love one another," to Jesus, meant "Love one another," not "It is wrong to murder millions but okay to murder one." Or "Atom bombs are wrong but bows and arrows are okay." Jesus was not concerned with the laws or arithmetic. To him, one person was the whole human race. Now, I know I will be taken to task by the atheists, the humanists, and the utilitarians. They will say that there is a vast difference between killing one person and wiping out the whole human race. And of course they are right, as any sensible person would agree. But not Jesus. He would not be drawn into that kind of specious argument. To the atheist, "Love one another" is a worthy sentiment, but one that is impossible to put into practice in the world in which we live. And with the enormous nuclear arsenals just waiting for some lunatic to press the button and blow us all to kingdom come (figuratively speaking, of course), the sentimental Sunday school platitudes of Jesus are not sufficient to prevent the human race from destroying itself. In this twentieth-century nuclear age, Christ's simplistic well-meaning aphorisms have no relevance.
Me:	What you have just said only strengthens my argument. The only way we can ensure that the human race survives to "love one another," is to destroy all nuclear weapons. That surely makes sense.
Myself:	Agreed. But that is substituting "survival" for "morality." I mean, where do you draw the moral line between killing one person and killing the entire human race? If it is morally acceptable to kill one person, why not two persons, two hundred,

306

two million, two thousand million? Where do you stop? When you have run out of people to kill? Because there is no moral logical limit. It is as morally wrong to kill one human being as it is to kill the entire human race. You see, I am talking about morality not expediency. Now, if you do it Christ's way, you don't get involved in the problem of where to draw the line between what is morally acceptable and what isn't, because the killing doesn't even start. Whose way then is the most sensible?

Me: Look, are you against nuclear weapons or not?

Myself: I am. But if you get rid of the world's total atomic armaments, the moral problem will not be touched. And even if we put morality on the backburner for the moment, the problem of war will not be solved. We will simply revert to the good old days of a conventional world war every twenty years or so.

Me: That's nonsense. We have come a long way since 1945.

Myself: You must be joking! Were it not for the atom bomb, the Americans and Russians would have been at each other's throats many times during the past forty-odd years. Have you forgotten the Berlin blockade, the Cuban crisis, the invasion of Czechoslovakia, of Hungary, of Poland? You are surely not suggesting that men have suddenly found a miraculous moral formula for settling their differences without resorting to the use of force? Because if you are, just take a look around the world today. There are more wars in progress, more acts of terrorism and violence than at any time in man's history. How's that for moral progress? If you think that the unprecedented period of peace that Europe has enjoyed since the last war is due to man having reached a higher moral plateau, and not to his fear of the ghastly consequences of

307

	a nuclear conflagration, then you have a much higher opinion of human nature than I have.
Me:	What cynicism!
Myself:	I'm sorry, but when you've been around as long as I have, you are apt to notice that the cynic has a lot to be cynical about.
Me:	I've been around just as long as you have, and I must say that I find your cynicism quite appalling. Frankly, I would have expected something better from a Christian.
Myself:	Criticism accepted. Strike my last remark from the record.
Me:	Let's get back to the crux of the argument. Are you suggesting that if Christ were alive today, he would approve of atomic weapons and oppose efforts to get rid of them; and that he would say that it was no more wrong to wipe out the entire human race with nuclear bombs than it was to kill one person with a bow and arrow?
Myself:	No, for the simply reason that you couldn't catch Jesus with that kind of question. I believe he would have responded with a parable, the essence of which would have been "Love one another," which, as I say, is an absolute command. Now if you say that it is an impossible command, I agree. But the fault lies with us not with Jesus. Exactly what Jesus meant by "Love one another," is for each of us as an individual wrestling with his or her own conscience to decide. Sometimes it is easy; often it isn't. For instance, in the last war, Dietrich Bonhoeffer, the German Christian martyr, took part in the plot to kill Hitler. His conscience told him that this was the right thing to do. But how did this square with "loving one another"? Was he loving Hitler by trying to kill him?
Me:	We seem to be going round in circles.
Myself:	I know. That is the trouble with Jesus. You keep coming back to the beginning. In the beginning was the Word . . .

| Me: | You're getting me even more confused now. |
| Myself: | Me, too. |

This internal dialogue between me and myself shows the dilemma that Christians face when making choices. Jesus lays down absolutes; and then leaves it to each of us to interpret these absolutes as best our fallible human nature will permit. I know it is wrong to kill, but is it wrong to kill one evil person if by doing so the lives of thousands of innocent people are saved? Is a soldier justified in killing a terrorist engaged in murdering and maiming scores of innocent men, women and children? If a madman were about to press the nuclear button, would I be justified in shooting him dead? In other words, does the end justify the means? Christians have always believed that it doesn't. Were Bonhoeffer and his friends wrong, then, in plotting to kill Hitler? What they planned to do was wrong, but were they wrong in planning to do it? I do not know. It is not for me to judge the actions of men much better and braver than I.

You may be wondering where all this philosophizing about violence and war is leading us. We do not live in an ideal world of gentle, loving, and forgiving creatures. And it's no good pretending we do. But we have to start somewhere. And it would be a mistake to assume that because we can't change human nature overnight, we can't do anything. There is something we can do. Right now. We can see ourselves as we really are, and not as we like to think we are. Whilst we are so certain of our own perfection, we are less likely to show a spirit of tolerance and understanding towards those whom we believe to be less perfect than we are.

Those whom we perceive to be our enemies, may be wrong. They may even be evil. But if we are to live in peace, we should first make an effort to remove the mote from our own eye, before demanding that they remove the beam from theirs.

Thankfully, there has been a dramatic improvement in East-West relations in the past few years. No longer are we living on the daily knife edge of nuclear annihilation. It is fervently to be hoped that the new processes of democratization taking place in the Soviet Union and other Eastern bloc countries will prevail, and that we will all seize the opportunity of making the world a safer place in which to live.

Whatever our individual views on nuclear disarmament, we would all agree that it is in everyone's interests for the insane arms race to be halted. Now that the climate of fear, mistrust and hatred has improved and the sterile deadlock broken, we have at last a chance of breaking the pernicious habit of settling our disputes by force, and of getting used to the idea of peace. Now, perhaps, peace might become addictive and world disarmament a real possibility.

Of course, peace in Europe is not world peace. But it is a step in the right direction. If the West and the Soviet Union can find a way of accommodating each other's hopes and fears, and of working together for peace, then it should have a tremendous psychological effect on the rest of the world. Pupils are never on their best behaviour when they see the teachers fighting amongst themselves.

And so it may be that the very instrument of destruction that has brought the human race to the verge of extinction, might prove to be our salvation. For what we cannot bring ourselves to do out of love, we may be forced to do out of fear.

The message is there, writ large, for all to see. Ignore it and our civilization could come to an abrupt end. Can man really be that wicked, that stupid, that insane?

What we desperately need is breathing space; a probationary period of a few hundred or few thousand years to allow our spiritually to catch up. Perhaps we may be granted this time. But if we are, we shall have to earn it! And we won't earn it unless we make a determined effort for peace. Simply to be prepared to fight for freedom and democracy or whatever is not enough. In the long term the disease of war can only be eradicated by a massive change of heart.

And that means mine and yours.

Hate and aggression are endemic in the human soul. But so is love. And therein lies the hope for mankind. We must give love a chance. Allow it to grow. To spread from one individual to another, from one nation to another. Love is God's presence in man, the most powerful force in the Universe, the only thing that is seen to make complete and utter sense.

"Love one another" is not a sugary sentimental slogan, a redolent echo from the swinging sixties. It is a cry from the cross. The ultimate expression of faith. What binds man to man, and man to God. "Lovingness," says Malcolm Muggeridge (*Conversion: A Spiritual Journey*), " ... [is] an awareness of having, with others, a common purpose and a common destiny; seeing fellow human beings, whoever and whatever they may be [yes, and that includes the Nazi goons—E.C.], as belonging to a family to which we all belong, love being what binds us together, besides binding us to God, our Creator. Love, that is to say, is not only the condition for a perfect relationship between God and man, but also unfolds the essential nature of God Himself, manifest to us in our mortal existence but transcending our mortality."

What is love?

I would like to relate a story told by a Jewish lady who was incarcerated with her daughter in a Nazi concentration camp during the last war.

The woman managed on one occasion to get hold of a bowl of soup, which she gave to her daughter. But the daughter refused it, insisting that the mother had it instead. Neither would give way, until they realized that this would mean that both would be deprived of the soup. So they agreed to share it, taking alternate spoonfuls. But the daughter noticed that the mother was taking a smaller amount in her spoon. So she refused to eat anymore; and the mother followed suit. The only way they could resolve the problem was to each feed the other, and so every spoon was full.

The two women survived, and when the camp was liberated by the Americans shortly afterwards, some of the demented inmates set upon a German woman and tried to kill her baby whom she was walking in a pram. The Jewish mother was distraught. "This can't be right," she screamed. "The baby is innocent!"

An American padre came by with some GIs. "How did you manage to preserve this love?" he asked the woman. "I think it was love that preserved me," she replied.

If the reader wants an example of the power of love, he need look no further.

Another example: As an ally of Nazi Germany in the last

war, Rumania, too, was guilty of horrendous attrocities against the Jews. Towards the end of the war, when the Germans had been all but brought to their knees, Rumania severed her alliance with Germany and decreed that any person concealing members of the German army would be liable to the death penalty. A number of German girl soldiers (Blitzmädchen) appealed to Pastor Wurmbrand, a Rumanian Christian Jew, to shelter them, to save them from being deported to Russia. "Naturally," said the Pastor, "we did so." (Source: Richard Wurmbrand's *Christ on the Jewish Road.*)

Why "naturally?" Would it not have been more natural for a Jew, half of whose own family had been murdered by the Nazis, to hand over Nazi soldiers to the Communists? What's natural about risking your life to save an enemy? A friend, yes. But an enemy?

Finally: On Sunday November 8, 1987, an IRA bomb exploded at a Remembrance Day service in Enniskillen, Northern Ireland. Eleven innocent people were killed and sixty-four injured. A Mr. Gordon Wilson and his daughter, Maria, a twenty-year-old student nurse, lay buried beneath the rubble. Unable to move, they held hands, until Maria died. Her last words to her father were: "I love you very much." Next day, Mr. Wilson, in a TV interview that touched the hearts of the whole nation, if not the world, said: "I prayed for the bombers last night. I prayed that God will forgive them." No one who saw the broadcast will ever forget the anguish and pain etched on the face of this saintly man, and his plea for forgiveness for the men who had taken the life of his beloved daughter. There was no bitterness, no hatred—only love for the loved one he had lost, and forgiveness for her killers.

A year later, in memory of the occasion, Mr. Tom King, the then Secretary for Northern Ireland, said: "Mr. Wilson's broadcast was a shining example of Christian love."

The most remarkable aspect of this story, it seems to me, is not so much Mr. Wilson's love and forgiveness (we expect this from saints), but the fact that we lesser mortals (including Tom King), who cry out for justice and revenge in the face of inhuman attrocities, are able to recognize the authentic voice of Jesus; that, in spite of the fact that we want retribution, in our hearts we know it to be wrong. This I find the greatest hope for humankind.

The future of the world is in the balance. Never before has man been so truly master of his own fate. The age of reason has come and gone. The age of reckoning—the age that will separate the men from the apes—has arrived. That good will triumph in the end, I do not doubt. In the words of Jane Gow, wife of the British M.P. Ian Gow murdered by the I.R.A. twenty-four hours earlier: "We know that despite [the] seeming triumph of evil . . . right will always triumph. The ultimate battle has already been won." But that doesn't mean that the human species in its present state of anthropological development will be around to see it. It may well destroy itself before evolution decides that it is time for a new improved species to arise.

The case for pessimism is strong, and is encapsulated in this prophetic passage from the Victorian novelist George Gissing's *The Private Papers of Henry Ryecroft,* published in 1903: "I hate and fear 'science' because of my conviction that, for long to come if not forever, it will be the remorseless enemy of mankind. I see it destroying all simplicity and gentleness of life, all the beauty of the world; I see it restoring barbarism under a mask of civilization; I see it darkening men's minds and hardening their hearts; I see it bringing a time of vast conflicts, which will pale into insignificance 'the thousand wars of old,' and, as likely as not, will whelm all the laborious advances of mankind in blood-drenched chaos."

With two World Wars and Hiroshima yet to come, prescient words indeed! But from the same oscillating pen (ibid), these precious words of hope: "However one's heart may fail in thinking of the folly and baseness which make so great a part of today's world, remember how many bright souls are living courageously, seeing the good wherever it may be discovered, undismayed by portents, doing what they have to do with all their strength. In every land there are such, no few of them, a great brotherhood, without distinction of race or faith; for they, indeed, constitute the race of man, rightly designated, and their faith is one, the cult of reason and of justice. Whether the future is to them or to the talking anthropoid, no one can say. But they live and labour, guarding the fire of sacred hope."

It will be noticed that the agnostical Gissing doesn't mention God. He has no need to; his words are full of grace and godliness.

Is there any future for mankind? I believe there is. Not just because I am a supreme optimist (doom and gloom may reign in the short term but optimism must triumph in the end), but because I cannot believe that God would have gone to all the trouble of creating creatures capable of loving him and each other, and then let it all go to waste.

Love is the essence of the soul. It cannot be destroyed. And whilst there is just one human being on Earth capable of loving the Creator of Love, and of distinguishing between good and evil, right and wrong, then the human race will survive.

At least, that is my belief.

Addendum

This chapter has been somewhat overtaken by events. It was first completed way back in the dark days of the Cold War when Russia was an "evil empire" and Americans were "fascist bandits" and "capitalist warmongers," when the Eastern bloc countries were one vast prison camp, Soviet troops had invaded Afghanistan, and Cruise missiles were being installed on the continent of Europe, convincing many that the run-up to World War Three had begun.

Now that has all changed. The seeds of freedom and democracy are taking root (though some have fallen on stony ground) all over Eastern Europe and the U.S.S.R. A new era of reconciliation and understanding between East and West has begun. Peace at last is being given a chance. We have much to be thankful for. But we are not out of the woods yet.

With the coming of freedom and democracy have also come hatred, death and destruction. Ethnic violence and civil war have broken out in many parts of Eastern Europe and the Soviet Union. Atrocities being committed in some of the Asian republics of the Soviet empire are reminiscent of the worst excesses of the Nazis. There has been an upsurge of malignant anti-Semitism in Europe and outbreaks of Jewish programs in the Soviets. Even in the Western democracies, Jewish cemeteries have been defiled, tombstones daubed with swastikas, and newly-buried bodies dug up and desecrated. (The heart sinks; have we learned nothing from the Holocaust?)

Tyranny is dead! Long live tyranny! Yes, everything has changed—everything, that is, except everything. Unfortunately it will take more than the clinking of falling chains and the sniff of a ballot box to change the hearts of men. There is no direct correlation between freedom and morality. Freedom is a state of existence, not a moral or spiritual attribute. Free men are no less likely to commit evil deeds than men who are slaves. Indeed, more likely because the opportunities are greater.

Man's addiction to violence, coupled with his ability to destroy his own species, is still the greatest threat to the continued existence of humankind. The newly perceived problems of global pollution and ecological catastrophe, though daunting, are not insoluble. With intelligence and scientific know-how they can be solved. It will, however, take more than intelligence and scientific know-how to solve the problem of man's sinful nature.

Our condition is not terminal; it can be reversed. But it will need a lot of imagination and loads of goodwill. And it will require something else besides—a humbling of the human ego, a recognition that we are not, as is sometimes arrogantly assumed, the king-pins of the Universe, that we are, in fact, temporary tenants with nothing more than squatters' rights. We also need to understand that by rejecting God *in our hearts* we alienate ourselves from our spiritual roots. (It is in the heart alone that God is accepted or rejected. Atheists may think that by denying God they are rejecting God, but this is not always so; just as theists who profess to believe in God often prove by their actions that they are, in fact, rejecting God. "The gentle inquisitor cross in hand, [who] kindly burns his fellows and weeps for them" [Besterman, after Voltaire], is rejecting God totally and utterly, his rejection could not be more complete. In his hands the cross becomes an emblem of blasphemy. Injustice, fanaticism and cruelty, hallmarks of Christendom in the Middle Ages, have no place in the heart of a Christian. The Christian who celebrates the Eucharist with murder in his heart and blood on his hands, is not celebrating the Eucharist at all.)

Pollution of the human soul is a much greater threat to

315

humanity than pollution of the environment, and can only be overcome by bringing God back into the human arena. I am not talking here about going to church or singing hymns or "worshipping" God (all outward trappings of religiosity—nothing wrong in that), but of what goes on within the greatest cathedral of them all—the human heart. For it is here in the deepest recesses of the soul that the battle for survival will be fought and won or lost.

The nightmare of imminent nuclear annihilation, which has haunted us for over forty years, is now yesterday's bad dream. (Never mind that we still have enough nuclear warheads to destroy the world a dozen times over; never mind that for the inhabitants of Chernobyl the nuclear nightmare has already begun.) The war drums are silent, and swords, if not being beaten into ploughshares, are at least not being sharpened as ferociously as they were before.

What have we learned from all this? That it was the West's courage and determination not to give in to Soviet blackmail and aggression that finally brought the prospect of permanent peace within our grasp? That if we want freedom and democracy to survive we must be prepared to fight for them? That the only way to beat the bully is to stand up to him?

If that is what we have learned, then we have learned nothing. (We already knew, did we not, that in this world "appeasement," a lovely word that has acquired an awful meaning, only encourages aggression, that to dismantle one's defences is to invite attack, that to leave one's front door unlocked and unbolted is to attract the attention of every burglar in the neighbourhood?) The real lesson to be learned is that true freedom and peace reside in the heart. They are not achieved by force of arms or threats or political and economic reforms.

The difficulty that confronts the human race is that we live in two different worlds, on two different levels. The material world of the flesh insists that we, like all other members of the animal kingdom, in order to survive, must eat and drink and perform our bodily functions, satisfy our carnal desires, and carry out our reproductive duties. We have no alternative; we must obey the dictates of nature. This physical, nonmoral world demands that the fittest survive, that the strong be rewarded, and the weak be punished, that it is suicide for the lamb to lie down with the lion, that to turn the other cheek is to invite that that also be struck. The earthquake is oblivious of morality; the cruel sea knows nothing of right and wrong.

That is the way the world works. Dog is ordained to eat dog; lions are ordained to kill lambs; seas are ordained to be cruel.

In the other world which we inhabit—the unscientific supernatural world of the spirit—dogs do *not* eat dogs, lions *do* lie down with lambs, the strong are commanded to help the weak and take care of the sick. To turn the other cheek is not a fool thing to do but obligatory. And in this other world the redemptive power of love is absolute.

This dichotomy of two worlds existing side by side and constantly colliding means that, being both animal and spirit, with a foot in both camps, as it were, we are obliged to live in both worlds *simultaneously*. Hence the conflict. Our problem is: how can the human spirit rise above the demands and limitations of the selfish, greedy, hedonistic, hostile world, which is as much our home as the other supernatural world of the spirit? When these two worlds—one aggressive and nonmoral, the other spiritual and loving—are in direct competition, how are we to cope, what should we do? Fat lot of good it will do us to preach "love one another," when our enemies are standing on our doorsteps, waiting to break down our doors, rape our womenfolk, and kill our children. If that is what Jesus expected us to do, then he knew little of human nature.

Not being a professional theologian, I cannot answer this question. (If the professional theologians are honest, neither can they). Whether or not the human spirit can rise above the obligations of human animality, depends on the human in question and the strength and quality of his or her spirit. (For the author, for instance, it presents insuperable difficulties; but for someone like Mother Theresa, I doubt it presents any.)

There is no way that any of us, *on our own*, can overcome the "world of the flesh." But with help from "above," it can be done. It is for each one of us to decide how he or she can best tap into the rich source of universal love and goodness that is God, without which the world is doomed. Indeed, it is for each one of us to decide whether we want to.

Epilogue

I have been . . . haunted by the thought of how much there is that I would fain know, and how little I can hope to learn. The scope of knowledge has become so vast. I put aside nearly all physical investigation; to me it is naught, or only, at moments, a matter of idle curiosity. This would seem to be a considerable clearing of the field; but it leaves what is practically the infinite.

George Gissing

I hope that this book may have stimulated the imagination of those who feel that life is not just a meaningless meander through a purposeless Universe, that we are here for a reason, even if we do not know what that reason is.

"Man," wrote G. G. Simpson, "is the result of a purposeless and materialistic process that did not have him in mind. He was not planned." This I reject. Because it doesn't make sense.

I believe that everything—the Universe, life, death, joy, love, suffering, even evil—was planned. From start to finish. Everything is a purposeful part of the universal jigsaw. It all fits together. There is nothing, *absolutely nothing*, that does not make sense.

We are not, nor will be ever be, privy to the universal plan of the Universal Planner. The transient whiff of existence that we experience here on Earth is just a taste of things to come. What those things are I haven't the faintest idea. Nor has anyone else.

We do not know the meaning and purpose of life. But we may be sure that there is meaning, there is purpose. The nihilist, with his crazy notion of nothingness—no God, no good, no evil, no meaning, no purpose; and the atheist with his next-to-nothingness—no God, just nothingness incarnate, cut sorry figures. Even if they are right, they still cut sorry figures!

319

The nihilist is a self-confessed liar. "Those who deny Thee," wrote T. S. Eliot (*Murder in the Cathedral*), "could not deny, if Thou didst not exist; and their denial is never complete, for if it were so, they would not exist." And this from Berdyaev: "For man exists only if he is an image and reflection of God, he exists only if God exists. Let God be nonexistent, let man make of himself a God and no longer a man—his proper image will perish."

> If God does not exist
> Then man is God.
> And if man is God
> Then God help man.

"The Universe," wrote Sir James Jeans in his *The Mysterious Universe,* "begins to look more like a great thought than like a machine."

"In my youth," said Arthur Koestler (*Bricks to Babel, Epilogue,* 1983), "I regarded the Universe as an open book, printed in the language of physical equations, whereas now it appears to me as a text written in invisible ink, of which in our rare moments of grace we are able to decipher a small fragment."

The Universe is the universal whodunit. In the beginning, the scientists tell us, was radiation, helium and hydrogen (the "Physicists Trinity," as D. H. Jack liked to call them). "At the big bang itself," said Stephen W. Hawking (*A Brief History of Time*), "the Universe is thought to have had zero size, and so to have been infinitely hot." Now, physicists choose their words very carefully, they are not given to imprecision or hyperbole. So what, may we ask, does "zero size" mean? In physical terms, it means NOTHING. And "infinitely hot"? So hot that the heat CANNOT BE MEASURED. It seems to me, then, that if the Universe didn't physically exist and was so hot that its heat couldn't be measured then it was indeed nothing more (or rather, nothing less) than a "great thought." (Even the thoughts of mere mortals, which also do not physically exist, are sometimes too hot to handle—certainly some of Stephen Hawking's are!) If the Universe at the moment of creation did not physically exist, yet was infinitely hot, what better description could we have of an almighty idea, the only true miracle that has ever been performed?

Why did God create the Universe? Did he create it? How do we know it wasn't an accident? Quantum mechanics has demonstrated (or at least, scientists think it has) that events in the atom can happen uncaused. In which case, why not the Universe? What's good for the atomic goose is surely good for the universal gander. But then, does the Universe look as if it were uncaused? Admittedly we don't know what an uncaused universe might be expected to look like. But is it unreasonable to suggest that it wouldn't look like this? In other words, is it sensible to say that the Universe is a senseless creation? I do not think so.

Why life? Why human beings? Why were we put on this Earth? Simply to enjoy ourselves, to work, to make love, to suffer, to die? What of beauty, art, music, truth? Are these just phantoms of our imagination? And if they are, who created our imagination? Why do we imagine these things if they do not exist? Indeed, have we the ability to imagine things that do not exist? And what of the innocence and inquisitiveness of little children? Why are children innocent if innocence has no meaning? Why are they inquisitive if there is nothing to be inquisitive about? And what of love and compassion, goodness and morality? The questions are endless . . .

What has science to offer us? Nothing but facts. But what use are facts when it it truth that we seek? To discover how and when the Universe was created will not tell us why or for what purpose it was created. Nor will it bring us closer to the God who created it. If we are to "close the gap," it will be through the heart not the intellect that the gap will be closed.

And medical science? Well, even if we found a cure for everything, we still have to die from something. There is no cure for death, the Grim Reaper will never be made redundant.

Suppose that the human life-span is eventually extended to, say, one hundred years, two hundred years . . . and that poverty and starvation are finally eliminated from the face of the Earth (but not earthquakes, tidal waves and floods of course. We have no control over them.) What then? Will it make us better human beings? Indeed, will it make us happier? Will it make us turn our swords into ploughshares? Turn the other cheek? Love our neighbour as ourselves? It will not. It will have no effect whatsoever on the moral dimension of man. Man is not just a physical creation. (Better for him perhaps if he were!) Good health and long life are wonderful things. But they are conditions not conclusions.

What is truth? No one knows. We only see a part of the truth, a distortion of the truth. What is true for one person may be untrue for another. What is true in one circumstance may be untrue in another. Human beings perceive only their perception of the truth. The truth itself is unknowable.

The Universe is a mystery. Life is a mystery. And God is the biggest mystery of all. Don't, I pray, be deceived by the sometimes arrogant assertions of the scientists. They do not know, nor will they ever know, the answers to the most important questions in life. "Even if *all possible* scientific questions be answered," said Wittgenstein (*Tractatus*), "the problems of life have still not been touched at all. Of course there is then no question left, and just this is the answer."

"Between us and our God," said the ancient mystic, "there is . . . a Cloud of Unknowing . . . Of God Himself can no man think . . . He may well be loved but not thought. By love may He be gotten and holden, but by thought neither . . . The most godly knowing of God is that which is known by unknowing . . . Beat evermore on this Cloud of Unknowing that is betwixt thee and thy God with a sharp dart of longing love."

This Cloud of Unknowing also applied to Jesus. Not even he knew the whole truth, only the truth about God-as-he-relates-to-man. Jesus was a man reaching up to God, but a man nonetheless. He did what no man before or since has done: he accepted the gift of Sonship that God offers us all.

The Jesus of faith is not the Jesus of history. Even if the theologians were all wrong—yes, even if the whole of the New Testament were a fiction and no such person as Christ ever lived—we would still be left with the Jesus of faith. By believing in Jesus and the Incarnation, that Jesus came directly from God in order that we may reach up to God, we ourselves create the Jesus of faith. We internalize the spirit of Jesus, and in doing so the Jesus of faith becomes real in a way that the Jesus of history never could. I know that there is an apparent contradiction between this and what I said in Chapter 9 about belief in a mythical Christ being a superstition. Nonetheless, if a person believes in a myth with such intensity and conviction that it changes his whole life and enables him to reach up and find the true God of the Christian faith then that myth, FOR THAT PERSON, becomes true. Not historically true, but spiritually true. There is more to truth than historicity.

We are now at the end of our journey. Many questions have been asked. None has been answered. Because definitive answers are not available to us. Humankind is a fantastic creation; and for all I have said about the wickedness inherent in the human soul, there is, too, a wonderful reservoir of goodness, love and compassion that manifests itself in saints and sinners alike.

I believe that our purpose in life is to embrace good and reject evil, to love love and hate hate; in the words of Tolstoy: (*War and Peace*) "To love one's neighbours, to love one's enemies, to love everything, to love God in all His manifestations." That is not the whole story, of course. But then only the Whole Story knows what the whole story is. "As the sun and each atom . . . is a sphere complete in itself, and yet at the same time only a part of a whole too immense for man to comprehend, so each individual bears within himself his own aims and yet bears them to serve a general purpose incomprehensible to man." (Ibid.)

We do not know what God's purposes are, or what our role in the Universe is. "We live in a world of unreality and dreams," says Simone Weil (*Waiting on God*). "To give up our imaginary position as the center, to renounce it, not only intellectually but in the imaginative part of our soul, that means to awaken to what is real and eternal, to see the true light and hear the true silence."

This means humbling ourselves before God. For while man arrogantly imagines that he is the center of the Universe, that he is the fount of all wisdom, that he, the unraveler of scientific fact, is the revealer and indeed the creator of universal truth, then he will never be able *"to see the true light and hear the true silence."*

So it's back to square one. And to Sir James Jeans: "Things are not as they seem . . . we are not yet in contact with reality

323

[and] to speak in Plato's well-known simile, we are still imprisoned in our cave, with our backs to the light, and can only watch the shadows on the wall."

Being a Christian, however, I cannot allow Plato to have the last word. That must be reserved for Jean-Pierre de Caussade: "There is nothing that faith does not penetrate and seek out. It passes beyond darkness, and no matter how deep the shadows, it passes through them to the truth which it always finally embraces and from which it is never separated."

And so, the impenetrable Cloud of Unknowing which separates us from God is penetrated by faith and love. It is only by unknowing (and that presumably means by becoming as little children), by throwing off the shackles of egotism and intellectual nihilism, and filling our hearts with "a sharp dart of longing love," that we can hope to pass through the shadows, reach out to the truth, and touch the hand of God.

None of this I can prove. But then if I could, the truth wouldn't be worth knowing. If God does exist, you can bet your sweet life that he has made it possible for us, his children, to reach him. If he doesn't exist then I have wasted my time. Whether I am right or wrong, of one thing I am certain: *I have not wasted my time.*

> The good want power, but to weep
>   barren tears.
> The powerful goodness want;
>   Worse need for them.
> The wise want love; and those who
>   love want wisdom;
> And all things are thus confused
>   to ill.
> Many are strong and rich, and
>   would be just,
> But live among their suffering
>   fellowmen
> As if none felt; they know not what
>   they do.

In memoriam:

This moving poem by Shelley is reproduced here in memory of my late friend, D. H. Jack, one of whose favourite poems it was. Like Shelley, he had a passionate sense of social justice. Unlike Shelley, he was a theist and a Christian. To eulogize is to devalue—only silence can do justice to the memory. But through the silence I hear the words of Jesus: "He that believeth in me, though he were dead, yet shall he live: And whosoever liveth and believeth in me shall never die."

E.C.